Leadership for Institution Building in Education

Other Books by the Author

- *Story of EDUSAT*, Shipra,
- *Educational Technology: Knowledge Assessment (Ed).* Shipra,
- *Value Development for College Youth (Ed)*, Viva.
- *Education for a Global Society: Interfaith Dimensions (Ed)*, Shipra
- *Secondary Education: The Challenges Ahead (Eds)*, NIEPA.
- *Total Quality Management in Education*, Sage, Published also in Hindi, Gujarati, Marathi, and Bengali; Tamil.
- *Governance of School Education in India (Eds)*, NIEPA.
- *Education in India: Dynamics of Development, Shipra*
- *Education India: The Next Millennium,* ETMA.
- *Open Schooling: Selected Experiences (Eds)*, Commonwealth of Learning

Leadership for Institution Building in Education

(Revised 3rd Edition)

Marmar Mukhopadhyay

SHIPRA

ISBN: 978-81-7541-650-5

First Published in India in 2012

Leadership for Institution Building in Education

Published by:
SHIPRA PUBLICATIONS
H.O.: LG 18-19, Pankaj Central Market, Patparganj,
I.P. Ext., Delhi-110092, Tel: 91-11-2223 5152, 2223 6152
Br.Off.: 4617/18, Ansari Road, Darya Ganj,
New Delhi-110002, Tel: 6594 6453, 9810522367
E-mail: info@shiprapublications.com
www.shiprapublications.com

Dedication

At the Lotus Feet of
Our Gurudev
Swami Satchidananda Giri

Preface to the Third Edition

Institution building is both an art and science. For people with naturally endowed leadership qualities, it is an art. Others can learn from the experiences of the institution builders who made marks in shaping their institutions. Case studies of 15 educational institutions—schools, colleges and regional and national institutions, and universities—bring the rich experience of leadership and institution building to the doorstep of every head of educational institutions. Multiple case analyses provide an empirically tested Indian model of leadership for institution building.

This is the 3rd edition. Indication is, the book has been well received. Hence, I decided to come out with a revised third edition. I have added two more cases in the school section. Also, I have revised and updated certain chapters and added a brief note on my thesis, Graduation in Leadership.

I must acknowledge the editorial help of my colleagues in ETMA, Ms. Monika Rao Singh and Ms. Charu Dhungra in finalizing this edition; Sabyasachi Panja, Graphic Designer at ETMA for the cover design. Mr. D. Kumar offered to accept the responsibility of publishing this edition. I thank all of them.

I hope readers, especially heads of educational institutions, will find the book useful.

Gurgaon
5 February, 2012

Marmar Mukhopadhyay

Preface to the Second Edition

Empires rise and fall. That is the rule of history. Historians make the empires immortal by documenting the story for generations to derive lessons from. Similar are the stories of institutions. They take birth, grow to new heights, decay and degenerate; although they rarely die out, yet, their stories go uncelebrated. Many important experiences of development go unrecorded, depriving the successive generations of the opportunity to learn. This book is an effort to document the heroic efforts of some of the institution builders, who figure occasionally in the large tapestry crowded by millions of administrators. Capturing the process is not easy; but worth an effort.

The first edition of the book was published in 2004. At the instance of Dr. Pilooben Buch, I authored the book to commemorate the 20th anniversary of India's leading educational journal, Perspectives in Education, initiated by Dr. M B Buch, my academic preceptor. The book was not priced nor sold in the market. It was a gift to the subscribers of the journal. Since there is a dearth of well-documented case studies on the subject of leadership and institution building, a large number of institutions and individuals asked for a copy of the book. They did not have access to the book as it was not in the market. I conceded to the demand and decided to bring out a second edition, upgraded with a few more cases and analytical chapters for a larger readership. I have added more new cases. I propose to do a few more case documentations on institution building. But that is for the future. I have also added a new chapter on leadership ethics; I have added this chapter for more than one reason. Many of my professional friends insisted that I also document the stories of institutional decay and degeneration so that well-meaning learners learn to protect their institutions. My serious efforts to study the process of degeneration led me to one important conclusion—*at the core of institutional decay and degeneration is the crisis of ethics in leadership*. I have tried to capture that in the new chapter added in this edition; since these are negative stories, I have been hesitant in referring to actual episodes and cases.

I must admit that one of the major inspirations of this book was the affectionate reception of my book, Total Quality Management in Education in many countries of the world. I thank my readers who inspire me to undertake new initiatives of this kind.

I am indeed grateful to ICFAI for undertaking the publication of this revised edition. My special thanks are due to Professor N Rajshekar, Dean, the ICFAI University Press, who initiated the dialogue with me about this book, and Sri Ved Prakash who pursued the process to its natural conclusion.

Since I propose to pursue the subject in the near future, I welcome comments and suggestions from my readers.

June 23, 2006, **Marmar Mukhopadhyay**
New Delhi

Preface to the First Edition

Dr. Piloo M Buch deserves all the compliments and credits for this book. She asked me to undertake a 'project' to commemorate the 20th year of the journal, Perspectives in Education, the most important legacy of the legend of our times, Professor M B Buch. Grateful to Pilooben for the opportunity, I am happy to place this book in the hands of the readers on Professor Buch's birth anniversary. I thank Professor P N Dave, who has untiringly edited the journal and nurtured the legacy; my thanks are also for his foreword, adding value to this book.

Organizations also have life cycles characterised by birth or establishment, period of early and fast growth, time of stability, and organizational decay and degeneration, and resurrection. But unlike the experience of living organisms, organisations skirt death; they 'turn around'. But this depends upon the people in leadership positions. Organizational growth can happen at the hands of 'leaders', and not with the 'managers' or 'administrators'. Indeed, leaders are rare birds among many managers and still many more administrators. Leaders, though few, offer us a lifetime opportunity to learn—what they do to manage change for development.

For me, it was revisiting my favourite theme, management of change to which my mentor, Professor Buch introduced me decades ago. Here, in this book, I made an effort to learn the dynamics of leadership for institution building in education. My documentation is based on interviews with the institution builders. To that extent, these are largely self-reported—institution building as perceived by heads of institutions themselves. A few institution builders like M B Buch, Moonis Raza, Yogendra Saran are no more. Having had the opportunity of working closely with them, I read their life and style, the way I could. I prepared the draft, and got it reviewed and vetted by others who also knew these leaders either as admirers or critics. Such cases, either self-reported or reported by an admirer can never be objective, and I do not wish to claim to be one. Let that luxury be of the timid. As long as we are able to capture the spirit of the style, we stand to learn.

I had long cherished such a work. My courage and convictions were triggered off when I received an invitation from Colin Latchem and Donald Hanna to document my experience in building National Open School as its chairman for the international volume on Leadership for 21st Century Learning, that later got an important US award for the best book on the subject in 2001-2002. I am grateful to Professor Colin Latchem for granting me permission to reprint the case. I thank Professor Udai Pareek for his permission to reproduce his interview with Professor Ravi Mathai, the leader who shaped IIM Ahmedabad. I am grateful to all my respondents who readily agreed to be captured in this book.

I hope my readers will find the book as interesting as I found the work exciting.

October 9, 2004,
New Delhi

Marmar Mukhopadhyay

Contents

1
INSTITUTION BUILDING

The rise and fall of empires has been the well-known rhythm of history across the continents. Historians have taken special interest in observing, interpreting and documenting such great human experiences. Human civilization, knowledge seekers in particular, stands wiser and enriched through such documents. Such ups and downs, rise and fall are also experienced in educational organizations. At some point of time, an educational institution glows in all its glory, performs superbly, to enjoy great reputation. The same institution, at some other time looses the glamour and glory and gets merged with the crowd of ordinaries. Unlike the mainstream history, such ups and downs of institutions and their capabilities to stay at the top over a period of time go largely unnoticed and unattended. We know Harvard University manages to stay at the top of the list of Top 100 universities in the world; however, we do not know, why and how it manages to stay at the top when all other top universities exchange places and ranks in different years, except in 2010 when Harvard lost its rank to Caltech. We still do not know precisely why good institutes cannot become great institutes. It is important to learn why and how institutions develop and degenerate. In what circumstances such changes happen. We need to factor in the variables that contribute either to growth or degeneration. Because of absence of such circumspection, what a wealth of human experience and learning is lost every day, everywhere. Indeed, as Havelock lamented, how little of such experiences are documented for others to learn! (Havelock, 1973). If we knew how institutions are built, how developments are sustained, how self-renewal can become a culture, we could probably engineer sustainable growth in many institutions benefiting more students, and the society at large.

A large majority of our educational institutions at all levels—schools, colleges, universities, teacher education, technical and management institutions—are rigid, static, pre-occupied with the past, and are change-resistant. They are victims of their own self-fulfilling prophecy and complacency. They don't break open the cocoon of 'Good' where they have sheltered themselves with make believe game of being 'Great'. The IIT community did not take kindly the statements by the man of Infosys fame Mr. Narayan Murthy and Indian Minister Mr. Jairam Ramesh on absence of poor quality research in those institutes of national importance. A colleague professional, C R Mitra, former Director of BITS Pilani expressed the same sentiment, 'it is easy to assert that graduates from these institutions are world class professionals. ... in the domain of post-graduate education and research, the achievement of the undergraduate education has not been duplicated" (Mitra, 2007)[1]. They do not take feedback from outside howsoever well meaning they be, invest energy and resources in reviewing their goals, beliefs, values and cultures. There is no mechanism for review of performance and accountability, no meaningful HRD plan.

Researchers, however, have been interested in identifying, isolating and predicting factors that determine organizational change. In such researches, human endeavours and attributes occupy the central space, above other elements like infrastructures, finance, etc. of organizations and educational institutions in such researches. One unmistakable pointer of all such studies is to the characteristics and qualities of people in leadership positions—principals, vice-chancellors, heads of departments, etc. What research proves across cultures is the role of leadership in managing change and sustaining the process over a period of time. As this process of change grows in strength to move past the 'leader', organization becomes self-renewing. 'Leader' gets replaced by 'Leadership. The phenomenon of self-renewal is ascribed to process capability of the organization. Institution building aims at generating this 'process' capability of self-renewal. In this chapter, we will share our understanding of the process and importance of institution building for sustainable change and development of educational institutions.

Organizations and Institutions

The words 'organization' and 'institution', though used interchangeably, need to be differentiated in order to appreciate the importance of the process of institution building. Institution connotes several meanings in the social sciences as different from organizations. Social Science Encyclopaedia provides separate entries both on organization and institution. According to Kaiser (1985), "Organizations can be defined as resource pools. They come into existence when individuals place the resources available to them (such as skills, money, ...) under some sort of central control, rather than using them individualistically. Organizations must establish certain rules of the use and distribution of the resources. These rules may be based on an autocratic hierarchical principle, whereby one person assumes the role of central coordinator or they may be cooperative democratic, in which case all the members participate on equal terms in coordinating and distributing decision-making. Most organizations fall somewhere between the two extremes, and in reality an organization may combine hierarchical and market features".

Educational institutions—schools, colleges, universities, etc.,—have definite structures, defined relationships among various components; there is a set of written rules and regulations that guide the organizational activities and personnel management. Thus, schools, colleges, universities, etc., are organizations, though they vary in the degree of their degree of formality on the basis of relationships.

In formal organizations, relationships are well defined; there are fixed set of rules that leave very little space for interpretation and discretion documented in writing; such rules guide '*intra-organization procedures and structures*'. In formal organizations, jobs are well defined with associated authority and responsibility, making each incumbent responsible against a set of predetermined goals.

Informal organization is defined by the '*aggregate of behaviours, interactions, norms, personal and professional connections through which work gets done and relationships are built among people who share a common organizational affiliation or cluster of affiliations.*' Informal organizations may develop within the formal set up on likes and dislikes, feelings, emotions, friendship bonds, etc. They sprout and grow automatically without any formal resolution. Not based on any prescribed rules, here, people develop their own procedures and cultures (http://www.scribd.com, http://www.managementstudyguide.com)

Compared to organizations, institutions refer to "aspects of social life, in which distinctive value orientations and interests, centering upon large and important social concerns (e.g., education, marriage, property) are accompanied by distinctive modes of social interaction. Its use emphasizes 'important' social phenomena, relationships of strategic structural significance (Scheinder, 1964).

Institutions continuously evolve. Study of that process of evolution is important. From this standpoint, "institutions are simply patterns of behaviour which persist and crystallise in the course of time and to which people become attached as a result of their role in the formation of identity, or to investments of energy for social interests (Roy, 1985). Institution is a process. For example, family is an organization whereas marriage is an institution. Marriage as an institution is an important component of sustenance of families in society. The nature of marriage as an institution varies from one society to another, as much as the structures of the families and the roles of individual members vary from one society to another. But the institution binds and strengthens the structure of the organization. The term institution, as different from organization, denotes some special characteristics. Blaise (1964) identifies three common elements in the concept of institutions:

- Prescription of norms of behaviour;
- Their relative permanence, independent of individuals; and
- Their applicability to both a small group as well as to the entire society.

Selznick (1957) makes some interesting distinction between institution and organization:

Organization	*Institution*
A pre-designed system for coordinated activities, also an instrumentality for certain functions.	Responsive, adaptive organism to respond to social needs and pressures.
Strives to maximize efficiency and management—remains outside the system.	Adaptive proactive part of the community and larger society.

According to Ezman and Blaise (1966), institutions are "organizations which incorporate, foster and protect normative relationships and action patterns and perform functions and services which are valued in the environment".

Institution Building

Institution building implies the process of developing certain capabilities which makes the organization continue not only with its ongoing operations, but also innovate and continuously improve on its performance. To that extent, institution building is developing the process capability of the organization for self-renewal and traversing the path of continuing change.

"Institution-building is a continuous process by which educational institutions are able to build and strengthen an internal culture with values that help a dynamic functioning of the institution enabling it to achieve its objectives and have the right kind of impact on the environment. Thus, an educational institution with a strong institution-building base is never static and is ever changing". (T V Rao, 1990—www.eric.ed.gov ED331772)

These definitions of institution building focuses on process capacities of single institutions. A large body of literature is emerging on institution building in the larger social and national contexts. "Institution building is the creation of governance capacities. It entails the dismantling and reformation of old organizations and institutions— legal, administrative, economic as well as social— the improvement of efficiency and effectiveness of existing institutions, the restoration of destroyed institutions and the enhancement of authorities' professionalism". (www.sais-jhu.edu). In our context, institution building implies development of self-renewing and process capabilities of the system comprising the network of institutions.

The difference in the developmental experiences among the schools, colleges and universities is primarily due to the differential emphasis on and the different processes of institution building. A large majority of the institutions do not experience any deliberate and planned effort in institution building. Few institutions that experience growth and development indeed experience institution building. It continues to change and sustain change on the strength of its process capabilities; change seem to happen rather automatically. The term "institution building" has been used for the process of internal development of an institution as well as making external impact on the society" (UNESCO, 1982).

According to Pareek (1981), institution building has been used with two meanings. 'One meaning refers to the process of development of some institutions by an outside expert institution, as total systems, including the development of values and norms which is relevant to the type of work the institutions have been doing. The second meaning in which the term is used relates to the internal development of an institution to be able to play its role effectively'. Pareek also emphasized on "process of establishing or transforming an organization into an integrated and organic part of the community in a way that will help the organization play a proactive role in projecting new values and become an agent of change in the community". This is important since educational institutions are public institutions funded by public either directly through student fees or indirectly through public taxation via government.

Several important aspects of this definition are:

- Institution building covers both the processes of establishing and transforming an established organization;
- It makes the organization an integrated and organic part of the community;
- It helps the organization take on a proactive role;
- It helps the organization project new values; and
- It encourages the institution to become an agent of change.

Process/Strategies of Institution Building

Pareek (1981) proposed a cyclic model of institution building comprising idea formulation, preparation, innovation, consolidation, multiplication and review. Chowdhry (1977) proposed Master-Plan Approach and Organization-Around-The-Man Approach. The Master Plan Approach refers to development of a master plan and then setting up the institution. In the contrasting model, her emphasis is on human capability—building institution around individuals. While focusing on Homi Bhaba and Vikram Sarabhai, she points out their emphasis on human beings. In conclusion, however, she did not see these two approaches to be exclusive. Realistically, the question is where the emphasis is. In some cases, institution building is built around man with the necessary support for Master Plan Approach; in certain other cases, support is derived from the man within the Master Plan Approach. In the Master Plan Approach, the process is supposed to be contained by the structure, and the goal is relatively pre-decided. In Organization-Around-The-Man Approach, emphasis is on creativity and managing change through human excellence. Institution building covers both the processes of establishing and transforming an established organization. Pareek offers a framework for decision-making for institution building (Table 1.1).

Table 1.1: Framework for Decision-making

Framework	*Orientation*	*Relationship*	*Motivation*
Feudal	Ownership	Dependency	Dependency
Beaureaucratic	Rules and Procedures	Independence	Status
Political	Power	Clique membership	Power and affiliation
Managerial	Efficiency	Task interdependence	Creativity
Institution building	Effectiveness and health for organic growth	Achievement cooperation	Ownership

Pareek classified organizations into five frameworks, namely feudal, bureaucratic, political, managerial and institution building. In terms of orientation, the emphasis in institution building framework is on effectiveness and health for organic growth as compared to ownership, rules and procedures, power and efficiency in the other frameworks. The institution building framework is characterised by cooperation and achievement; and motivation is ownership of decisions, in general, and the organization, in particular. This framework provides institution building with a dynamic process, a process of adoption of innovation and management of change.

Clark classified organizations in terms of the state of growth, namely:

- Formative period: When an institution is conceptualized and first established.
- Rapid growth period: Three years of institution immediately after establishment, when it experiences tremendous energy and fast growth.
- Period of stability: After the initial period of establishment and rapid growth, institutions settle down and tend to continue within a dynamic equilibrium.

- Period of decline and decay: As the traditions set in, institutions tend to follow the traditions and appoint innovation; with the changing times, complexity and demand of the community and the client, the practices and programmes become inadequate; also institutions tend to lose energy.

Then, there is fifth stage; the stage of crisis when examinations schedules are totally disrupted, teachers are beaten to death by students, physical infrastructures of institutions are occupied by outsiders an goons, institutions are ruled by political leaders through shadows inside, teachers boycott classes and examinations at the slightest provocations, heads of institutions are humiliated and tortured, and so on.

There are implications for institution building at every stage of growth of an organization. The difference is in the nature of institution building at different stages of growth. The institution-building framework during the period of decline and decay has to be different than the institution-building framework during the formative and rapid growth period. The challenges of managing change in different stages of the organization are qualitatively different. An exercise in juxtaposition of these two models can provide an important learning opportunity (please fill the matrix given below).

	Feudal	*Bureaucratic*	*Political*	*Managerial*	*Institution Building*
Formative					
Rapid growth					
Stability					
Decay and decline					

Managing Change for Institution Building

Educational institutions are not static organizations. They too go through different states of existence, as mentioned earlier, namely rapid growth, steady state, reforms, crisis and organizational decay and decline. A large majority of educational institutions continue to function in a similar manner over a long period of time; in a way, they continue to stay in steady state or maintain status quo. They continue to practise the same process of admission of students, selection of the staff, academic time scheduling and assignments of classes to teachers, staff meetings, examinations, processing and management of finance, and even the same techniques of classroom transaction oblivious of changing times and practices. No wonder, they either show consistency in their performance in various areas like student results, organizational culture and climate, interpersonal relationships, etc. or decline due to mismatch of methods and processes with time. Since such institutions continue to do what they do, they continue to perform the way they perform. They indicate their pride in being 'consistent'—preserving themselves.

Such institutions remind us the story of a British inspector of schools who left India, in the late 1930s, and re-visited in mid-1970s as a tourist. During his tour, he visited some of the schools, especially the ones he used to visit during his assignment in India. At the end of his tour, he admired, 'how much India has changed! It is difficult even to recognize places where we used to visit every day." But, "I felt absolutely at home when I went back to some of the schools that I inspected in 1938-39. They are exactly the same. There is no change. I could recognize them from a distance and I really rolled back on time. They looked the same; classes were also held exactly in the same manner. If I was still an inspector, I could have given the same report that I gave in 1938; I just have to change the date."This experience is nothing unusual.

The colleges, we studied 30 or 40 years ago, function exactly in the same manner; they continue to charge the same fees; transact the same curriculum, dictate same notes except the pages are more soiled due to overuse and ageing, same pattern of examination. The schools and colleges lack missions and shared goals, collaborative processes; they are rigid, resistant to change, without any accountability and social commitment (Pareek's contention mentioned earlier).

The second type of experience in organizational change relates to the organizational decay. Over a period of time, outstanding institutions have degenerated and lost their reputation. The institutions that were well-known for strong academic traditions and culture, where the academic faculty were outstanding scholars, busy most of the time in teaching, research and scholarly discussions, now host teachers who engage significantly in non-scholarly pursuits, like private tuition, business-like textbook writing, share-broking, insurance agency, etc. Although, by convention, students are selected through the same process, they busy themselves with ragging, unionizing, etc. Many educational institutions, with great past and excellent reputation, have degenerated not only into ordinariness, but even below that. This would be evident in many institutions. For example, what is the condition of the school where Swami Vivekananda was a student and Pandit Iswar Chandra Vidyasagar was the headmaster? Calcutta University of Sir Ashutosh Mukherjee's fame is now struggling to find/regain a foothold. A university of Jamia Millia Islamia's standing and reputation had to appoint people from Army and civil services cadre to bring back to normalcy. There are many such instances where educational institutions of outstanding reputation have degenerated over a period of time.

The third variety of experience is that of organizational growth and development, which is the core of institution building. As compared to status quo, these institutions change with great enthusiasm, initiative, innovation and confidence. There are several varieties of experiences within the ambit of institution building.

One such core variety can be classified as an 'out-of-crisis' institutional transformation, though in strict sense of the term, it is just an initial step. In such a situation, institution building may imply a turnaround to normal functioning. There are several cases and experiences of this nature. Just to illustrate, let me refer to the experience of one of the central universities. After the retirement of the vice chancellor, the university was looked after by an acting vice chancellor who could not enter the campus until a senior retired army officer was appointed as its vice chancellor. When he joined, the examination schedules were late by more than six months affecting the future and careers of hundreds of young students in the university; students' hostels were forcibly occupied by outsiders who ruled the hostels; university land was forcefully occupied as slums under the patronage of political leaders. The '*General*' in the Vice-Chancellor declared the examination schedule within a few days of his joining; the student union leaders who threatened the vice chancellor with 'consequences' were rusticated forthwith. Examinations were held on schedule, results were published much before the normal time. The vice chancellor paid unscheduled visits to classes in many departments and faculties, noted teachers' absence and called upon them to take classes. In a sweep, he had all the unauthorized occupants of the hostel removed. With the help of the police, he got the slums removed from the university land, despite strong political opposition and resistance. The university had a turnaround and became once again a place of study as it should be. Nonetheless, university had to appoint an IAS officer to succeed, and more of them to follow.

The second core variety of experience is that of a steady transition of an institution from the status quo and the average to higher levels of performance. There are many instances of schools, colleges and universities developing their own self-concept and image. The institution makes a slow but steady change. It may take the form of a quantitative expansion where the institution increases the number of students intake. There can be qualitative shift to include introduction of new programmes and courses; improving student performance in the public examination; developing new areas of excellence like sports and games, arts and aesthetics. The institution experiences a positive change and development.

The third type of core change can be classified as repositioning of an institution. In this case, the institution makes a deliberate effort to change its processes and performance to equate itself with the category of institutions above itself. It tries to get the brand name which others enjoy. In the recent past, many educational institutions, schools in particular, have got ISO 9000 series certification. Many of the schools now affiliate themselves with International Baccalaureate Organizations. More and more colleges and universities are volunteering to get evaluated by NAAC is another instance of deliberate efforts to change, among others, processes and performances in the institution. Some institutes of higher education collaborate with foreign universities to change quality, reputation, and often marketability. These are instances of institution building for repositioning of the institution itself in a new class.

The other shade of institution building for repositioning is redefining organizational missions and goals, although there is no crisis in the organization. Generally, institutions perform much below their potentiality and they get used to it. In a personal discussion with the head of a state level institution in English Language Learning and Research, I mentioned that it was an under-performing institution.

Quality of its infrastructure, academic staff, programmes are enough to put this institution as one of the best in the country; and potentially an institution of globally comparable quality. But the institution is happy and satisfied with its performances dozing over its hidden potential. However, as such institution realizes its 'treasure within', it redefines its mission, its goals and work methods, and also the organizational values. It is another variety of turnaround without a crisis. One of the DIETs, in my experiment in TQM, that was down under with large but shabby campus due to non-availability of staff and funds and felt helpless, collectively discovered their might after the TQM experiment and converted the campus into the most beautiful one in the state.

The fourth and, indeed, the most outstanding experience is in the shaping vision of an institution. This may include all the three development experiences mentioned above; though it actually means much more. This is typically the case of the new institutions. The very process of conceptualizing a new institute is creative. It looks into the future, sets its models, defines its goals and its mission, and experiences a tremendous surge of positive energy. The institute grows fast. This experience of institution building is important not only because it is unmatched, but also because it seeks and tries to establish traditions and culture of the organization that shapes future life of the organization, but also pursue, promote and boost the philosophy of the institution. This is equally applicable in case of 'turn-arounds'. Experience of institution building in IIM Ahmedabad is the most fascinating example. The process capabilities developed during the leadership of Ravi Mathai still sustains the organization at the top of the pyramid of quality institutions in India. Institution building, has thus twin challenges—building process capabilities and sustaining them.

Conclusion

Institution building occurs at all stages in the life of an institution. Critical features of institution building at different stages are defining and redefining of goals, empowering people for self-regulation, creating a resilient and responsive structure, culture of innovation and change, a mentoring mindset and an inspiring leadership. The intriguing questions are: what inspires such a change? Why does it not happen to all institutions and all the time? Why is institution building such a rare experience? What are the turning points in the life of an educational institution? Is there a universal process of institution building or is it culturally embedded? These and many such questions form the backbone and inspiration of human endeavour to understand the dynamics of organizations. I would explore responses to these questions in this book.

The question that stares at our eyes is the role of head of a school or a college or a university in institution building. We know that the same institution with the same teachers, similar students, same or similar infrastructure and comparable financial provisions changes significantly with the change of head of the institution. Empirical evidence all over the world corroborates the role of leadership in the growth and development of an academic institution. So, also in its decay. With change of guard at the top, an educational institution either continues to function at the same level and style or tends to decay and degenerate or, takes a growth path. In order to understand the dynamics of institution building, it is necessary to understand the people in leadership positions, their styles and processes of leadership. Second important agenda of this book is to explore nature of institutional leadership and its impact on change. I also propose to study, in this book, whether there is any uniqueness in leadership style and institution building processes that are especially shaped by Indian cultures and traditions.

NOTE

1. Though Mitra condones the system saying, 'an endowed system with intellectual competence has been left without partners to secure the mission'.

2
LEADERSHIP IN EDUCATION

All educational institutions have certain leadership positions. Vice-Chancellors, Pro-Vice-Chancellors, Deans and Heads of Departments in the universities; principals, vice principals and heads of departments in colleges; principals and vice-principals, supervisors and heads of departments in schools are all examples of leadership positions. But, all those who occupy leadership positions are not necessarily leaders. Large number of them are '*Designated Leaders*' only ('leaders' because of designation i.e. they occupy leadership position by appointment); only few are '*Ascribed Leaders*' (who are leaders because others ascribe them the leadership role). Institutions grow when designated leaders and ascribed leaders find expression in one—head of the institution. Institutions maintain status-quo or decline when designated, but not ascribed leaders, occupy the leadership position in the academic institutions. Institutions grow when designated leaders are also ascribed leaders.

There are three roles for the people in leadership position in educational institutions. These are administration, management and leadership (Mukhopadhyay, 2005). Although each person in leadership position has to perform all three roles, their typology is determined by their dominant traits and tendencies that define their workspace (Figure 2.1).

- Administrators (dominant trait) operate within the small circle of laid down rules, regulations and protocols in the past.
- Managers (dominant trait) operate in a relatively larger workspace dealing with 'here and now' situations; they

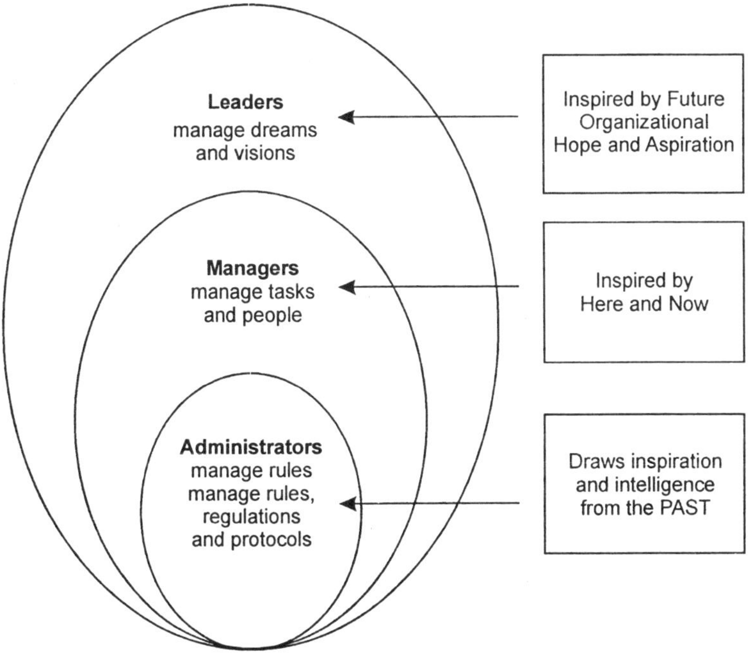

Figure 2.1: Workspace of Administrators, Managers and Leaders

subsume administrative concerns within the ambit of management of tasks and people as they exist.

- Leaders (dominant trait) create still larger workspace filled with organizational dreams and visions; they subsume both administration and management within the process of realization of their organizational dreams and visions.

Another meaning and interpretation of the figure above is administrators are rather exclusive; managers are partially inclusive as they subsume administration; leaders are inclusive as they subsume both administration and management. What changes are the perspectives.

Leaders inspire and influence people in the organization to cherish dreams, construct the future and move forward. "Leaders create and change cultures" (Schein, 1992); managers live with them. "Leaders are also people who have the capacity to motivate and inspire others to think beyond their current frameworks to what is desirable, necessary and possible. They enjoy the spirit and energy, creating optimal environment for information, quality and enterprise. They change mindsets and practices and gain cooperation and commitment, even in an environment initially characterized by low trust and low morale. They redefine and reform organizations" (Latcham and Hanna, 2001).

Robbins and Finley (1997) credit organizational change to 'talented leadership', whether at the top levels of the organization or at the team levels. Institution building which is a creative process of organizational change is directly related to leadership, if not restricted to only 'talented leadership'. For institution building, then, having leaders in leadership positions is a necessary condition. Extending the argument further, a 'non-leader' as head of an institution spells the beginning of the end of the organizational decay.

Choices for Leadership Positions

Leaders in leadership positions can be by design or by default. Leadership positions can be by designation or by ascribing. The corporate world and even private enterprises in education choose persons with leadership skills and qualities for leadership positions. The choice of leaders for leadership positions in such cases is by design. This is not so in the case of state-funded and state-controlled institutions. The selection and placement of people in leadership positions in the state-managed schools, colleges and universities do not take into account leadership skills as a requirement. Exceptions apart, the appointments in schools and colleges to the position of headmaster or principal are by and large, according to seniority. Even in the case of selection, it is done at best on the basis of academic merits; other significant considerations like acquaintance and proximity to the centres of power, dominate the selection process. The appointment of university vice-chancellors and heads of national and state institutes has steadily changed, especially during the recent years, to by and large a political process. Thus, most of the cases of positioning of leaders in leadership positions are largely by default—more of a chance, if not accident.

Further, unlike in the corporate sector, there is hardly any provision or practice of leadership development—capacity building of people in leadership positions in state institutions. Orientation and training of vice chancellors are unknown; NIEPA's programme for college principals, the only one of its kind, covers about 100 principals a year, with a potentiality of covering the existing 20,000 colleges only during the next 200 years! Fortunately, there is some rethinking about reconstructing Academic Staff Colleges. The story is worse in the case of heads of secondary and elementary schools. Majority of the head of institutions, hence, continue to either administer or manage conventionally, by imitating the existing practices of their predecessors. No wonder, a large majority of the educational institutions continue to maintain the status quo or even decay out of the system fatigue of managing the status quo. 'Leadership' is rather unknown and not experienced in a vast majority of educational institutions.

The issue becomes alarming, if we view this situation against the backdrop of what we understand today about the dynamics of management of change based on research literature. Research literature on the management of innovation and change is almost unanimous that the attributes and style of the person occupying the leadership position exert the single largest influence on the process of change—growth and development of an institution. Several Indian studies have indicated the different types of personal attributes of people in leadership positions that contribute directly to the organisational growth (Mukhopadhyay, 1981, 2005). Latchem and Hanna (2001) summarized their learning about leaders, especially of open learning systems, under a few heads like values and beliefs, characteristics and behaviours, and strategies for change. Leaders differ in their ethics and values, their skills and strategies from their counterparts, and they also differ in their learning skills. Getting leaders by chance or by accident is risking the institutions, a great deal.

Let us revisit the issue of leadership for institution building as it exists in the contemporary literature. In a way, I am revisiting the issue a third time, but with a difference.[1] While I have consistently adopted a qualitative approach to the understanding of leadership in management of change in education, some of my predecessors in Indian research on management of innovation and change used quasi-scaling technique, promoted by Everett Rogers in early 1960s, with the advantage of quantifying a qualitative issue.

In presenting my thesis, I have an important opportunity of mapping my findings and learning in the overall framework of contemporary leadership theories as they evolved over a period of time.

Organizational Life and Leadership

Leadership (effectiveness) is also related to the stages of development of an organization. Organizations are conceptualized and established, they grow, stabilize and decay; they redefine goals, tasks and processes, and begin a new journey. As mentioned in the previous chapter, Clark classified organizational life into four periods, namely Formative, Rapid Growth, Mature and Declining.

Clark's conceptual model provides a meaningful basis for studying institution building and role of leadership therein. There are, experiences, though rare, of organizational rebirth; a paradigm shift in organizational mission, goals and activities. This may or may not be related to organizational decay or decline.

The important contention is that the role and the requirement of leadership qualities may not be the same. Those leaders who are credited with institution building from the stage of conceptualizing,[2] or at the budding stage, may not be equally effective in cases of institutes that are stable or institutes that are 'at risk' and require a turnaround. This demands deeper probing into the dynamics of leadership in institution building.

Leadership Typologies

One of the commonly known typologies of leadership is authoritarian, democratic and laissez-faire. The heads of institutions of the first category decide what to do, when to do, how to do, etc., all by themselves and instruct others to carry out. Here, subordinates or followers have all the responsibility without any authority.

The heads of institutions of the second category pose problems to others in the organisation, ask their views, seek solutions and ideas, formulate solutions on the basis of their views and get them revalidated; they also seek others' views on how to do, when to do, and even who would do. Here people share dual responsibilities of decision making and implementing.

The heads of institutions of the third category leave things to happen. There are interesting variations among the members of the last group. One category of heads does not take decisions, does not take interest in the institution; these heads are more concerned about their own personal interest, and allow the institution to drift. They allow others also to nurture their own personal interest over, often against, the interest of the institution. There is yet another important category of heads that allows and encourages people to take decisions and implement, carefully delegating both responsibilities and rights to individuals in the organisation. This category of people can be classified as Delegative, rather than Laissez-faire leaders.

Baddaracco and Ellsworth (1989) offer another typology for understanding leadership roles. Leadership roles are guided by one of the three philosophies namely political, directive and value-driven:

1. The political leader is a strategist. He/she adjusts his/her vision of the future and mutually defines goals with the inherent resistance to change within the organization. He/she is aware and conscious of such resistances.
2. The directive leader directs the organization towards a well-defined goal based on SWOT that is assessment of organizational strengths, weaknesses, opportunities and threats. He/she takes key-decisions personally and relies upon the structure and the system to control decisions while challenging the conventional wisdom.
3. The value-driven leader is a pace-setter, leading by example, through walking the talk. He/she demonstrates values for the followers, emphasizing the overall organizational purposes rather than one's own interest.

One of the important contributions to the understanding of leadership is the situational leadership theory by Hersey and Blanchard (1992). They identified four styles of leadership based on the combination of leader's concern for task, and concern for relationship. The style takes shape through interaction of these two concerns. Although the concern for task and the concern for relationship form a continuum, the authors dichotomised each one of them into high and low. Accordingly, they identified four styles, namely

- directive (high concern for task but low concern for relationship);

- coaching (high concern for task and high concern for relationship);
- supporting or participating (high concern for relationship but low concern for task); and
- delegating style (low concern for both task and relationship).

In the **directive style,** the leader tends to dictate.

In the **coaching style,** he or she primarily acts as a coach to ensure accomplishment of goals. Alternative description is 'selling' style where leaders acts like salesperson convincing followers or subordinates about a new idea instead of forcing them to accept. This is an important style for the heads of institutions for introducing innovation and change.

In the **participating style,** the leader involves himself or herself along with the followers in actually carrying out the tasks with the main objective of keeping the people happy.

In the **delegating style,** the leader trusts his/her followers, and allows members to take responsibility along with rights to innovate, change and redefine their roles.

Everyone in leadership position displays a personal style by his/her preference in various situations. What distinguishes a leader is his/her effectiveness in choosing the style according to the demands of the situation, thus calling for flexibility. Moving from directive to the delegating style through coaching and participating styles is guided by the task-maturity of the followers; but follower's task maturity is what the leader perceives. The perception itself emerges from the leader's own world-view. This theory is situated 'here and now', living from moment to moment. Also, it takes a static view of leader-follower relationship.

Transactional and transformational leadership concepts accommodate the dynamism of unfolding relationships between the leader and the follower. In transactional leadership, leaders empower followers with greater access to information and participative decision making. Transformational leadership goes a step beyond. It visualizes transforming the followers into the second and the third order leadership roles in the organization with several implications for institution building. It builds succession, reducing the risk of organizational degeneration with change of guard in leadership position. It also lays the foundation of a self-renewing organization.

Most important of all, it ensures continuity in the ongoing cultural transformation of the organization.

The emotional intelligence guru, Daniel Goleman (2002) has made a refreshing contribution to the understanding of leadership and the dynamics of relationship between the leader and his/her follower in his books, Primal Leadership and The New Leaders. His basic thrust is on 'leading with emotional intelligence' by generating resonance with the followers. Accordingly, he classified leadership styles into resonant and dissonant styles. Visionary Leadership style is the most positive, as it moves people towards shared dreams, when changes require a new vision and a clear direction.

1. Coaching style is highly positive since it connects personal goals with organizational vision.
2. Affiliative style makes positive impact by connecting people to each other.
3. Democratic style also exerts positive impact since it values people's inputs and gets commitment through participation.

Goleman et al., classified Pace-setting and Commanding styles as dissonant styles, although such styles are relevant and can be effective in certain situations like high quality results from a motivated group or in kick-starting a turnaround.

Power and Authority

Organizational leadership is the function of official position and personal skills. As mentioned earlier, official position makes one a 'Designated Leader' through placement in the organizational hierarchy, coupled with financial and administrative powers. In hierarchic organizations with bureaucratic administration, position plays the most significant role. Personal skills of influencing and leading are not necessarily linked with the official position. Every individual, whether a head of the institution or otherwise, possesses a certain amount of personal skills to influence others; we will call it power, but not authority. Leaders tend to use their positional advantage and personal skills for influencing differentially in different situations. For example, authoritarian style indicates higher use of authority and democratic leadership is characterised by greater use of power.

According to Indian scriptures, human nature is governed by three qualities namely *Sattvik, Rajasik* and *Tamasik*. According to this theory, every individual has all the three qualities but in different proportions; also in the same individual at some point of time one quality may be dominant over the other two.

Sattvik qualities are knowledge, illumination, sense of duty without attachment,

Rajasik qualities are action, high energy, urge to dominate others and material possession, etc.

Tamasik attributes are lethargy, inertia, ignorance, lack of interest, etc.

The dominance of the *Rajasik* quality is likely to make one an authoritarian leader; the *Tamasik* quality is likely to make a person laissez-faire, and *Sattvik* quality is likely to make a person democratic and delegating, and inspiring. The theories of power and authority fit into this Indian paradigm very well.

People in authority, namely the head of institutions have both personal power and authority. Those who are strong in power and have the ability to influence people, very rarely or reluctantly use authority. In fact, they do not need to. People weak in personal skills and influence tend to use authority more. If leadership is influencing people to reach the collectively defined goal, personal 'power' is more powerful than 'authority'. Institution builders use more of power, and less of authority.

Inspirational Leadership (Secretan, 1999) and Spiritual Leadership (Fry, 2003; Sanders, 2007) added new dimension to the thinking of leadership. Lance Secretan discards visioning and strategic planning as old story leadership. He also discards the classification of a leader and a follower. He bids goodbye to the word 'follower' in preference for 'percener', not just as a new word but as a new expression—changing from follower to percener or partner, is a shift from unequal to equal relationship. He contends that each one is a leader and proves his point by raising different situations and roles in life; thus, leadership is hidden in everyone. A P J Abdul Kalam, the scientist former President of India asked the same question 'why wait for someone else to lead, why not you lead yourself?' (Kalam, 2002.)

The old story of leadership ends with motivating; the new story is all about inspiring—beyond motivating. Secretan asks: "What caused the followers to dedicate themselves with such passion to the visions of Christ, Gandhi, Confucius, Martin Luther King, Mother Teresa and Nelson Mandela?" "They were inspired, not motivated". We know that Martin Luther King did not say, "I have a strategic plan!" and Mother Teresa did not have a 'quality programme'. She did not need one. "Inspiration does not depend on power relationships: on the contrary, when we are inspired we are truly empowered. To inspire others, we must create an environment in which people sense a power beyond that of another human being; a higher power, a divine influence from deep within, causing them to be infused with a breath of God. In other words, we must become as effective in engaging the energy of the soul (inspiration) as we have become in engaging the energy of the personality (motivation)". Secretan's theory gets summarized into two questions—'why can't we see God in others?' (Implying, then we don't need to manage), and leader to percener question, 'I am your leader, how can I serve you?' instead of the old story question, 'I am your leader, how can I teach you?'

Almost all these theories are derived from on research on male (sample) leaders. With the increasing number of women assuming leadership roles, there is an emerging women's voice on leadership theory. Dewan (2004) does a comprehensive review of the research and writings on the theme. A competent summarization of this issue has been done by Latchem and Hanna (2001). The issue is more about the difference of impact of male and female brain, the logical-rational versus empathic-emotional attributes of male and female brains respectively. Goleman and Secretan built an effective bridge. Women with large female brain are endowed with greater potentiality of developing resonance; the natural mother-being in them with empathy makes them spiritually richer to be inspiring. No wonder, a large majority of male celebrities identify mother as their source of inspiration (deBono, 1985).

Just as there is relevance and importance of the concept of 'women's voice' in leadership, there is need to consider the issue of 'eastern voice' as compared to western voice (model) of leadership. All these theories are set into western society and organizations. From the standpoint of theory of Transactional Analysis, leadership behaviour is guided by the life scripts of leaders as scripted by their families and society in their early childhood days. Is that valid enough for Indian and Asian societies and organizations, when the 'Geography of Thought' differs between Asians and Americans? (read as Westerners) (Nisbette, 2003). This question needs to be explored.

Conclusion

There is a fairly large body of Indian research literature on leadership, in general and in education in particular. Almost all research studies and assessments of leadership skills and styles are based on the use of tools made in the west like Leadership Behaviour Description Questionnaire (LBDQ) and Leadership Effectiveness and Adaptability Questionnaire (LEAD) Questionnaires. Just as the FPS system cannot generate data in centimeters and grams, the leadership measurement tools developed in the western world have only helped measuring Indian leaders against western norms. Indian leaders have been measured against 'initiating structure' and 'consideration' in LBDQ or in terms of the four styles proposed by Hersey and Blanchard in LEAD Questionnaire. Such measurements are inadequate to represent ethos, culture and intricacies of Indian leadership in Indian institutions. Deriving strength from the western researches, it is important and necessary to carry out qualitative analysis of leadership behaviour of the Indian leaders in education to understand what leadership attributes and styles work in building Indian institutions. In this book, my primary effort is to search for styles of leadership that are effective for Indian institutions through case studies of those who have successfully led institution building process.

NOTES

1. In my first study, I carried out case studies of sixteen schools identified through case nomination; I used a number of research instruments and tools and compared the two sets of schools—innovative and non-innovative against the set of criteria measured with the research instruments. Leadership, as measured by LBDQ, was one of the variables. This was way back in 1972-75 (Mukhopadhyay 1981).
   I revisited the issue of management change and leadership in my study on Management of Change: A Diagnostic Study for UNESCO: Bangkok
   I revisited the issue of management of change in the late 1980s (Mukhopadhyay, 1989). Case studies were done on innovations, institutions,

states/societies (e.g., universalization of basic education in Kerala). Based on the multiple case analysis, my major effort was to generate an Indian paradigm of management of change, where leadership figured as a major determinant of management of change.

In this second revisit, my focus is singularly on leadership, and leadership for institution building only. Hopefully, this will provide consolidation of our learning on what styles are relevant and work in building Indian institutions.

2. G Ram Reddy for conceptualizing and leading Indira Gandhi National Open University in the first five years; Moonis Raza for rebuilding NIEPA as a research institute; Gen. Zaki for pulling out Jamia Millia Islamia for putting the university back in rail from complete anarchy and non-functioning.

Case Studies

3

SCHOOL AS INSTRUMENT OF SOCIAL CHANGE

Udang High School

The community leaders decided to set up a high school in Udang in 1933. Since there were no qualified persons around, they invited Sri Nrisinha Parasad Mukhopadhyay[1] from another village to head the school. The new headmaster's vision was much more than school as a place for transacting curriculum. School was an instrument for energizing and transforming the community. This story brings into focus how a rural school was designed to act as a hub for rural transformation through leadership development among students, alternative pedagogy to suit learning of rural children, involvement of the community for infrastructure development, encouragement of school students and teachers in disaster management in rural areas. The story also brings into focus the lifestyle of the headmaster and the teachers as role models, with their concern and empathy for rural children and the community at large.

Childhood Development

Late Sri Nrisinha Parasad Mukhopadhyay (b. 1901) began his life as an orphan; his father expired just before he landed on the earth. He grew up in utter poverty and deprivation but under the competent care of his grandmother. Although he could manage to attend the local school, he had to be a self-learner for his collegiate education. Mukhopadhyay passed his BA with distinction from Calcutta University, a rare feat those days. With his consistent, excellent, academic background, he could have found a job in the British government and lived a life of comfort and ease. When he was asked why he chose teaching in a rural school rather than accepting a comfortable assignment in Calcutta, his response was, "government can always get highly qualified people, though they do not actually require great scholars. Schools in Calcutta have many highly qualified locals. There are only a few in rural areas. If highly qualified rural students migrate to Calcutta, who will teach the rural children? Yes, I wanted to teach, and teach my rural children. Not that I did not know that life would be difficult in rural areas. I decided to share my life and learning with my fellow rural brethren and serve them." Mukhopadhyay, then 32, was heading a school in his native village, about 14 kilometres from Udang. He was invited by the management committee of Udang High School to head the institution and build it up. He accepted the invitation. As he joined the school, one of the villagers offered him a mud hut as his residence where he lived his entire life.

The school is located in the village Udang in Howrah district of West Bengal, bordering Medinipur. The school was established in 1933. Mukhopadhyay was the founder headmaster and he served it from 1933 to 1962. Udang and the surrounding villages housed both Hindus and Muslims; indeed, a poor community comprising largely of landless laborers or poor marginal farmers. There was hardly any amenity for decent living. There was no electricity, no water supply except one hand pump for the entire village. The nearest metal roads were seven kilometers away on one side and about 10 kilometers away on the other. There was no medical facility except for one Licentiate Medical Practitioner (LMP) and a few quacks. Though there were a few primary schools strewn around in the cluster of villages around Udang, this was the only high school, without basic amenities like classrooms, laboratories, staff room, library, toilets, etc. There was just one big hall partitioned into four classrooms. There was no provision for schooling of girls in the entire area.

Besides being poor, the local population was illiterate, superstitious, and furthest from scientific knowledge. People walked miles together; a few could afford a cycle rickshaw or a boat. Except in the school, there was hardly a newspaper; radios with antenna—a wire/cable hung from one tree top to another or on two long bamboo poles, another cable connecting the radio to the antenna was a rare distinction for the rarest of the families. The large majority of students were first-generation learners without any possibility of academic support at home; without the basic economic background to buy textbooks, exercise books or even to pay the minimum charges of the school. Students were advised and taught to write with pencil first and then with ink pen (made of bamboo branches), so that the same paper might be used twice. Some re-used the used papers upside down and wrote in between the lines with a different ink, using the same paper a third time.

Missions

The headmaster articulated his missions on many occasions. However, his missions were much more visible from his actions. His believed in the inseparability of the school from the local community. He did not see the school as a campus where students from the community came and learnt a few subjects for the board examination. For him, the school was an instrument of change and transformation of the local community where, rather incidentally, some meaningful learning of subjects also happened. The important implication was his concept of education being incomplete, if the school and its students did not provide social leadership for alleviating the living conditions and improving quality of life of the community.

His second important mission was to develop and/or adapt the pedagogical processes to the given socio-economic framework, so that children might be able to sustain through the process of schooling under dire poverty, on the one hand, and lack of academic support at home, on the other.

With this socio-economic backdrop, the missions of his school so far as the students were concerned, were to develop life skills, concern for others and the community, and leadership qualities. For teachers, his missions were to develop empathy for the children and the rural community; to see themselves as agents of rural transformation rather than constrain themselves to the concept of classroom teachers.

In building these missions for the school and the community at large, he not only involved the teachers, but also the community leaders. As the subsequent strategy definition and description would indicate, instead of professing his missions to other teachers and the community leaders, he set examples by practicing himself both at school and at home. He consulted, discussed and mentored the community leaders to think beyond themselves and their power structures to be able to serve and benefit the rural community. His most powerful ally was the local, only qualified medical practitioner from Udang, who later grew as a political leader as well as a person of high ethical standard. Initially, several teachers had to be brought from outside the village. But as the school started functioning, students started passing out; old teachers either retired or returned to their own native villages; many of the past students joined the school as teachers. They shared common values and ethics practised in the school. Mukhopadhyay was their teacher. For them, he was more a pace-setter and 'guru' rather than a headmaster or leader, as understood today. The remaining teachers, who were not directly his students, also treated him as if he was their teacher as well.

Actions and Strategies

The actions of the headmaster did not necessarily indicate any planned strategy. His actions were primarily guided by his convictions. Let me recount some of the important but uncommon activities practised in the school that contributed to the achievement of the missions.

Life Skill Education and Leadership Development

Saraswati Puja is celebrated as a festival all over West Bengal. Celebration includes installation of idols, organization of the religious aspect of the puja (worship), decoration of the school, celebration of cultural week and the feast involving all teachers and students. While such celebrations are common in all the schools, what was uncommon here was the way the celebrations were organized. All events were organized by the students. Teachers and the headmaster were invited as guests. A few of the teachers, however, helped in the cultural programme by directing the drama, preparing students for the recitation competition, etc. As a matter of practice, the entire responsibility of such events in the school was with the senior students of the top two grades.

i. They planned all activities in great detail; if necessary, they consulted their respective class teachers.
ii. They prepared the budget and the entire cost of the

celebrations was borne by contributions from the students and the teachers. In order to generate the revenue, they fixed a target of collection from each class with the stepped-up contribution from the lower to the upper grades.

iii. The organizing team was divided into smaller groups of three to four students. Initially, they would visit each class. Keeping in view the target to generate revenue, with the advice of the class teacher, contribution for each student was fixed. While fixing the contribution, the economic background of each student was borne in mind. As a result, students in the same class paid differential contributions. Those, who could, paid higher than the average of the class, whereas those who could not, paid less, or did not pay at all. While fixing the amount of contribution, they also fixed the date. All these were recorded in a temporary hand-made register. The monitor collected the money from his classmates, and handed it over to the organizing committee when they visited the class. As a result, both the monitor and the organizing team monitored the collections regularly, initially once a week and then, daily as the puja drew nearer.

iv. In the night before the puja day, members of the organizing committee involved a few of the old students of the school, and decorated the whole school building. The school wore a festive look. They also installed the idol. On the next day, they fixed the priest, bought fruits, sweets, etc.

v. The invitations for the puja and the cultural festival were circulated to all parents and other members of the community. The students got these done, either handwritten or printed, and distributed it through the students in various classes.

vi. The cultural programme normally consisted of recitation, elocution and theatre. These were also organized by the senior students. This involved not only acting, but also constructing the stage, inviting people to witness the cultural function, etc. Teachers prepared students for such cultural shows.

vii. The feast was a simple community lunch cooked in the school for all the 300-350 students. Students bought vegetables and cereals, cooked, served and cleaned up the premises. Teachers joined the feast as invitees, rather as special guests. Some of the old students made themselves available to work with the students.

viii. Just as the organizing committee mobilized revenue and spent it, so did it maintain expenditure accounts meticulously. They submitted the accounts at the end of the event.

ix. The school celebrated many other functions like Independence Day, Republic Day, etc., though on a comparatively lower scale. The practice was the same: students were the event managers. Teachers were guides or guests.

Such student-managed activities provided them with training in some of the important life skills like planning, budgeting and accounting, management of men and material, managing small and large events. It also built affiliation to the school where they perceived ownership because of the participative process.

Another incident was of great importance. The school was housed in one single hall partitioned into several classrooms. It had no facilities for drinking water, toilets, laboratory, library, etc. One of the classrooms housed the school office, staff room, headmaster's office, and the library partitioned by office almirahs. In this situation, the school received a government grant for the construction of building. The total grant was just enough to construct one all-weather room. However, what resulted out of the grant was a two storeyed building with six all-weather classrooms. This miracle was the outcome of conviction, leadership and concern for the village children.

The headmaster consulted the teachers, local leaders and some of his old students, how to make the best use of the grant received from the government, given the difficult condition of the school. The discussion led to identification of cost of different items like materials, labour, transportation, etc. It was collectively decided that the entire amount of the grant money would be used to purchase the building materials, particularly such items that could not be mobilized from the local community like iron rods, cement, etc. It was decided to mobilize the community's contribution for bricks and sand. Old students offered their services for transportation of material and labour. Some of them worked as labourers. However, they needed a mason so that the building could be constructed with adequate safety. Interestingly, the doctor was a competent mason and he offered to be the second mason. The headmaster became the labour manager and leader. According to the practice in the area, the labourers received wages plus food. As the work started, it took the shape of a festival where current senior students and local old students—more than 100—joined hands with one professional mason and the doctor turned mason. The building was constructed within a short time. As the things started moving, the villagers poured in with eatables like coconut, puffed rice, tea, gur, etc., for the 'labourers'. The cost of the food was completely neutralized. In this festive looking event, not only the headmaster and the doctor were involved but steadily all the teachers got involved, along with their normal teaching work in the school.

In these villages, the road conditions were extremely poor. During the monsoon, most of the village roads were under water; people would walk on a piece of bamboo laid on the bamboo crosses just above the water. The school students reconstructed those roads at the end of every monsoon. Similar festive and sporting spirit could be witnessed when students undertook maintenance of village roads. In all these actions and activities, old students were an inseparable component; they got involved voluntarily without even being called or invited. When the students participated in reconstructing local roads, householders joined and supported them with food and beverages.

Academic Discourses

Another unique activity was the celebration of birthdays of great sons and daughters of the country like Gandhi, Rabindranath Tagore, Subhash Chandra Bose, Vivekananda and others. These functions were also open to the community. There was a serious academic dimension to such events. Teachers, the community leaders, the doctor and the headmaster made a well-orchestrated symposium by presenting the lives and contributions of these great men and women. Quite often, the headmaster and the medical doctor delved into the philosophic aspects of the issues in great depth, at times much beyond the comprehension of the audience. During a discussion, the headmaster mentioned that it was not true that he was not familiar with the difficulty of the audience. He did it with full consciousness and with the purpose of creating an understanding among his students and parents about the nature of academic discourses which the villagers do not have access to. 'This had to be done by the teachers'. His main contention was that such academic discourses were necessary not only for the development of the students, but also for opening up their minds to higher levels of understanding.

Disaster Management

The villages obviously did not have any provision for management of flood and fire, epidemics and other such disasters. It was a conscious decision of the school to take a lead in disaster management. Because of poverty, exceptions apart, all village homes were mud-huts, with thatched roofs. This was equally true of the houses of the headmaster and the other teachers of the school. Fire during summer days, hence, was not uncommon. Whenever there was a fire, the students of the senior classes would rush out along with the teachers and douse the fire with the help of the past students. Floods warranted much greater management skill since it affected large number of villages at the same time. The school building was the only building which could sustain the fury of the flood. Students evacuated the people and housed them in the school building and served them with food and water. This was equally true in the management of epidemics. All these student activities were carefully nurtured as a part of school culture.

The student leadership was utilized for academic management of the institution. A strike was called by the All Bengal Teachers Association (ABTA). This school refrained from joining such strikes since it affected the students. Because of this reputation(!), the leaders of ABTA decided to land into the village and ensure that the teachers join the strike. They spoke with the headmaster; he settled a contract with the leaders that the teachers will join the strike, if the school would not be closed. The leaders of the ABTA were rather baffled, how could a school run when the teachers were on strike. The headmaster pleaded that this to be left to his solution. He argued with his moral conviction that teachers have every right to demand for quality living but students have every right to get their dues. The school functioned full day. On the previous day, the headmaster and a few senior teachers called the monitors of the senior classes and informed them that all the teachers would be on strike. They would stay outside the school. But the school 'must run normally' and the students of the two senior-most classes were to take the classes. The topper of grade X, the highest grade in the school was to act as the headmaster. Students quietly organized themselves and created teams of two's. They created eleven such teams which were equal to the number of the teachers in the school. They prepared the absentee timetable and moved into the classes. They started with the usual prayer, where the monitor of the top grade performed the function of the headmaster and others took over the roles of other teachers. According to the headmaster's instruction, it was not just engaging the classes, the student-teachers had to actually transact curriculum with all sincerity and competence at their disposal.

Situational Pedagogy

Switching over to conventional areas of schooling, namely classroom instruction, the headmaster initiated innovative pedagogical processes, particularly in teaching of english to the rural children. He shared the subject (English) at the top two grades with one or two other teachers. He used to teach one single prose piece, rather drama, in nine long months. The remaining four pieces were taught by him in the remaining fifteen months. Other teachers taught poetry, grammar, translation, etc. He used this particular piece to teach linguistics in an applied situation, rather than teaching it as a drama and literature. Since drama comprises dialogues, it was useful to develop functional skills among the rural children. Also, this particular approach was used to supplement learning of grammar, syntax, etc., in applied situations. This was an important departure from the teaching of the subject in most other schools.

Absentee time table is common in all the schools. The headmaster shared significantly the absentee time table load with other teachers since he had more free periods than the assistant teachers. He shared the load for two main reasons. Firstly, it gave him an opportunity to keep track of the academic aspect of the school in various classes. Secondly, he set standards of teaching. Since he taught every subject very well, some teachers were afraid of being absent, lest the headmaster should take the class and be compared with their teaching skills and competence, by the students.

Some of the other actions and activities were guided by humanitarian considerations. As mentioned earlier, the majority of the school children came from poor homes. They could hardly afford even notebooks and textbooks. The headmaster, with the help of the teachers, decided to make a multiple use of exercise copies and books. They impressed upon the students to write on the exercise copies first in pencil and then with ink pen over the pencil writing. Thus, the same paper could be used twice. The second innovation was about the textbooks. Those days, there were no set government textbooks. Schools were free to prescribe textbooks published by private publishers. Because of the business interest, every school was under pressure to change the books every year. With the consensus of the teachers and the local leaders, the headmaster set guidelines that textbooks should not be changed for five years. His contention was that a textbook could sustain five years of reading; it can pass from one hand to another and serve five batches of students. Thus, at the cost of one textbook, five students can complete their studies. He encouraged the students to pass on all the books to the students of the next class, and those who do not have anyone to pass on, were encouraged to deposit the old books in the Book Bank of the school. The complimentary copies of the textbooks supplied by the book sellers were kept in the library for consultation.

The teachers' salaries were meager; but the more serious problem was that of irregular payment. The payment was made when government grants were received in the school every quarter. The local collections, through token fee or as development fee, were extremely small. Till the quarterly installment was received, teachers used to share their local collection, which often used to be just a few rupees. All teachers, including the headmaster, belonged to poor or lower middle class. Despite their own poor conditions, the school maintained a humane practice. When the annual results were announced, results of many students were withheld because they did not pay their fees, though it was a small amount. Since all the teachers and the headmaster knew the exact financial background of each and every student, they knew that the defaulters would not be able to pay the fees. The headmaster initiated the process of writing off the fees of defaulting students against his own salary. This contribution, every year, amounted to two to three months of his salary. This practice was adopted by other teachers, especially the local teachers, who had been his students. There were occasions when the headmaster took a moral stand that since teachers themselves were ill-paid, they did not need to pay for the students from their own salary. Teachers politely turned down on the ground that the headmaster himself was not in a sound economic condition. This act of empathy and concern for the students was further extended by the headmaster by picking up poor, meritorious students at risk and housing them in his own home, sharing the meager resources like food, clothing, etc., of his own children and other members of the family.

The headmaster learnt and developed a roaring philanthropic (free) homeopathic practice. Literally, his village home would be full of patients every day. They would be his students, teachers or parents of his students. Not only the treatment was free, but medicines were also free—medicines bought by the headmaster. When asked, he responded: "for learning well, they need to have good health. How can I teach them if they are not in good health?" Generally, villagers were in poor health—malnutrition complemented with unscientific health practices. "I had to learn homeopathy to help them manage their health better. The villagers could not afford costly allopathic treatment and medicine." Unlike other local doctors and quacks, the headmaster read extensively and intensively physiology, biochemistry, materia medica, psychology, etc., to prepare himself. He had regular discussion and consultation with the local doctor. He based his treatment on full scientific basis. This was another indication of his social concern and support to students and the community.

Deciding the Strategies

It did not appear that the headmaster had a strategy at all. He worked according to his convictions and his understanding of the needs of the students. The important difference was that he could separate out the developmental needs of the school from those of the parents and the community at large. He hardly ever recognized the boundary between the school and the community. In all major actions like construction of the building, managing the school and teachers strike, he invariably consulted the community leaders and his old students. His basic approach was collecting the ideas for solving the problems and consolidating them in a synthesized manner and putting them on track. While he put it on track, he was hardly ever seen active, except for his personal presence on many occasions.

Managing the Resistance

All his actions for building institution could be classified into three different areas. These were programmes of educational or pedagogical nature, development of life skills and leadership among students and social actions. Because of his overwhelming scholastic stand and his personal relations with the teachers, who were mostly his own students, there was hardly ever any resistance. Because of his seasoned understanding of human psychology, almost like a thought-reader, he counselled the teachers and coached them for better performance, not only in the classrooms, but also on human behaviour.

Similarly, he hardly faced any resistance in achieving his ambition of developing life skills and leadership among the students. Being a rural area with poor economic conditions, manual labour and hardwork of the children and the youth were common. And, these were appreciated much more than the academic or theoretical skills. Also, because everyone was involved, the headmaster often withdrew himself from action, except providing inspiration. He actually mentored leadership, while himself remaining in the background. This involvement of the people and their perceived involvement in the major developmental activities of the school automatically neutralized the resistance.

He, however, faced strong resistance, including outcasting of his own family for social action programmes. Despite being a Hindu brahmin, he practised Sarva Dharma Samabhava. He encouraged the students from both Hindu and Muslim communities to feel equal and share. He encouraged sharing of food by the members of two communities. He practised it right in his own home. This was done at a time, when the caste structure among the village Hindus was very rigid. One example will illustrate the point. The headmaster's daughter wanted to marry a boy from a non-brahmin caste. While there was tremendous resistance from the villagers, he personally stood and solemnized the marriage. The local brahmins outcast his family. Outcasting implies that the barber, the washerman and such other skilled workers will not serve the outcast family. Brahmins, the priests, will not worship and do the rituals in marriages, deaths, etc. Instead of bowing down to these pressures, the headmaster encouraged his children to learn washerman's work and cutting of hair at home. Slowly, the resistance reduced. Such resistances were also visible in the election of the School Managing Committee, organization of school feasts, etc. He simultaneously used his persuasive skills. Although he failed sometimes, he pressed it hard and moved forward. This was, however, possible, because the brahmin community was in a minority compared to non-brahmins and the muslims. Obviously, the majority of the villagers was on his side.

Leadership Style

Although he was in action, he confined himself and lived in the conceptual world. This is important to understand his leadership style. During one of my personal meetings with the headmaster, I asked about his role models and inspiration. He said: "it is a combination of Gandhi, Tagore and Tolstoy". When asked why he needed a synthesis of three such great persons in the world, he mentioned that all of them, despite their greatness, were human beings. Hence, they are achievable. However, 'when you generate an idea which is a synthesis of the three, it is not achievable, but a goal or ambition worth pursuing. What is important is the honest pursuit of the goal, rather than reaching the same'. In a way, he fully subscribed and practised quality (of life) as a life journey.

When Gandhiji died, the headmaster observed a full 13-day mourning. He followed exactly what a son in his community would have followed in the case of death of his own father. When he was asked why he was observing fast and rituals of mourning on the death of Gandhiji, he replied, "If Gandhiji is the Father of the Nation, aren't we all his children? If the father dies, isn't it the duty of the children to observe mourning, praying for his soul to rest in peace? Since I am a part of the nation, he is my father, too."

These two episodes indicate the depth of his life and his living in the conceptual world connected with the divine. He inspired others by opening up his own life as a book to be read by all. In other words, he basically set the pace, without insisting on others to follow him. However, at every opportune moment, he coached and counselled the teachers as well as students and even parents to follow certain basic principles in life. In this pace-setting mechanism, he not only set pace for academic excellence, but also for a strong sense of ethics, values and concern for others over self. The students, teachers and members of the local community not only remembered and adored him, but also sought his guidance and inspiration throughout his life even after his retirement as head of the school.

He practised the inspirational style of leading the school which transcended the local community as well. The inspirational style of leading was strongly backed by his staying in personal excellence. While he expected personal excellence from everyone in the school, he hardly ever insisted that they should follow him as a model. On various occasions, he used coaching and counselling as an important tool for mentoring leadership among the teachers and students.

Learning from the Experience

When Mukhopadhyay was compared with other teachers and headmasters who followed him, his towering presence as a scholar and as an ethical being was evident. As a result, his style of management was much more personal than organisational. Similar management is possible only when a headmaster provides such a towering presence. This was manifest from the slow but steady decline of the quality of schooling, ethics in management and personal conduct in the years that followed.

Although the spirit of his action was not sustainable, because it was more personal than institutional, the practices initiated by him still continue. For example, students are still in the leadership role in every major event and social organization in the school and the community; however, in the earlier situation, teachers, though not prominently, played a proactive role in nurturing the students into the leadership role. Compared to them, the teachers today are much more laissez-faire and are not pro-active in nurturing the students. They have converted themselves into onlookers of student-initiated activities.

Stylistically, the spirit of service was the back-end support and activities were the front-end. Although the front-end has been maintained, there has been a crisis in the back-end of the movement. It has sustained the activities including community involvement in school activities and extended the boundaries of the school as a community centre. This important concept has stayed back, though it has lost much in spirit.

NOTE

1. Also see *Ancient Indian Education: A Plea for Reintroduction as a Liberating Education from the Decadence of our Times* by Late Sri Nrisinha Prasad Mukhopadhyay (A Shipra Publication in 2004).

4
COURAGE OF CONVICTION
SHREYAS HIGH SCHOOL

Shreyas High School, Vadodara is distinguished for some of the world class educational facilities including a cricket academy, a state of the art audio-visual centre and computer centre. It began from a scratch in a hired government godown and then, from the premises of another sister school. Government apathy for the guiding socialist philosophy, local competition, small ambition of people around, ... nothing could deter Rajnikant Jani, the architect of Shreyas. This is the story of institution building through courage of conviction and well-designed strategic interventions.

Early Development

Shri Rajnikant Jani lost his father when he was seventeen. He was then only a matriculate (passed 10th level examination of the Board of Secondary Education, Gujarat). His father was a primary school teacher; the economic background of the family was rather poor. In order to maintain and support his younger brothers, sisters and mother, he had to, as a compulsion, take up petty jobs. After losing his father, he kept on picking up odd jobs, joining different factories and establishments, at remunerations not enough to make the two ends meet. Under such desperate conditions, Rajnikant met his neighbour, principal of Sharada Mandir High School in Baroda. The principal was sympathetic, but because Rajnikant was not adequately qualified, he could not offer him the job of a teacher. He was offered a clerical job in the school. The job got him a foothold, and he was able to fulfil his family responsibility.

Rajnikant was an ambitious young man. His job as a clerk allowed him enough time to pursue his studies further. While working in Sharada Mandir, Rajnikant did his graduation, post-graduation and a degree in law. After working for sometime as a clerk, Rajinikant was offered a teacher's job by Sharada Mandir. The new assignment was satisfying. According to Rajnikant, since he belonged to a teacher's family, teaching came to him naturally. He was, however, very emphatic to go on record that he did not join the profession out of love for teaching. It was the situation which compelled him into teaching. Setting up a new school is the story now.

After completing his education including post-graduation in law, Rajnikant wanted to join MBA in the western California University. For that, he required to be a first class postgraduate in India. He requested the principal of Sharada Mandir for more free time so that he could study better to get first class in the postgraduate programme. The principal of Sharada Mandir, in the interest of the school, could not oblige him. Rajnikant held the principal responsible for not permitting him to go and study in the USA, which was his ambition. This antagonized the principal of Sharada Mandir, who had helped him in a crisis. His poor economic condition stood in the way of nurturing his dream. He recalls the influence of his friend Pandya in the next course of action. Pandya and Rajnikant were once travelling together by train from Mumbai to Baroda. Pandya exhorted him to give up the idea of leaving the country and set up a school instead. The seed of establishing Shreyas School was thus sown.

Because the principal of Sharada Mandir did not sanction leave for studies, which, in Rajnikant's view, stood in his way of realizing the dream of studying in USA, he became a disgruntled teacher in Sharada Mandir. Another 6-7 teachers joined him. Although this was the underlying reason for Rajnikant's dissatisfaction with Sharada Mandir, there was another important reason for him and his colleagues. It was the financial exploitation of the teachers and the high-handedness of the school management.

Meanwhile, Rajnikant came in contact with local leaders of the socialist movement led by late Shri Jai Prakash Narayan, Ram Manohar Lohia, Achyut Patwardhan and others. The local leader of this socialist group was Shri Sanat Mehta, who later became a minister in Gujarat. This exposure to the socialist ideology also could have triggered off his reaction to the exploitation. When he set up the new school, Shreyas, initially, 3-4 other teachers left Sharada Mandir and started working in Shreyas. Rajnikant and another disgruntled teacher continued to be in Sharada Mandir, despite discomfort, for reasons best known to them. The possible reasons were the financial security of service in Sharada Mandir, and the maintenance of a low operational cost of Shreyas School.

The principal, of Sharada Mandir was equally uncomfortable with these disgruntled staff, because, they often became the source of problem. The tension in Sharada Mandir drew the attention of certain other principals in the city. One of them intervened and asked Rajnikant to leave the school and take up Shreyas on a full time basis. Rajnikant heeded his advice, and left Sharada Mandir to take charge of Shreyas, little realizing the struggle ahead.

The major problem of starting a new school was the space. As a matter of coincidence, another school on a private initiative, Jeevan Sadhana, was vacating its premises in the government godown to shift to its new building and campus. Jeevan Sadhana was started by people inspired by socialist thought and was led by Shri Sanat Mehta. In view of the ideological identity, Shri Sanat Mehta allowed Rajnikant to start his new school in the government godown vacated by Jeevan Sadhana. Shreyas commenced its working in 1965 from the government godown. The trouble was waiting. The then Gujarat government was not kind to the socialists. It asked Shreyas to vacate the godown under the pretext that the government needed it. Shreyas management refused to vacate. The Gujarat government filed a petition with the court which, in turn, asked Shreyas to vacate. Not knowing where to go, Rajnikant approached Shri Sanat Mehta. He offered Shreyas the premises of Jeevan Sadhana building in the morning shift. Shreyas was re-born in Jeevan Sadhana campus in the morning shift and Jeevan Sadhana continued in the noon shift—the same campus and the building with two schools under different managements. Rajnikant never missed an opportunity to express his gratitude to Jeevan Sadhana and its leader Shri Sanat Mehta, that not only allowed him the space but also the furniture, equipment and every other facility, almost free of charge. Shreyas was running a Gujarati medium school. In the same building of Jeevan Sadhana, another English medium school Vidya Kunj was also functioning in the morning. Later in 1967, Shreyas started another English medium school as well.

Mission/Conceptual Dimensions

It seems the mission of the school was linked to the beginning of Shreyas and the personal life and experiences of Rajnikant. On the one hand, a sense of achievement through Shreyas against missing the opportunity to study in the USA and on the other hand, the impact of socialist party and thought were important determinants of the nature of the school and its management to be. As mentioned earlier, Shreyas was set up by a group of teachers who came out of Sharada Mandir and one of the reasons for dissatisfaction was their financial exploitation. As a reaction, Shreyas was set up as a school "by the teachers, for the teachers", where teachers could not be exploited and would also enjoy job security. Teachers were at the helm of management of the institution. Accordingly, when the Trust was registered, all the teachers were members of the Trust. There was no industrialist or businessman on the Trust board, as it was customary with other schools in the city. Accordingly, the mission was to set up a school that did not exploit teachers; a school by the teachers where the teachers did not have to worry about security of service and financial security of their family, so that they could devote their full time and concentrate on the education of children.

Related to the concerns of exploitation and security of service of teachers, the second mission was to create a school that did not generate personal profits for the members of the Trust, which was, otherwise, common with the private schools in Gujarat. This was primarily to ensure that the vested interests did not take control of the school and hamper its growth and development.

The third mission was to create a school of distinction, with excellent facilities. Since a majority of the institutions suffer from paucity of facilities, which becomes a serious problem for its quality and development, Shreyas' mission was to set up a school with first-rate facilities in every department of the school. Interestingly, all the articulated missions were woven around the management of the school—its nature being defined by management parameters.

Strategies and Actions

The teachers looked for three inter-related benefits in Shreyas. Firstly, they wanted security. This was assured by their involvement as member Trustees of Shreyas Education Trust. The second important demand was participation in the management. To fulfil this ambition, Shreyas introduced 'Headmastership' by rotation, so that everybody had an opportunity to participate in the management of the school, but within the prescribed norms of Gujarat government. Thirdly, the teachers needed additional income or financial support to manage their families, particularly, since the school had decided to ban private tuition, and not to share the surplus earnings with the trustees. As a strategy, Shreyas initiated an English medium school in 1967. The English medium school charged slightly higher fees than the Gujarati medium school. The teachers in the Gujarati medium school were drafted for teaching in the English medium school too, on extra payment. This compensated their need for additional earning. Also, this enhanced their self-respect that they could teach in the English medium school. Further, there was a demand for sharing of power and becoming the principal of the school by rotation, Rajnikant discussed with all the Trustee teachers about the legal requirements for recognition of the Board and approval by the government. According to the required qualifications, Rajnikant was the only person with the postgraduate qualification. Hence, he was the solitary qualified contender for the post of principal. Only when Rajnikant retired, another teacher could become the principal of the school.

As mentioned earlier, because of the socialist background, the school had all along a tussle with the state government. It took almost 10 years to get into the good books of the government. Two important strategies adopted by Rajnikant seem to have worked to bring down the animosity of the state government. Firstly, Shreyas ensured that the education provided to the students was of high quality. This emphasis was a part of both the mission and the strategy. The high quality education creates a supportive community of parents; it builds a new culture and reputation. Parents' opinion matters even for the political masters. The second important strategy was involving eminent educationists of Baroda and Gujarat with the school. For example, Rajnikant involved, among others, Prof. M B Buch, the undisputed educational leader of his time. On the one hand, with their advice, the school found quicker ways of building quality of education; on the other hand, their reputation became a stumbling block for the government to harass the school. The end-result of the struggle was recognition of Rajnikant by the state government. He was selected and nominated by the Gujarat government for the National Award of Best Teachers. This was both a recognition of Rajnikant as an individual and of Shreyas as an institution.

There were series of other actions that contributed to the growth of the institution. One major effort was developing a mechanism for monitoring and managing learning. The main approach was to administer tests to students at the end of a unit, a month and other periodicities. The results of the tests were to examine the students from more than one angle. The conventional use was to provide a feedback to the students on their performance. The next use was diagnosis. But the most unconventional and innovative use was to diagnose teacher competence and effectiveness in dealing with the subjects. The step that followed was providing remedial learning for improving the general performance of every student. Instead of carrying it out in an informal or casual manner, the entire range of activities took a formal shape. Shreyas established a Research and Development Cell to conduct and manage these activities. The professionals in the cell carried out analysis of the data under the active advice and guidance of academicians like Prof. Buch; records were maintained carefully. The primary concern was ensuring learning among the children.

There was something unusual in this school. In a small city like Baroda, the school created some world-class infrastructure, which is rare to find anywhere in the country. One such facility is its Computer Department. About 15 years ago, Prof. M B Buch, a member of the Board of Trustees of the Shreyas Education Trust advised the school to introduce computer education. The main agenda was that every student in the school must not only be familiar, but also be skilled in utilizing computer as part of the life skill. Initially, the computer education was introduced from standards III to VII; subsequently, to standards VIII to X and then to standards XI and XII. While computer education is common in almost all schools today, what is different here is its approach, beginning with the junior grades. With a sound logic and argument that as they grow up, they are continuously and consistently exposed to higher and newer skills in computing. The other new feature is the infrastructure. The computer lab is housed in 2900 sq. ft. area with 40 sets of computers which were upgraded to a new generation computer system based on client/server architect consisting of 100 clients/nodes connected with a server. The lab supports education of 5,277 students. It has all the possible accessories and modern gadgets. The computer lab was built at a cost of Rs. 30 lakhs. The lab is open and available to everyone from 7.30 a.m. till 5.30 p.m.

Another important modern facility is the Audio-Visual Room. Again, audio-visual rooms with certain facilities are common in many of the private schools in the country. The difference is in the quality of the hardware and more so, the quantity and quality of educational softwares. Without getting into the details of the list of hardware, it would be enough to say that almost every possible equipment is available in multiple numbers in the school. It has over a period of time developed a stock of several thousand educational software in video and CD-ROM. These audio-visual facilities are available for the use of teachers and students. Also, it is possible for the teachers to take the equipment and the software into the classes.

The third most significant infrastructure is the Shreyas Cricket Academy. I was given to understand that it is the second best Cricket Academy, next to that in Bangalore. Of course, it is unique for any school in India. This was inspired possibly because of the fact that the ace Indian wicket keeper Kiran More was a student of this school. Baroda has also produced a couple of other world class cricketers like Anshuman Gaekwad. The Academy has turf wicket, close circuit camera for observing the stance and actions of the batsmen and bowlers, a mini pavilion to watch, a Gymnasium for fitness management, theory room with books as well as media material for the budding cricketers to read and enrich. Beyond this physical infrastructure, it has several coaches and consultants, including Kiran More himself.

The interesting story behind this world-class infrastructure is its inspirational philosophy derived from the socialists. As mentioned earlier, it was decided right in the beginning when Shreyas was being established, that it would not be a commercial enterprise; surplus revenue as profits would not be shared among the members of the Board of Trustees, which is, otherwise, common in the privately managed schools. In order to remain competitive and not be looked down upon Shreyas charged the same amount of fee as charged by other private schools. But in Rajnikant's own analysis, there was a difference between the cost of education and the fee charged. The difference was Rs. 100 per student in Gujarati medium and Rs. 200 in English medium. This difference generated a substantial amount of extra revenue for the school. A major question was: what to do with this excess? If it was put in a bank, it would accumulate to a huge amount, which was not necessary to provide security to the teachers and the school. On the contrary, it might attract the trustees to share the money, defeating the very mission of the school and its socialistic objectives. It learnt the trick from its own experience.

The school was originally started, as mentioned earlier, in a government godown. When it was moved out, it took shelter in Jjeevan Sadhana. Since the Trust did not have any industrialist or businessman and all the trustees were teachers, there was no easy access to resources for infrastructure development. Shreyas had to use its own resources, derived primarily out of student fees to construct the building. The building came up in phases, depending upon the availability of funds. But all that money management and development of the school building was carefully and efficiently planned. This experience of money management was important and came handy to the development of world-class facilities. Despite its reputation in the city, as a matter of principle, Shreyas did not charge higher fees from students compared to other schools in the city. In order to maintain its social parity with others, it could not charge less either. Since the difference between revenue and expenditure was not shared by the trustees, there was a surplus accumulating each month. The Trust ploughed back the revenue into development of its own infrastructure. This was justified in simple logic that 'it is students' money, they pay for it, and have every right to have world-class facilities'. This served a dual purpose. It kept the trustees away from sharing the surplus and maintain the management principle on which the school was started; and the school built world class facilities.

Management of Resistance

Although many of these institution building experiences appear to be smooth, they go through a series of resistance management experiences. Shreyas' experience was not different. Sometimes, resistance was being managed successfully, sometimes, the programmes had to be withdrawn.

Its first teething trouble was from the state government. Moving out of the government godown, seeking refuge at Jeevan Sadhana, which was already hosting two schools, is a significant and successful experience in resistance management.

Shreyas began an R&D Cell, an unusual activity for a school of its kind for management of learning. The data that was generated shed light on the performance of teachers, although that was not the objective. This was resisted by the teachers in many ways. The effort in managing learning was also affecting their private tuition market. For assessing the paper of every test, teachers were paid an amount of Rs. 5 or 10 which made a significant amount of earning but it also amounted to monitoring and management learning. Some teachers criticized it, some sabotaged it by not doing the job properly. Finally, the project had to be shelved because it was not fulfilling its purpose. And, R&D Cell was dismantled.

Similarly, though there was a well-developed infrastructure of audio-visual aids, actual transformation of the classroom was not perceptible. The classroom instructions continued to be as conventional as they used to be in the early years of Shreyas without such facilities. On the contrary, the school seemed to have lost the enthusiasm of the teachers.

This is, however, not true when it comes to the Computer Centre and the Cricket Academy. Computer Centre is continuously on high demand from the students. However, the response of the teachers was again not encouraging. Cricket Academy is very popular and on demand. There is a general pattern so far as these innovations are concerned. Innovations that were directly related to the students' lives are highly appreciated, adopted and internalized. Innovations that influence teachers' lives, particularly, their vested interests like additional income through private tuition, or demand of additional and unconventional work are resisted.

In the initial phase, all the teachers were recruited by the Trust.

However, at a later stage, with the change in the rules and provisions by the Gujarat government, all such privately run schools had to appoint teachers recruited by the government. Since Shreyas was a government aided school, it had to fall in line with government rules and regulations. Many of the teachers brought with them the normal culture of being overprotected by the government provisions, coupled with an attitude of not working and even shirking work. As a result of this, the school faced serious problems. In order to handle this new generation problem, Rajnikant, initially as a principal, then, also as chairman of the Management Trust, after his retirement, took a rather strong stance. To cite one example, there was a good, and popular physics teacher. He was busy throughout the day and late in the night in private tuitions, earning a huge amount of money. When he reached the school, he was exhausted and drained of. His practice was to hide in the dark room of the Audio Visual Centre, arrange a couple of chairs in a row and sleep. He was identified, confronted and served notice. During the discussion with Rajnikant, a mix of frustration along with enthusiasm could be noticed.

Leadership Style

This school with good quality and some of the world-class infrastructure, which could be built from the scratch indicates the leadership style of Shri Rajnikant. Although there were several mechanisms indicating a democratic, participative process, his goals were fixed and people had to contribute and adhere to the organizational goals. There were not enough points to differ with Rajnikant; to that extent his style was that of directing. Secondly, despite resistance, he protected the ideals of the school set up with socialist philosophy and thoughts thus, deriving appreciation and admiration from his colleagues, friends and students. Yet, he was uncompromising. It was a curious mix of admiration and discomfort of his colleagues coming together.

His emphasis on productivity is another important attribute of leadership. He was uncompromising also with regard to work targets and quality. As mentioned earlier, he consulted and associated several educationists and managers of education systems of repute in the city with the school. Together, they generated a collective leadership of a different genre where a majority of the people was not employees of the Shreyas Education Trust. The eminence and reputation of these individuals provided a new set of unwritten rules and statutes to the school.

Rajnikant, by his own admission, changed his leadership style, coping with changes in the social milieu for more than three decades. "I have changed my leadership behaviour. I have developed tolerance. But now I understand that there is a limit to tolerance. The period for tolerance is over. So, now I have become somewhat harsh, but my harshness is with modesty, love and affection. These are in my favour and the results are good."

Learning from Experience

There are several important lessons for Rajnikant. Although the philosophic inspiration that laid the foundation of the institution was socialist thoughts, it was not easy to orient and convince all the stakeholders to such kinds of thoughts. Since the sharing of the profit was banned, teachers demanded alternative sources of earning. The English medium school was started primarily to provide a second channel of earning to the teachers. Rising above self is much easier said than done. The school went through several phases of difficulty. A slightly weaker determination would have slipped Rajnikant off his feet and students to give up the endeavor. The patience and determination, coupled with important strategy planning, helped his entire effort survive. Through strategic intervention, good intention and efficient management of money, it is possible to create high-quality infrastructure; but that does not necessarily ensure the change of attitudes and values of the teachers to make use of such facilities and get involved in the quality. The democratic leadership is an admirable phenomenon and a process, but it cannot be the panacea for all situations. In the interest of the institution, it may sometimes be necessary to adopt a harsh and directorial style of leadership. In a summative estimate, it is difficult to classify the effort that has gone into the building of this institution as either success or failure. There are definite indicators and stories of success; but they could have been more and better.

5
BUILDING CASTLE FROM THE RUBBLES
Bharatiya Vidya Bhavan

Vidya Bhavan, Delhi, was facing some serious problems when Dr. M P Chhaya was called upon to take charge of the institution by the authorities of the Bharatiya Vidya Bhavan. He took it up as a challenge. Banking on his long experience as a teacher in a residential school and as principal in a leading school in Delhi, he set out to chart a new chapter for Vidya Bhavan by involving teachers, students and parents in policy making, planning and managing the school. A large number of participative innovations changed the enthusiasm and culture of the institution. This story captures the spirit and the actions that brought success; Bhavan was no more struggling for existence. It was much beyond—a quality school to reckon with.

Early Development

Dr. Mandlik P Chhaya lost his father at the age of 10. His father, an honest, God-fearing, and hardworking person was Mandlik's role model till then. He encouraged Mandlik to be independent in his daily chores as his mother looked after her two younger daughters.

He recollected how his parents treated him, when he, as a young child, stole 25 paise coin to buy some sweets, which left an indelible mark in the genesis of his personality and character. 'They called me and without losing temper gave me lots of sweets.' I told them "I cannot eat that much." They said to me that there was no need of searching a coin to buy the sweets. That was an important message. Mandlik apologized and his lesson of honesty started.

After the death of his father, Mandlik's mother took charge of the family and asked Mandlik to help her look after his sisters and their studies. He started sharing responsibilities with his mother. As the family shifted to his grandparents' house, he learnt to share with his cousins and nieces, some of whom were younger to him. He helped his cousins in studies; Mandlik believes that the seed of love for teaching was probably sown then. His grandfather's principles had a tremendous impact on him, in conducting himself with dignity and decency in the family.

Motivation for the Job

Mandlik worked in Rajkumar College, a 100-year old residential school, in Rajkot, for 17 long years. As a teacher in a residential school, with all his enthusiasm and love for teaching and students, he participated and assisted students in a variety of co-curricular activities including sports and games, hobby clubs, etc. Instead of being a usual one-dimensional teacher, Mandlik learnt to be an all-rounder. He served Mother's International School, of Sri Aurobindo Ashram, Delhi for two years as principal. Unlike Rajkumar College, this school was guided by Sri Aurobindo's spiritual, cultural and educational philosophy. As a good learner, Mandlik had a new and important orientation of education here with certain higher values. Also, he tasted success as a principal here.

Dr. K M Munshi, the founder president of Bharatiya Vidya Bhavan asked him to join Bhavan at Vadodara. But, then some problems were there at the Bhavan's school in Delhi. So he invited Mandlik to Mumbai and asked him to take up the school in Delhi and improve it. Dr. Munshi mentioned that the task was challenging. Mandlik accepted the assignment also because there was challenge in it. He joined Bhavan's school in 1969 and worked till 1987. He welcomed crisis as an opportunity. To overcome the crisis, he initiated a number of innovations and experiments.

Vision

Mandlik's vision was to develop the school as a (man-making) centre for development of human qualities in the students. His total focus was on all-round development of students with human values, self-discipline, leadership qualities, etc. Associated visions were modernization of classroom instruction, capacity building of teachers, involvement of parents, teachers and students in school management for achieving excellence. Probably, influenced by his experience in Rajkumar College, he wanted to create the ambience and programmes of a residential school in a day school.

His past experience in the two schools shaped his vision of development for the Bhavan. At Rajkumar College, he learnt how to integrate the co-curricular activities in the school curriculum. From Mothers' International School and visits of Sri Aurobindo Ashram, Pondicherry, and personal discussion with The Mother, he learnt about integral education and the integrated development of the child and how to build it up in the school programme. During these 20 years, he had been exposed to many Indian public schools, in particular the Doon School, where he spent a month for a physics course and a few schools in Europe in 1965. Mother's International School was also an experimental school of NCERT. When he was the principal, Mandlik came in close contact with the experts of NCERT for the new experiments and projects for the classroom teaching. The most significant influence was that of eminent educationist, Dr. M B Buch, one of the leading experts in NCERT, who was my guide for all the new experiments we did in Bharatiya Vidya Bhavan.

Strategic Planning

Mandlik did not seem to have a strategic plan in the usual sense of the term. He had no well-researched blue-print. He had a clear vision, gut feeling and courage to experiment, backed by his rich experience. His focus was on developing his students in the physical, mental, intellectual and spiritual domains with values of Indian culture, patriotism and universal outlook.

Accordingly, the instructional strategies were reconstructed to include cooperative learning projects and problem-solving activities, discussion, role play, inquiry, decision-making, etc. Conventional classroom lecture was reduced to the minimum; wherever necessary, classroom lectures were supported with educational technology.

For development of non-cognitive skills, a comprehensive plan was developed comprising activities including outdoor games, indoor games, athletics, yoga, NCC, scouts and guides and adventurous activities, house system, debates, recitation, declamation, music, dance, painting, clay modeling, dramatics, band, celebrations of religious, national and cultural festivals, creative crafts, class magazine, wall magazine, school magazine, etc.

Programmes and activities such as performing manual work individually and collectively, acquaintance with the world of work and community services, participation in productive work and for vocational preparedness were also introduced.

Programmes and activities such as morning assembly, nature study, study of philosophy of major religions, reading of biographies and autobiographies, stories from various scriptures, devotional songs, meditation, yoga, exposure to real life situations, satsang, caring and sharing of activities, activities for developing civic sense, narration of real life experiences and examples from practical life, self-assessment and evaluation, taking cognizance of strengths and weaknesses of the self, constant self-correction and improvement, practising values in school environment, etc., were introduced for moral development.

Leadership development was achieved through a three-tier leadership training, in the school, in the classroom, and at the house level. There were four monitors in each class—one boy monitor and one assistant boy monitor, one girl monitor and one assistant girl monitor. They were changed every month, so that every student got a chance to be a monitor in a year. There were twelve house captains in each house—one boy and one girl each as captain, assistant captain, cultural captain, assistant cultural captain, game captain, and assistant game captain. Half of them might be changed at the end of every year, so that continuity might remain and many students would get leadership training. At the school level, the leaders were school prefects. They were appointed from the final year class. They did not belong to any house and they were to control and guide the activities of the whole school. The various leaders at the school level were head boy, head girl, assistant head boy, assistant head girl, cultural boy prefect and cultural girl prefect, assistant cultural boy prefect, assistant cultural girl prefect, sports boy prefect, sports girl prefect, assistant sports boy prefect, assistant sports girl prefect.

Students participated in all activities through houses and they were guided and controlled by the house captains and school prefects under the guidance of the teachers. They were also included in various school committees with the teachers. This gave them the highest exposure to day-to-day running of the school.

Although the school premises are generally used for six hours a day, Bhavan initiated a large number of activities like music (vocal and instrumental),- various types of dances, painting, clay modeling (ceramics), photography, commercial art, dramatics and theatre art, home science crafts, typing, shorthand, computer science, yoga, scripture classes, foreign languages, management classes, craft classes, coaching classes for various games and sports, coaching classes for all India competitive tests, etc., after school hours. Faculty members were hired from the school staff as well as from outside on part-time or hourly basis. Bhavan offered diplomas after completion of the course.

An important element of development of Bhavan was development of teachers through their involvement in decision-making. Every month at least one staff meeting was conducted. Agenda of the meeting was circulated well in advance. Fair and frank discussions among the staff members were encouraged leading to collective decision-making and ownership among the staff members.

Regular minutes of every meeting were maintained and circulated to every member of the staff. Suggestions given by the majority of the staff members were actively considered by the principal for implementation. Staff meeting was a vital mechanism for revitalization of the school organisation. This involved the staff and reduced most of the confrontations with them.

The regular weekly or monthly meeting was designed as an effective way to improve instruction. Emphasis was more on frequent departmental or small group meetings to deal with specific tasks concerning group members. To make the meetings focused, agenda was developed jointly by the faculty and the principal. The all-inclusive faculty meetings were a necessary part of the school and they sometimes exceeded one per month. It provided Mandlik with an opportunity to promote esprit de corps among teachers to feel part of the overall school effort. Innovations were introduced through the faculty meetings; it provided a clearing-house for the exchange of ideas and gave the faculty an opportunity to participate in curriculum and other policy matters of the school.

School-based In-service Education

It was difficult to provide in-service training to all the staff by sending teachers to outside agencies. Instead, Bhavan planned school-based in-service programmes for all teachers spread throughout the year, according to the convenience of the school, one-and-a-half hour to half-a-day each time. It covered a variety of subjects like improvement of school programmes, innovation in classroom teaching, professional development of teachers, improvement in school administration, etc. These programmes were handled by the staff members themselves, invited experts from outside, etc. The detailed training programmes were prepared well in advance in the beginning of the year so that all were aware about their responsibilities and of the need to be prepared.

In scheduling such programmes, participants' convenience and availability were also seen. One solution to the problem was to provide released time for the training sessions by devoting an afternoon of a given day in each month to the in-service programme. Another practice was to extend the school year by reducing vacations or by simply adding more working days to the school calendar.

A special staff meeting used to be organized every year. In this meeting, teachers were asked to identify various functions of the principal and competencies required to run the school effectively. Brain-storming sessions were conducted in this meeting. The ideas generated were recorded on the chalk board; these were then grouped into various categories such as administrative functions, financial functions, managerial functions, day-to-day functions, etc.

Teachers were divided into teams to work for each of these functions. There were different committees comprising 2 to 3 teachers. They met periodically, discussed how to perform the function and how to develop the competency required for better functioning of the school. They maintained the minutes of their meetings. The minutes books were retained with the principal for follow up action.

Every year, a few members were rotated among different committees so that, in some years, they would have the experience of handling various functions of the principal. This involved the whole staff in running the school; they developed professionally and their leadership skills were honed.

Creche

Lady staff members of the school faced problems of looking after their infants at home while they were on duty at school. They were under tension and could not give their best in the class. To solve this problem, Bhavan set up a creche in the school premises in a well-ventilated small room, equipped with necessary things to look after small babies. Social work department looked after the creche. A trained aaya was employed; the expenditure was shared by the teachers who used the facility. Teachers could visit their children during their free periods.

Parent-Teacher Association

Bhavan involved parents in school management by organizing parent-teacher meetings regularly. This built a bridge between parents and teachers for better understanding of each other's problems. Parents were useful in collecting the funds for new projects, strengthening library, organizing school functions, social service activities, arranging educational excursions and tours, career guidance, placement of students, etc. They were not allowed to interfere with the school administration and management, but were actively involved in the developmental activities of the children.

Taking the People Along

Teachers, parents and students were allowed to visit the principal freely in their allotted time slots. In the staff meeting, parents meeting, prefects and monitors meeting, there were open and frank discussions; there was an environment of give and take, no snubbing at any stage.

It took sometime initially to create such an environment. Whenever something went wrong, the practice was to sit down together and thrash out the differences of opinion. If the principal himself was found wanting, he would accept and mend his ways. There were occasions when several meetings were required to sort out the problems. There were frank, one-to-one talks as well. This worked so well that Mandlik never had to use punishment or threat to any staff member any time. The bottomline was a value system right from administrative staff to teachers and parents.

Managing Resistance

When any new thing is introduced the resistance is likely to be from management, teachers or parents. Before introducing an innovation, Mandlik used to plan it at his level first and anticipate the possible resistances. To overcome these resistances from any quarter, the principal used to call the meeting of the teachers and explain the new idea and examine their pros and cons before implementation. There was an open discussion, where every teacher was asked to express his/her views. With due modifications and consensus, planning for implementation was done. Everybody felt that they were implementing their own new idea. Then, it was taken to the management and after considering their views, it was placed before the school PTA executive body. After amending the proposal, if needed, it was sent to the parents in the form of a circular. There was hardly any resistance after going through this process. All the old and new programmes were regularly evaluated at the end of every year; and with any amendments needed, they were introduced in the next academic year.

Leadership Style

Mandlik's leadership style was democratic in developing new programmes and working methods, but firm (autocratic) in implementation. He built harmonious teams and mentored strong human relationship. He personally practised and demonstrated human values and self-discipline. He maintained himself as a learner.

An event would depict Mandlik's undisputed leadership in the school. There was some difference between Mandlik and the management of Bhavan with the change of its director. Mandlik resigned from the stewardship of the school. Not only teachers and students went on strike, but also the parents joined in boycotting the school—'no child without Mandlik as principal'. Mandlik's own appeal to parents and teachers not to harm education of the students did not yield results. The management had to backtrack.

There are several factors that shaped his leadership style, e.g., struggle for survival in early childhood, nurturance in a joint family, role models among elders. Other influences were from his working life and experience. As a life long learner he made the best use of the opportunities that came before him.

Success and Failure

Education is a slow process and its growth is not easily visible in the initial stages. It takes about two years of meticulous planning, scrutinizing, implementation, evaluation and refining wherever needed. Mandlik got positive feedback from the third year onwards. He was highly successful in whatever small or big innovative programmes that were implemented. The feedback from students, teachers, parents, management and the community was very positive and encouraging. Bharatiya Vidya Bhavan school progressed significantly during those 18 years. Students' population grew from 600 to 2400. There was hardly any turnover of the members of the staff in the last 15 years. Nine of its senior teachers were selected as principals in reputed schools in India and gulf countries. Bhavan staff members were invited as resource persons in various schools, subject associations, CBSE and NCERT. Students who passed out from this school were highly successful not only in academics, but also in their personal life with their value system and character.

His success was recognized when Mandlik was invited to join as an educational advisor to Navodaya Vidyalaya Samiti, government of India and was told that his work in Bharatiya Vidya Bhavan was responsible for that offer.

His Learnings

To build an institution, Mandlik summarized his learnings in the following terms:

- Be democratic in taking the decisions and autocratic in implementation.
- Take the people together, making them into a harmonious team, working just like a joint family.
- Maintain strong human relationship.
- Be open-minded.
- Believe and practise human values, and, therefore, be self-disciplined.
- Be a lifelong learner.
- Active involvement of staff members and delegation of powers.
- Involve parents as partners in school development.

6

WAKING UP THE SLEEPING GIANT

National Open School of India[1]

National Open School (NOS) was established in 1989 for providing educational opportunity to youth and adults who could not take the advantage of the conventional formal schooling. The NOS has been functioning as a large school, though it has a qualitatively different potential. Based on a meticulous SWOT, the chairman provided a new vision to NOS to emerge as a national resource centre for promoting open schooling in all Indian languages through state-level open schools. It dreamt of carving out a leadership position for India in open schooling in the world. This story brings out the strategies of collective visioning representing national and international ambitions capacity building of staff, building process capabilities through a series of internal reorganization and interventions. Just as the benefit of NOS has spread to every nook and corner of this large country through programmes in various regional languages, the institution has also emerged as a key player in open schooling in the international arena. It was singled out for its being highlighted in the report of International Commission on Education for 21st Century by UNESCO.

The Assignment

My first induction to open education was through a magazine, 'Pratyayan'. The Editor of the magazine, I guess, invited my teacher Dr. M B Buch to contribute a paper on open education. Dr. Buch asked me to contribute, and I did. This was sometime in early 1970s. Little did I realize then that I would have the opportunity to work in open education at national and international levels. My second induction to the subject was in the All India Association for Educational Technology (AIAET), at the instance of Prof. S S Kulkarni, who is regarded as the father of educational technology in India, where open and distance education are important areas of activity; and I had the privilege of leading AIAET as general secretary and president for eight years. I made sincere efforts to learn the subject; edited a few titles and authored a few addresses and papers. I was exposed to some of the stalwarts in educational technology and distance education in India and the world. The effect was both humbling and inspiring. The novelty of the endeavour and the challenge in the field attracted me.

I joined NIEPA with my specialization in educational management in 1983. I was keen to relate my interest and budding specialization in distance eduçation and specialization in management, organizational behaviour, in particular. With the encouragement of the then director of NIEPA, Prof. Satya Bhushan, I conducted several programmes on planning and management of distance education for the directors of the institutes of correspondence courses in the conventional universities in the mid-1980's. We also conducted programmes on research in distance education. These programmes and research activities in distance education deepened my interest in this new venture. NIEPA opened a full-fledged department on educational technology and distance education, which I was asked to head. I was still not exposed to open schooling that was slowly taking shape.

My first exposure to open schooling was when Fr. T V Kunnunkal, the then chairman of National Open School invited me to present a paper at a SAARC Conference in Open Schooling at India International Centre, New Delhi. The deliberations in the conference left an indelible impression on me about the social need and relevance of open schooling with its tremendous potential for delivering quality education to all those who remain deprived of educational facilities for a variety of reasons, across the SAARC countries.

Accepting the Assignment

Against the backdrop of my exposure to open education mentioned above, let me recount the situation that led me to the assignment as chairman of National Open School. My early school education represents the typical Indian school education scenario—less than 25 per cent of the students admitted in grade I reach grade X, and less than 50 per cent succeed to get through the Board examination; about 87.5 per cent of them drop out before completing their secondary education. In my case, only four out of 40 of us in grade sixth (I began my schooling in sixth grade only) survived our village schooling and sailed through the board examination. Surprisingly, out of the 'surviving four', I am what I am, another is now a British citizen and world famous medical scientist and AIDS Consultant. Being a villager with intense relationships among families, leave alone classmates, I knew all those who dropped out at great depths. For, we grew up together. Many of my classmates who are now rickshaw pullers, bus conductors, farmers or barbers had no dearth of talent. One classmate who stood first in our class, till the seventh standard, completed his schooling only as a school drop-out, and became a refrigeration mechanic. There are innumerable such cases. No, it was not economic condition alone; there were important 'schooling' and 'neighbourhood' factors that contributed much more to the phenomenon of dropping out at a stage when they were themselves not decision makers.

By extrapolation, I liked to believe that I knew all those who dropped out of the Indian school system. It is a large untapped potential with alarming underachievement! I felt that NOS was designed for people like my classmates and friends who were either unsuccessful in the traditional educational system, or had to leave due to a variety of schooling and neighbourhood compulsions.

Fr. Kunnunkal, the first chairman of NOS and a member of the Search Committee appointed by government of India, asked me if I would be interested in the assignment. It was challenging, it was attractive—heading a national institution meant for millions of school drop-outs like those who were my own 'classmates'! Further, the NOS was structured with endless autonomy—chairman was head of the society, the policy making body, and head of the Finance Committee and Executive Committee. Chairman was also the chief executive. Hence, he/she got full authority and responsibility for everything from policy making to implementation. It is a very rare phenomenon in Indian institutions.

I had a discussion with the Search Committee, chaired by Prof. G Ram Reddy, a doyen of open education, the then chairman of UGC. During the discussion, I elaborated on my vision as to what could be done with such an institution. I guess it impressed the Committee; it recommended my name to the Appointments Committee of the Cabinet (ACC).

I was invited in 1992 by the Appointments Committee of the Cabinet of the government of India to chair NOS for a three year term—1993 to 1996. At the same time, I was also selected for the prestigious Ravi Mathai Chair at the Indian Institute of Management, Ahmedabad. This position was more attractive in terms of status and salary. I shared my dilemma with Sri S V Giri, the then education secretary to the Government of India. His advice to me was, "With your value systems and your concern for the rural poor, I feel, you will enjoy working and shaping the National Open School more, and through it, serving the cause of many, 'your friends' too". So, I decided to take up immediately the less attractive, but more challenging work with NOS.

My Vision for NOS

The first director, Prof. O S Dewal had laid a solid academic foundation to the open schooling with scientifically developed instructional material. Fr. Kunnankal, had provided a systemic structure to NOS, as it was separated from CBSE that carefully nurtured the school at its embryonic stage with Dr. Dewal at the leadership position. With these two leadership contributions, NOS was already functioning as a nation-wide school, designing curriculum, preparing course material, conducting examinations and certifying. And, its enrolment was growing every year. My acquaintance with NOS, though limited, gave me the perception that it was working as one of the other 100,000 schools, though on a massive scale, offering programmes through distance education. For me, it was a sleeping giant—an institution with tremendous potentiality to transform life of the millions. Not by directly delivering education, but by being instrumental in generating a movement, a network. I saw the need and potential to develop NOS as a national institution of open learning that could act as a laboratory or a resource centre for quality open schooling. I also believed, we could build an open learning movement at the school level by developing a network of state open schools through which learners could learn through their mother tongue, and that we could become the largest open school and the world leader in the field. Such a vision might be construed as a personal ambition rather than an institutional vision. However, except for the international dimension, this vision was actually a synthesis of statements and recommendations by various Indian committees and commissions appointed by government of India from time to time.

Systems theory teaches us the critical importance of the environment in which systems are set. NOS, and specially I, was fortunate. At that time, the University Grants Commission was headed by the legendary distance educator, professor G Ram Reddy. Education secretary; Shri S V Giri, was also a strong supporter of open schooling. The Education Division of the Planning Commission was headed by Dr. Chitra Naik, an educator of great stature, committed to the cause of education of the deprived and the poor. The positioning of these three dynamic people at the three most strategic positions in the government provided the most congenial external environment for optimizing the internal capabilities of the open schooling venture.

Stepping Stones

As soon as I joined the NOS, in 1993, I reviewed all the reports of the various committees and commissions referring to NOS, and also examined all the internal documentation and operations relating to the setting up of NOS in 1989 as an autonomous organization, in pursuance of the 1986 National Policy on Education by the Ministry of Human Resource Development, government of India. The findings were rather unnerving. There were clear mismatches between the expectations and operating realities. The expectations were that the NOS would function as a leader in open learning. In practice, it restricted itself to the delivery of courses and conduct of examinations like any other school. The courses were comparable to those in conventional institutions and the instructional material rich in content and structuring. However, the production quality was poor.

The tutors, the lowest level of academic staff, were bright young men and women with consistent first class academic career, almost all of them. They consistently performed well, despite being poorly paid. But the heads of departments were weak—academically as well as managerially. The organization itself was weakly structured by placing the academic staff at a low level.

The Open School had been experimented with since 1979 as a project of the Central Board of Secondary Education (CBSE) and was later amalgamated with the NOS. NOS comprised three departments: academic, examinations and administration, but it was still perceived by the staff primarily as an examining body, as a legacy of its birth in the CBSE, which is an examining body. There was a total absence of research and development activities. It was almost impossible to monitor the quality of education and also that of the examinations. As a consequence, despite being comparable in academic standards, NOS qualifications were not recognized for admission by many conventional universities, though my predecessor had made a beginning in this direction. I thus faced the need for structural and process interventions, resistance in the organization, and a requirement to take risks.

I felt there was sufficient solid ground to build upon and we drew up a plan that envisaged NOS facilitating the establishment of 20 state open schools, offering programmes through regional languages and the NOS itself becoming a National Institute of Open Learning[2] with a strong research and development base to provide professional support to the state open schools. A draft document on the proposed NIOS was developed by a Committee chaired by Dr. Chitra Naik, and Prof. G Ram Reddy, Sri S V Giri and Prof. Ram G Takwale, the then vice-chancellor of YCMOU as members. I was member-convenor of the Committee. We began our journey by 'redrawing the map' in the minds of NOS staff. Slowly but steadily, the academic staff embraced the new vision, and NOS administration followed suit. The NOS examinations department, however, was recalcitrant and it proved a tough nut to crack.

Strategies for Plan Implementation

Fortunately, there were several vacant academic staff positions. In making these appointments, we gave emphasis to qualifications and qualities equivalent to universities and were able to recruit staff of high caliber—the new recruits came with their doctoral degrees from eminent institutions like IIT Kanpur, JNU, etc. Another major shift in staffing was the recruitment of engineers, agricultural scientists, paramedical scientists and home scientists to strengthen our work in vocational education.

To build up our research and development activities and to augment the academic staff, we designed major projects in Human Resource Development, Assessing and Enhancing Learning Skills, Policy and Planning, Regional Languages, Question Banking and Examination Reforms, Life Enrichment Programmes, and an Open Schooling Magazine. We secured funds from the government of India for these projects, each with its own professional staff and director. This gave us about 30 additional academic staff members.

Another major exercise was selecting and accrediting the study centres. Several unscrupulous agencies with commercial agendas had managed to enter the network of the NOS study centres, alongside institutions that were genuinely committed to the poor and the educational drop-outs and that had good buildings, laboratories, libraries, workshops and well-qualified teachers. There were also private schools running a parallel fee-for-service 'open school stream' for regular day pupils who found difficulty with science and mathematics. The main functions of the study centres were to provide personal contact programmes, distribute learning materials and offer counselling services. We established criteria to determine the quality of the physical and human resources, and those centres that fulfilled our criteria on paper were inspected to verify the written information. The inspecting team was particularly assiduous in assessing the teachers' disposition towards open learning. This review process brought about a major change in the level and quality of the centres. Today, there are more than 1,000 centres across India.

NOS used to function only from Delhi. The importance of regional centres for coordination and monitoring of quality had long been recognized and we proceeded to set up regional centres in Calcutta for the eastern region; Pune for the western region; Hyderabad for the southern region; Agra for the northern region; and Guwahati for the north-eastern region. Each centre had its own director—typically, a retired educational administrator—5 to 10 staff, standby stock of course material for any crisis in delivery, computers, audio visual equipment, fax, Internet, etc. This structural reform substantially strengthened the quality of regional support.

Enrolment in NOS was growing but there was still a perception that its programmes and qualifications were inferior to those of conventional schools. We therefore, undertook a major exercise involving the University Grants Commission to gain recognition from the universities, Indian Institutes of Technology (IITs) and Boards of Secondary Education. This effort yielded significant results, with NOS certificates recognized by all Boards of Secondary Education, the IITs and more than 150 of the 200 universities. This led to a further increase in enrolment.

With the increase in enrolment and the need for qualitative improvement in the self-learning materials (the curriculum had already been revised), I challenged the academics to develop new look, quality materials that were pedagogically sound and attractive to the learners, something they responded to magnificently and accomplished within six months. Until this time, our programmes had been delivered primarily through print and face-to-face. We now developed audio and video programmes, installed a Digital Multimedia Centre, and experimented with voicemail.

To upgrade the quality of the Personal Contact Programmes, we devised modularized training programmes on tutoring, cooperative learning, problem-solving, counselling, etc., for the part-time staff in the accredited institutions and study centres and delivered these through print, supported by face-to-face and interactive television teaching.

To orient our students into the philosophy and strategies of open learning, we gave each enrollee a specially developed free book, Open Learning: How to Make Best Use Of..., available in English and Hindi. We also initiated a glossy quarterly magazine, Open Learning, featuring social issues such as AIDS, gender equity, etc., biographies of inspirational individuals such as Jawaharlal Nehru, Swami Vivekananda and Rabindranath Tagore, subject-based enrichment articles and tips for examinations, which was supplied free to every student for one year.

We developed a large number of vocational courses in agriculture, technology, paramedical studies, home science and information technology, and introduced a system wherein students could combine academic and vocational studies towards their examination. This upgrading of the status of vocational courses radically changed students' choices in favour of vocational courses.

Finally, we addressed the issue of providing programmes in regional languages. Until that time, NOS had offered programmes only in English, which helped drop-outs from English medium fee-charging schools, and hindi, which supported poor as well not so poor drop-outs among hindi speaking people, particularly in Delhi and its surrounding areas. Within two years, thanks to the fine efforts of our young staff, led particularly by Dr. Rajesh Kumar, our entire secondary education programme was translated into Malayalam, Tamil, Kannada, Telugu, Bengali, Manipuri, Gujarati, Marathi and Urdu and were getting converted into other languages including Assamese, Oriya, Nepali and Punjabi.

We planned that NOS would concurrently work with the state governments to set up state open schools, then, hand over the regional language programmes to the state open schools and withdraw itself to provide only English and Hindi programmes. Each state open school project needed careful consideration of the organizational design, staff structure, staff induction and career paths, selection, establishment and accreditation of study centres and quality assurance, and required state subsidies for the education of girls, for the economically and socially deprived and the physically and mentally challenged. We were able to launch programmes in Bengali, Urdu and Kannada and establish state open schools in Haryana, Madhya Pradesh, Karnataka and West Bengal. Andhra Open School was already offering education up to eighth standard, NOS offered secondary education material in Telugu. Subsequent to my departure, state open schools were set up in Kerala, Punjab and Gujarat and there was a renewed interest in such systems.

Winning People Over

Besides vision building, developing process capability was the major challenge. I invested much of my time, energy and professional skills in building confidence and professional competence in the staff. The academic staff in NOS comprise: the core full-time academic staff who are largely responsible for curriculum design and material development; the subject experts and courseware authors drawn from various universities and schools; and the counsellors and tutors in the study centres and teachers in the conventional schools.

With respect to building confidence in the internal staff of NOS,

I started involving them with senior external experts, giving them national and international exposure, requiring them to produce reports and write professional literature outside courseware authoring, and take over as project directors in order to broaden their horizons and giving them a break from their normal duties. For example, I have personally witnessed NOS academic staff providing logistic support to the SMRC Conference on Open Learning in 1990 without any involvement in academic aspects. International travels were restricted to chairman and heads of departments. First time in 1994-95, we deputed four academic staff members to present papers in an open learning conference in New Zealand. There were several such activities to open them up and build confidence. It took more than 18 months to pull them out of their cocoons and make them believe that 'they have all the talents and they can make the difference'.

With the courseware authors, we held meetings about the new perspective and philosophy of open schooling, the directions we wanted NOS to take and the need for quality in content and material. These were well received by the academics who came from the formal system and were largely critical of the standards of the open learning system. For the study centre personnel and teachers, we conducted workshops on management issues and student support.

Our endeavours were largely successful with the internal staff, but less so with the study centre coordinators and tutors, possibly because they were involved in conventional teaching throughout the week and found it difficult to switch over in the evenings and at the weekends to the new instructional strategies for NOS. It is always harder to inculcate new values and practices in part-time, distant staff.

Utilizing my acquaintance with university systems and scholars, we involved national experts in various NOS activities. When I invited a vice chancellor and two senior professors to join an NOS committee, one of my young colleagues asked, 'Sir, will such eminent people come to NOS?', to which I replied, 'Yes. They will. If they don't come for NOS, they will, to help a friend in NOS.' Involving senior academics from various states of India demonstrated that quality cannot be compromised, and thus, in a way, I exposed my colleagues to academic stalwarts in their respective fields and broadened their vision. This breadth of contact with the intellectual community of the universities was significant in developing and carrying through the new NOS vision. Also, it repositioned NOS as a major national institution in the comity of academicians, more importantly, among my own colleagues.

Such involvement also helped to inform opinion leaders from the conventional system. For example, the eminent economist educationist, Professor Tapas Mazumdar, wrote several newspaper articles on open schooling and its potentialities that made uninformed critics rethink the whole issue. This strategy also helped us in getting NOS qualifications recognized, since the very people who assessed quality for equivalence and recognition by the universities were serving with various committees of NOS.

Management of Resistance

The main problem arose as a consequence of examinations having formerly been the dominant activity of NOS. The controller of examinations enjoyed the extraordinary powers vested in his office, reinforced by powers of financial privilege. For example, there was a practice of flying squads visiting examination centres to check copying and other malpractices. The controller was empowered to draft anybody from the organization without prior approval of the concerned head of the department and reward them with a token honorarium—something I learnt when my personal secretary was drafted without my consent!

The shifting of emphasis to the academics created an identity crisis in the Examinations Department and there was tremendous resistance, not only within the Department, but also from those outside it, who derived financial benefits from its activities. At one stage, the Examinations Department even declined to conduct examinations in regional languages. Clearly, this was a situation that had to be challenged.

Other resistance came from within the Executive Committee of NOS. Certain members had little understanding of the open learning systems and the interests of NOS. They looked upon the new vision as a personal agenda to enhance the careers of certain people within the organization.

There was also external resistance. Recasting the rules of accreditation impacted negatively upon many commercial entrepreneurs who joined forces against us, particularly when we were compelled to take action to assure quality. For the very first time, examinations in several centres were cancelled for mass copying and mismanagement. As is typical in the Indian socio-political scene, our opponents ran to the politicians, including the ministers, accusing the chairman of all sorts of misdemeanours. Fortunately, Ms. Selja, the then Minister of State in-charge of NOS, stood by the decision.

As a student of management of change, I knew I faced two options—to use power-coercive strategies that are here and now with poor sustainability, or normative re-educative strategies which are sustainable but are long-drawn-out. Someone on a three-year contract, I was presented with this dilemma. In the end, I chose the normative re-educative process, wherever this was most suitable—where minds were open like academic staff—and used power-coercion, wherever I considered any investment in the re-educative process as futile, like examination department. For example, despite relegating administration to a secondary position, behind the academic functions, I found that the head of Administration was talking of the new vision and I decided to work through the issues with him and his staff. But the Examinations Department brushed aside all new ideas and presented me with little choice but to use my authority to get things changed.

The major and most expensive resistance was to the idea of converting NOS into National Institute of Open Schooling. This decentralized networking model of open learning would have significantly affected the vested interests. Hence, various forces like examination personnel, study centre managers, a few other disgruntled staff in administration and academics, and a few members of the Executive Committee joined together to resist the idea. There was very little time left to manage the resistance; my contract period was coming to an end. On my departure, the idea was shelved by my successor; it was reopened by my grand-successor. And, NOS has been reconstituted as NIOS.

As an illustration, when the Examinations Department refused to conduct examinations in regional languages, we got it done through the regional directorates. When the publication unit expressed its inability to reduce the price for computerization and page-making of material under the pretext that the printing press did not agree, we set up our own DTP facilities; all the printing presses agreed to the new NOS rates which were more than 40 per cent less than they were paid earlier.

Leadership and Management Style

As a professional in educational management, I know that it is difficult to pinpoint principles of management that shape an individual's management style. Human beings are essentially value-configurations and their core values are developed in early childhood. In the years of pre-adolescence and adolescence, these values are strengthened or weakened through contact with the alternative value systems of peers, teachers, the community, and so on. In my own case, having been born and raised in a rural society that is largely homogenous in its value systems, characterized by cooperation, helping others, sharing resources despite poverty, and mutual love and trust, the values inculcated in my home and childhood days were reinforced by the wider community.

At NOS, my leadership style was guided by the situation and by my accountability to the students. I made serious efforts to base decisions on facts; for example, redefining the vision of NOS in the light of the recommendations of various commissions and the internal capability of the staff. My second principle was to share the vision, albeit, not always successfully. My third basic principle was to involve all of the organization, create a sense of purpose among the staff, give them latitude and recognize their efforts and achievements. To illustrate this latter point, between 1979 and 1992, only the NOS chairman or heads of departments went abroad for study visits or conferences. Between 1993 and 1995, seven junior academic staff were funded to attend professional conferences in New Zealand, Australia and other countries and present papers. These staff brought great credit to NOS and the approbation from overseas experts really enthused and encouraged them.

Stylistically, I had vision with impatience. I tried to take people along. If they joined the journey, I was thrilled. If they resisted it, I carried it out putting them aside. Thus, there was a significant production emphasis.

Moral values strongly determined my leadership style and action. For example, if there was a clash between the administrative principles and moral values, I chose the moral stand. For example, my predecessor had offered a higher scale to the academic staff. After my joining, there was a government order to place them back on their old scale and recover the payments made. I continued to pay them what they were getting, though I implemented the GO by putting them back on the scale. When after a lot of efforts and persuasion, NOS was permitted to buy a new vehicle, it was as per normal administrative practice, placed at the disposal of the chairman. The chairman's used car was to be given to the director (Academics). I asked the office to send the new car to the director who had so far been provided with a hired car. There were several occasions when I came under pressure from the politicians and bureaucrats asking for actions that would affect the interest of NOS. I politely refused.

Success and Failure

Referring back to our vision, NOS was able to set itself on a journey toward quality and spearhead the open schooling movement in India by promoting programmes in regional languages, professionalizing open schooling and developing a network of state open schools. Another major achievement was the recognition and acceptance of NOS by the universities and the employers, on the one hand, and the learners, on the other. Enrolment increased phenomenally. However, compared to the estimated number of out-of-school youth, the present coverage is far too small. But then, how can an institution enroll three million people and offer education in 16 different languages?

The NOS also scored on the international front. The Report of the International Commission on Education for the 21st Century to UNESCO, Learning: The Treasure Within (Delors, et al., 1996) featured NOS. The Commonwealth of Learning invited NOS to edit an international publication on open schooling. The UK Open University uses NOS as a case study in its international postgraduate programmes in open learning. NOS was involved in drafting the UNESCO policy document on open and distance education. As chairman, I was elected to the vice-presidency (Asia) of the International Council for Distance Education (1CDE). And NOS has successfully hosted several international conferences and study visits on open schooling. I made presentations on NOS and Indian open schooling in several international forums in UK, USA, Switzerland, Norway, Egypt, Philippines, etc. In short, NOS has emerged as one of the world's prominent distance education institutions and a leader in open schooling.

But there have been lost opportunities too. During 1993-96, we made a significant effort to develop courses in regional languages to accelerate the development of a state open school network. Ideally, there should have been twenty such schools as projected in our perspective document. Only a few could be established. Unfortunately, this policy was reversed on my departure, and as a result, the open school movement slowed down. We also failed to provide sustainability and challenge to the newly equipped staff. Many of the competent staff left NOS for better opportunities.

Lessons Learnt

Running such a massive institution with such a radical philosophy was certainly a rich learning experience. Let me list a few major lessons I learnt about institution building:

- Articulate a vision that will not limit the growth of the institution and that, rather than using apologetic terms like 'second chance' education, make bold statements, e.g., 'alternative education of high quality'.
- Give careful thought to organizational design that can accommodate the future.
- Ensure the pay, status and conditions for your staff to enable you to recruit and retain the very best people as managers, course developers, teachers and tutors.
- Ensure that the state takes responsibility for providing funds for at least eight years of schooling and is equitable in supporting those who attend regular schools and those who take to open schooling. Open schooling can be self-sufficient, but should be funded through a mix of students' fees and government grants to subsidize the education of girls, of learners from the economically and socially deprived communities, and the physically and mentally challenged.
- Make sure that the open learning system is twice as good as the formal system, because open learning systems are always suspected of being of poor quality. Involve outstanding scholars in curriculum development and take meticulous care of every aspect of the pedagogy and materials.

- Be constantly vigilant and monitor quality at every delivery point and make sure that learners are never exploited. The 'outreach and reputation' of an open school depends upon the study centres and the study centre network must spread to every part of the country and the centres and their staff must be selected with care.
- Deliver your programmes through multi-channel learning systems using the available interactive technology to ensure outreach and participative learning.
- Offer a choice of courses and modules, time-frames, learning modes, credit accumulation, etc., but once the choice is made, ensure that quality is non-negotiable.
- Foresee and assess organizational dynamics as innovations are introduced and make strategic plans for strengthening the proactive forces and dissipating the resisting forces. As Lewin (1997) shows in his Field Force Analysis Theory, innovations disturb the dynamic equilibrium of an organization and simultaneously activate proactive and resisting forces.

On the latter point, my interactions with institutions in the western world, particularly in the United Kingdom and United States, and my studies of the management of change in education in India, reveal that the former have a greater capability for introducing and sustaining innovation and change, regardless of the quality of the CEO. Indian organizations are far less formalized, and hence, far more person-dependent. Their growth and development, and decay depend largely upon the CEOs who tend to employ bureaucratic methods that suit those leaders who are weak in their ability to influence people.

For many senior academics, a contract as a CEO of an open school is a break from routine and a stepping-stone to a more attractive position, rather than a target in itself. Therefore, the first and the foremost requirement in selecting such a CEO is to ensure that he or she has a genuine commitment, indeed, emotional attachment, to the educationally disadvantaged and the open learning system. The CEO also needs skills in envisioning and developing a shared vision, strategic planning, human resource management, mentoring, interpersonal relationships and linking with external agencies, national and international. Academic credibility is another necessary condition.

The chairmanship of NOS is a three-year contractual position and the incumbent has no role whatsoever in choosing his or her successor. Such a lack of continuity is a serious threat to NOS. Every chairman tries to prove his or her mettle in three years by adopting short-term strategies for faster results rather than planning for long-term institution-building. As a result, there are major pendulum swings in policies and programmes every few years. This must be a matter of serious concern.

NOTES

1. This is the modified version of my contribution in Latchem, Colin and Hanna, Donald, (eds), Leadership for 21" Century Learning, London: Kogan Page, 2001. Cases on NOS, authored by me, are also published in Open Schooling: Selected Experiences edited by Mukhopadhyay, Marmar and Philips, Susan published by COL, Vancouver in 1994 (the case is used by UK Open University as course material), and in Multi-channel Learning: Connecting All to Education edited by Steven Anzalone and published by EDC, Washington DC, in 1995.
2. NOS has now been reconstituted as National Institute of Open Schooling (NIOS) as visioned by me with the advice of an expert committee; but it was effected by my grand-successor (my successor's successor).

7
BACK ON RAIL
Case of a Kendriya Vidyalaya

Kendriya Vidyalaya Sangathan (KVS) is an autonomous body under the Ministry of Human Resources Development, Government of India, presently running about 1000 schools in the country including a few schools abroad. The schools are primarily meant for wards of transferable Central Government employees who are very often transferred from one place to another. In order to provide uninterrupted, uniform education to their children, the KVs have common syllabus, books, test, and examination schedules. The curriculum is broad based and includes, apart from teaching, co-curricular activities, games and sports, art, dance, music, indoor and outdoor activities.

Entry into the KVS

Ms. Savita Kapoor, principal of this Kendriya Vidyalaya (KV), NOIDA completed her post-graduation from one of the well established and reputed Indian universities. The discipline was good and all classes were held regularly and punctually. According to Savita, this made them disciplined, self-dependent and confident.

Savita was advised to take a up a teaching career by the Head of the Department of her university. Soon after, she joined KV as a substitute teacher for one who was to get married and shift out of the city, after discussions with the principal and then an interview at KVS headquarter in Delhi. Savita was issued an appointment letter appointing her as an ad-hoc PGT (Chemistry) at KV; she joined in October. Later, she was again interviewed for regular appointment in

March and her appointment was regularized as a PGT. She 'liked the environment at KV, students were bright and from Air Force background. I started enjoying my work and was soon well-accepted by the students, parents, my principal and my colleagues'.

Savita traced three major sources of her motivation, namely i) her predecessor had set-up a high standard of teaching and was a popular teacher; ii) the Chairman of the Vidyalaya, who was a Group Captain, while addressing the staff meeting appreciated her performance and conveyed his happiness for maintaining the same standards as had been set-up by my predecessor; and iii) guidance of the principal, a respectful and a decent person. After her marriage, she worked in several other cities than her native place or her husband's working place.

As Principal

Savita was selected as Principal through open selection. As per the practice, she went through a three-month induction training along with a batch of 43 others at KVS training centre. After completion of the training, she was posted to a KV away from her husband and children. It was a new school with about 450 students that gave her a good exposure and insight into school administration. Since she was alone there, she spent most of time in the school, trying to shape it as per her vision and ideas. Only after about three-and-a-half years, Savita was transferred to her home town and joined a one of the biggest KVs in the Country, then. This was a unique school in the sense that apart from the main school running from class sixth onwards; it had three primary branches located at distances of 2-3 kilometers from the main school. As she had to monitor these three branches, she learnt driving and became self-dependent for commuting from one place to the other. There were some deep rooted problems in the present KV because of its strength (more than 3000), size and the distance at which the three branches were located. Because of the size of the school, there were many problems; she became well versed with rules and regulations, learnt to solve problems and to handle difficult situations. The other three schools where she worked as principal were equally challenging. One of the three schools was again a very big and difficult one that gave her many sleepless nights.

Early Years

Savita was born to average middle-class parents in a family of seven members including four younger brothers. Savita was the eldest and the only daughter; hence 'highly pampered'. The family lived in its own big house. Her mother was a very religious and pious lady. She would get up at early in the morning, perform 'puja' for about two hours, and would work for almost the whole day. All religious functions were celebrated with great fervor. Her education was only up to class five, but she had very high aspirations for her children; and was a great motivator. Savita's father was a self-made person who worked as professional building contractor. The parents were 'very loving and caring persons and provided us a secure childhood and a congenial environment. They gave us all the opportunity to do anything we wanted to, guiding us at every step with positive inputs. Being the eldest, I would help my brothers in their studies while they would bestow all their love and affection to their only sister'.

Savita studied at a Arya Samaj Trust School that provided a congenial learning atmosphere while inculcating high moral and social values; there used to be a period for 'moral education' imparted through lectures, and narration of lives of great saints. '*Havan* was performed in the school every Saturday; all students would participate in it. Most of the students learnt the mantras by heart'. On the academic side, 'teachers were sincere and dedicated'. There was a spirit of mutual help and compassion in the school. While all the teachers were excellent, two of them left indelible influence on Savita The English teacher guided students in their educational and personal problems. The Chemistry teacher was responsible to developing liking of the subject in Savita.

Vision for the School

According to Savita, 'my vision of a good school was based on my personal experience of working in a number of KVs, visit to some public schools in Delhi during my training as Principal at the KVS, and visit to some of the best schools in the U.K.' I had been selected by the CBSE to undergo Advanced Training in Science Teaching at Chelsea College, London for one academic year. On the basis of my performance in this training, I was invited by the Chelsea College for a three-month term to develop a Teachers' Guide for teaching Science at the plus-2 stage in India. During both these visits, I was attached to some of the good schools in England. In addition, I visited some good schools and attended a number of conferences and seminars on school education in India as well as in England. I had imagined developing a school wherein the focus would be on 'learning' and not on teaching; the students would develop their well-rounded personality; they would imbibe moral and social values on their own (rather than being taught); would be self-disciplined and confident to face any situation in any environment; would develop a sense of cooperation and competition: they would be good in studies also. I dreamt of making my KV, as one of the best schools in the area, of which the parents, the students, and the society would be proud to be associated with. I wanted to transform this KV, into an institution of excellence, with good infrastructure, a beautiful garden, well thought out co-curricular activities, and respectable academic standard through professional training and growth of my teachers. This vision was the result of my exposure to some of the best schools with which I was associated during various training programs. I also got opportunities to visit various schools as a member of inspection team. The workshops and seminars which I had attended broadened my horizon and enriched my experience. All this rich experience, I gained as P.G.T. and as Principal was translated into practice in my KV'.

NOIDA: A Challenging KV

Posting at this KV was perhaps the most challenging assignment of my entire career. On the joining day itself I got a fair idea of the difficult task ahead. With firm determination and great confidence I stepped into the school. With my experience of working in big KVs (3000 plus students) and small KVs (450 students), I had set up my mission of achieving high standards of academics, a conducive environment for the all-round development of students, a neat and clean school plant with a beautiful garden where all children would love to come. This was to be achieved through my concerted efforts, involvement of my staff in planning and execution of various programmes, support from KVS authorities and from my Vidyalaya Management Committee (VMC). The students were to be involved in decision making and suggesting various ways and means to improve things. The house system was to be made functional, co-curricular activities were to be carefully planned to inculcate high value system, academic enrichment, awareness of Indian culture and developing leadership qualities among them. The community resources were also to be exploited (for rain water harvesting and in developing a garden etc). The parents were to be voluntarily involved in school affairs. Issue: How could all this be achieved? Did the Vidyalaya really achieve all this? How?

First Day

On entering the Principal's office at KV (strength about 3000) on my first day, I found a group of about 10-12 persons surrounding the Principal in charge and discussing about Annual Examination result at a very high pitch. In between, there were some hot exchanges of words. The situation was not very pleasant. They were demanding that some students of Class XI who had failed in the Annual examination be passed because some similar cases were declared pass after the announcement of the Annual Examination results. This drama continued for quite some time. The group consisted of some senior teachers, parents and members of the society and a news reporter who shot a couple of questions at me as soon as I was seated.

"Madam, your school does not have drinking water, what will you do about it?"

The second question was "The students under question have been failed intentionally, will you pass them?"

In the afternoon when I went to submit my joining report to the Chairman, VMC who was a senior officer, he requested me that a new VMC may be constituted immediately and its meeting be held.

Issue that challenged me were how do I answer such questions of parents and teachers or why is the Chairman in such an urgency to constitute the VMC?

Vidyalaya: The Way It was

It was a big school with strength of about 3000 students. It was a seven-section school imparting education in all the three streams, Science, Commerce, and Humanities. The Vidyalaya was running in two shifts with staff strength of 130 members; the Primary Section would run in the second shift. Both, the front and the rear side of the Vidyalaya building, there was large space (belonging to the Vidyalaya) which was all barren with wild bushes all around. The assembly mud-ground was big enough to accommodate all the students of the Secondary section at a time. The school building was spread over three floors; the ground floor housed the office of the Principal, the two vice-principals, staff room, administrative office, three science labs and classrooms for 11th and 12th classes. Library, a store room, and classrooms for 9th and 10th classes were located on the first floor. The second floor accommodated the art room, the music room, the labs, and classrooms for classes VI, VII, and VIII. The labs were well-equipped but poorly maintained with worn-out furniture.

The Vidyalaya was managing seventeen buses that had been hired by it for transportation of students residing in different parts of NOIDA.

Soon after my joining the Vidyalaya, I tried to take an overall view of the whole scenario. I took several rounds of the school, met my staff members, interacted with students and parents, observed the classroom teaching; saw the labs and library, etc before the school closed for summer vacation in the first week of May. This gave me some idea of the institution which I was to Head.

Another thing which drew my attention was the cleanliness of the whole building. The ground had polythene bags flying all over. The classrooms, the corridors and the stairs had their own share of layers of dust. The cobwebs could be seen in every nook and corner. There was stink all around as the sewers were blocked.

The building gave an old look because of the lack of maintenance. The front and rear stretches of land gave a deserted and depressing look. The students would bring-in a lot of dust and mud with their shoes into the building from the kucha assembly ground. Inside the building, patches of cement were coming out, the live electrical wires were hanging in the corridors, classrooms and toilets as almost all switch boards were broken. The fans were non-functional; the roof top was full of old broken furniture.

Another thing that attracted my immediate attention was indiscipline among students and some staff members. The late coming was a routine. The teachers normally avoided going to their classes. The students used to roam about in the corridors. Some of them were very destructive. The furniture in the classes was broken. The overall scene was very depressing.

On seeing the toilets from inside, I found that more than half of them were dumped with condemned articles and locked. The other three or four toilets being used were stinking because of poor maintenance and non-availability of water therein; the WCs and washbasins were broken/damaged. The Safai Karmcharis (6-7 of them) were not to be seen anywhere. I came to know from parents that students would avoid using school toilets as they were very unhygienic. The staff normally used toilets of the staff quarters located on the school campus. At times, in urgency, some of the teachers would use the toilet inside the Principal's office.

The positive side of the, it was encouraging to observe that students in general were very bright; they came from good family background and were highly receptive. I met them in small groups and talked to them at length. It gave me a fair idea of how the things were moving. I conducted regular meetings with monitors, prefects, and captains. This helped the students to open up and I came to know about their problems, their expectations from the school and the areas which needed my immediate attention. This helped me in planning the future course of action and students also opened up and felt that they can also contribute significantly in improving the functioning of the Vidyalaya and they slowly developed a sense of belongingness. This helped in reducing the damage to school property which was completely controlled after some time.

There were about one hundred thirty staff members. Some of the teachers were outstanding while some other were very good and rest were mediocre. Among the teachers, there was a strong group of teachers who were trouble-makers and would create a lot of indiscipline in the Vidyalaya. Other teachers were scared of them.

Another Incident

After about 15 days of my joining the school, another incident happened. A post-graduate teacher (PGT) was transferred on public interest as there was a vigilance enquiry going on against him prior to my joining. The teacher refused to accept his transfer order and left the school in a huff. He was relieved in absentia on the same day as per the KVS rules. The next day he came to the school and demanded that I receive his half day casual leave application for the previous day which I refused. He created an ugly scene. He entered the Vice-Principal's room where the Principal and the two Vice-Principals were in a meeting. He bolted the room from inside wanting the Principal to accept a letter from him then and there. I told politely but very firmly that he should immediately open the door else he would face a strict disciplinary action for this act. He refused to oblige. After a while he opened the door. The two Vice-Principals were so horrified that they declined to give anything in writing. Though he stopped coming to the school, he refused to accept any papers sent by office and continued staying at staff quarter and created a lot of nuisance in the Vidyalaya. A group of about 30-40 parents met the Commissioner, KVS and requested that he may be retained as he was a very good teacher. An enquiry was set-up by Commissioner, KVS. Assistant Commissioner, Delhi Region was sent to the school to conduct this enquiry. He talked to the students of Class XII whose parents had gone to the KVS; not a single student spoke against the teacher. They were sent back to their classes. After some time, the monitor of the Class came back and requested that he would like to talk to the Assistant Commissioner. He gave full details of the incident as to how the parents were sent to KVS. Other students then opened up. All of them narrated the entire episode in writing. The students mentioned that the parents were called at home by the concerned teacher in the evening and were forced to go to the Sangathan the next morning. He also arranged taxies for their transportation. The narration given by the students also went against the teacher along with the report of his earlier conduct of not accepting the transfer order. To these were added the incidents of creating a scene in the Principal's and Vice-Principal's office and sending parents to Commissioner's office to plead his case. For about seven to eight months he remained absent from duty as he did not join the place of his posting. Finally, the Assistant Commissioner constituted a Committee that included his representative and some senior teachers of the school along with the Office Superintendent of the Vidyalaya. The members of the Committee were sent to his residence after confirming that he was present at home. When they knocked at the door, the concerned teacher himself opened the door and was stunned to see the members of the Committee along with relevant papers. He had no choice but to receive all letters. After this he joined his place of posting and the disciplinary proceedings against him continued. Later I came to know that his services were terminated from KVS.

New Strategy

After these experiences over a short period of time, I decided to formulate a long term strategy for the management of the Vidyalaya and to find solution to the immediate problems faced by the Vidyalaya and to make a quick start. The summer vacation was just 10 days away. I immediately started with a series of meetings with staff in general, subject committees in particular and with primary teachers separately. I also called a series of meetings of Group 'D' employees and *Safai Karmcharis* (staff incharge of cleaning the premises) and allocated them their duties floor-wise. It was made clear in the meetings that they had to sincerely perform their duty.

Cleanliness

The first and the foremost important work was the regular cleaning of the Vidyalaya building. The *Safai Karmcharis*, were asked to give their requirements of cleaning material and also report any problem they face. They informed me about the acute shortage of water for cleaning the floor and toilets. This problem solved by procuring large drums for storing water. The concerned staff started storing water in these drums. The cleanliness work started in right earnest. The work of all the *safai karmcharis* was closely monitored and supervised by a small committee comprising teachers and students; they were counseled as and when required. Within a few days the school started looking neat and clean.

Drinking Water

The next important issue was solving the problem of drinking water. Pending finding a long-term solution for continuous supply of drinking water in the Vidyalaya, a number of large '*matkas*' (earthenware pots) and plastic 200 litre plastic buckets were immediately purchased. One of the sincere group 'D' employee was allocated the duty of managing drinking water arrangements. This gave some immediate relief to the students.

Late Coming

Some of the teachers and other staff members were habitual late comers. This was checked; and I set my own norm. As per my practice earlier, I reached school ten to fifteen minutes before the start of the school. The teachers started coming in time as they knew that I would 'welcome' them at the gate. They understood that the Principal, who could reach the school well before time after driving a distance of 35 kms from Delhi, meant business. This message was loud and clear and it worked.

Going to Classes

Another message which was clear to the staff was that they have to take their classes regularly and punctually. The two Vice-Principals, who had, perhaps, never shouldered any administrative responsibility earlier, were fully involved in the administrative process. I gave them the responsibility of monitoring all activities on different floors (there were three floors including ground floor). Before the school closed for summer vacation most of the teachers started going to their classes and teaching work started in right earnest. The Vice-Principals were requested to maintain complete record of their observations during their visits to various classes. They would discuss these observations with me regularly. After observing a particular class the concerned teacher was also apprised of the notes prepared during class observation for follow-up work. The next task was taking action against the non-performers: the case of non-performers; those who did not budge in spite of my polite message were asked to explain their conduct in writing and a suitable action was initiated against them. This was an eye opener; they never expected that a soft spoken Principal could be firm also. I made my action plan for the whole year with the help of my two Vice-Principals and senior teachers who were in charge of their subject committees and other committees. As soon as the summer vacation started the teachers and Vice-Principals proceeded on holiday.

Attention towards Office

This was the time to pay attention to my office, I found out that all important office jobs like school fund, Vidyalaya Vikas Nidhi, service books, and other important files were under the charge of one person who used to undermine the presence of other members of office staff. Though there was an Office Superintendent, three UDCs and three LDCs, all the important work was under the charge of one UDC and others were either free or were given petty jobs. It was quite intriguing to observe this. However, before going into the depth and trying to know the reason for this dominance by an individual, the first thing I did was to ensure equitable distribution of work through an office order in writing and started regular monitoring of the work allocated to each member of the office staff. This was done on the basis of my own assessment of the capability and capacity of the individual members of the staff. The Superintendent was made responsible to check the cash books, accounts and other office routine before it was put up to Principal. This made everybody, except the person who was earlier dominating earlier, happy as they felt that they were also equally important members of the staff and they started contributing their best in the management process. Late coming among them was also checked. The office work became smooth and the pendency of the work diminished significantly.

Repair and Maintenance of School Plant

The next big issues concerned electrical repairs, availability of pure drinking water and cleanliness of the school building. These works were urgent in nature as students' health was at stake. Without fans it was almost impossible to sit in the classrooms during summer. With the help of the Chairman, VMC, the electrical repair work of urgent nature was got done during the vacation. The Head Water Works Department was invited to visit to the School and his help was sought in getting the uninterrupted supply of water. On the basis of initial technical survey and testing of the quality of the underground water, we got a submersible pump installed in the Vidyalaya. This initiative and immediate implementation of the decision by the Principal solved the perennial water problem of the school permanently.

The VVN budget was prepared and got approved from the Chairman of the Vidyalaya. For other major works for which the funds were not available, a request was made to the KVS for sanctioning and releasing funds. The construction related requirements were also sent to the KVS and the works were assigned by the KVS to government construction agencies for the purpose. All the toilets in the Vidyalaya were fully repaired and made functional for use of the students and staff. All broken fittings were changed; whitewash and painting work was undertaken. The school wore a different look. A beautiful garden was developed, the whole building was painted and polished and it was kept neat, clean, and tidy. Most of these things, particularly, availability of pure drinking water and neat and clean toilets for the students and staff, were completed during the vacation. When the school reopened after the vacation, the students and staff were pleasantly surprised and believed as if a miracle had happened in the Vidyalaya during the vacation. The students and parents were extremely happy.

On my recommendation, KVS initiated disciplinary action against those staff members who were undisciplined and were non-performers. Some of them were transferred. All these actions had a positive effect on others and they all started working and took their work seriously, shouldered all responsibilities in respect of the work assigned to them.

Academics and Co-curricular Activities

Simultaneously, the academics improved and the House system started functioning. The co-curricular activities were systematically planned for the whole year. The games and sports facilities were provided. Some coaches and artisans were engaged and students started enjoying these activities. A major change was observed in the functioning of the school, its infrastructure and other activities. It was comparable to best of schools in the vicinity. Two computer labs with total 40 PCs of latest configuration were set up. The library was given new furniture; new books were purchased as per the requirement of students. An audio-visual room and a junior science lab were established. VMC was constituted and all important matters were discussed and necessary approvals were taken.

The new look and content of the Vidyalaya became a talk of the town in the whole of NOIDA.

Monitoring the Academics

The subject committees were constituted and senior most PGT was made in charge of the subject committee. The meetings of the subject were held twice a month to discuss various issues related to the subject. These meetings were also attended by the principal and vice principal from time to time. They were made responsible for the term-wise split of syllabus, its coverage monitoring the class and home work and project work. The vice principals made their time table for class observation and noted their observations in the Performa meant for the same. The teachers were apprised of the no tings made for follow-up. The unit tests and examinations were conducted regularly and at the scheduled time. The result were compiled and announced on the dates fixed for the same. The students notebooks were regularly checked by the vice principals. The teacher's diary was regularly written by the teachers and checked. The overall monitoring was done by the principal.

Parent Teacher's Meetings

The parent teacher's meetings were held at regular intervals. The parents were apprised of the progress of the students. A day was fixed for the parents to meet the principal to discuss any problem related to their ward. The circulars were sent apprising parents about various activities of the school. The parents were actively involved in the activities of the school. This helped in significant improvement in the academics and overall improvement of the discipline of the students.

Vidyalaya Management Committee

The VMC was constituted and its regular meetings were held. All the financial approvals were taken from VMC. Their guidance was taken on the various issues related to school. The cooperation and help extended by the chairman and members of the VMC played a significant role in the overall improvement in the overall functioning of the school.

The Career Counseling

A qualified Counselor was engaged for the Vidyalaya for helping the students to solve their personal and academic problems.

The Lesson Learnt

After my transfer from this school when I look back and think what more I could have done? The following things come to my mind.

- With my strong academic background I could have contributed more significantly to strengthen the academic standards of the school in general and week students in particular.

- The vice principals should have been made more involved in improving the academic standards of the school and should have been made more accountable.
- More sports facilities may have been provided.
- I should have managed my time in a better way.

NOTE

1. Original contribution came from Ms. Savita Kapoor, then Principal of Kendriya Vidyalaya, Noida in the given format.

8

BRICK BY BRICK TO THE TOP

DAV Public School, Gurgaon

DAV Public School had its modest/naïve beginning in 1985 in Gurgaon in a hired one room tenement. It all began when Ms. Anita Makkar, then PGT (Maths) in Hans Raj Model School in Delhi had to relocate herself to Gurgaon because of her marriage. To her question, 'what should I do now?' her mentors in DAV asked her to start a school. A devout follower of Swami Dayananda's philosophy, Anita started with fumbling feet her school in a 250 yard house with one table and a chair, 'she had no experience how to run a school, leave alone start a school'. In due course, her mentors' confidence in her capability proved to be right. Her fumbling feet soon walked with confidence without looking back. Today, DAV Public School in Gurgaon is the largest school with 4200 students, 235 teachers and 150 other staff members. The school has been ranking at the top of more than 600 DAV schools all over India for the past ten years consecutively, according to the performance analysis by the DAV Managing Committee for qualitative and quantitative analysis based on the degree of merit of students performance.

Located in a 5 acre land in beautiful surrounding away from the concrete jungle of Gurgaon and 'far from the madding crowd', school is protected on two sides by lush green HUDA Park and HUDA Nursery; third side opening on to the busy road. In the lush green, amidst the chirping of birds, prayer meetings with chanting of Vedic Hymns brings in a rare spiritual experience with rejuvenating and inspiring vibes among all the denizens. Within this serenity, DAV Public School is a state of modern school preparing students for the future.

School is equipped with modern Language Laboratory, Computer Labs, Biology, Physics and Chemistry labs, Conference Room, Junior and Senior Libraries. The sporting spirits find equal opportunities. The school displays two basket ball courts, a volley ball court, a badminton court, a skating rink, cricket field, a fully functional gym, table tennis room, yoga room and a cool, blue swimming pool. The DAVites at Gurgaon excel in sports and win many tournaments at the State Level and National Level, be it in Athletics, Volleyball, Table Tennis, Cricket, Swimming or Skating. School has won many other awards that include best CBSE teacher award, national teacher award for Anita.

Getting into the Job

For her, it was 'really strange'. She was working with Hansraj Model School, Punjabi Bagh under the DAV management as a Post-graduate teacher in mathematics. According to her, 'I was not given a choice, nor was I asked. I was simply told that here is a small 250 yards house in the interior of Gurgaon; here is a table and a chair, for which I had to pay later, and just about Rs. 5000 to start the school'. There was no questioning, nothing, rather she was asked not to question the decision. Anita was a passionate teacher; she would spend all her spare time with children.

Early Years

I had a very good childhood. I was born and brought up in Delhi. Father, member of Indian Economic Service was a major influence; he retired from the Planning Commission. He was always concerned about our education and stressed upon the fact that the girls have to be independent, 'must stand on their own feet'. We are two sisters, both of us are working, today she is Director (South East Asia) in World Bank with International Finance Corporation. A lot of independence was given to us; I don't think we give that much independence even today. I guess, those times were different; it was safer; there was less distraction. Focus was always on studies. I did my college from Delhi University. Mother was a homemaker. She provided the support at the home front. She kept us rooted while our father let us dream. We were studying for the sake of learning and studying only. There was lesser competition, no rote learning or stressful learning, not for competition with each other. For reminiscent Anita, 'we were fortunate to be in those times.

I did my initial schooling from Raghumal Girls School, in Cannaught Place but later we shifted to Naraina. So I did 10th and 11th from a government school at PUSA Institute. There was a good crowd with children of the scientists; and good influence.

I did my masters in Mathematics from Hansraj College. I had two choices, either I pursue English or Mathematics. My father influenced me to take Mathematics. It was a valued subject.

Beginning of the Journey

Twenty five years ago, public school education was nowhere to be seen here in Gurgaon. There was one Convent School, the oldest school in Gurgaon. Very small proprietary schools had sprung up but were at the initial stages. When we came, we had a solid foundation behind us, an organization to support us. So we had all the wherewithal of books, pedagogy, and the basic framework.

So First of all, I had to see from where the children would come—the neighbourhood. So we put up some banners, advertised in the newspapers, sent out leaflets, etc. We immediately started to enroll children, and recruit committed and sincere teachers. Once the enrolment started, we began to look for more land. That time HUDA allotted land on the basis of the reputation of the management at a very reasonable rate. So, I started going to HUDA office. I must have traveled to HUDA office, Chandigarh about a hundred times. May be my age was on my side, I had the zeal. I was young, idealistic and enthusiastic; I had that drive.

We started with one residential building in 1985, for kindergarten, lower KG till class four. And then we acquired a couple of other buildings, till we got this land from HUDA in 1987, when we were running our school in six buildings.

Right from the beginning, academics has been our strong point;

till today it continues to be the priority. As a DAV institution, Indian value system has always been important to us. Education is a serious business. While one should enjoy learning, it should not become entertainment. Students come to school to learn, not just for social interactions. This is something inculcated into our children's value system right from day 1.

In 1990, we shifted here in this campus; we had 5 rooms, one library and one lab. By 1998, we had a separate kindergarten because we wanted to give special place to our little ones. It's very close by in Sector14 itself. It's a very cozy and comfortable, and looks inviting to small children.

Also, my conviction is we must give something to the society as well. I had in mind orphans or the mentally challenged children. And here, with this management, I got an opportunity to do that for the mentally challenged children. So in 2003, we started a primary school in Sector-10A, and in 2004 we started a special wing. Today we have 100 children who are either mentally challenged or spastic or have cerebral palsy. We try to integrate and include them wherever we can. Last year nine of my children have done their 10th from National Institute of Open Schooling.

Before constructing this special wing, we visited different centres of education for the differently abled children. We contacted special educators to know how to design programme for these children; what exactly do we look for, how do we go about it, and what kind of teachers do we hire. Once we set the wheel, the momentum grew. There are 14 passionate special educators for 100 children.

Last year (2010) we started another school on Sohna Road. It's going to be a big school. Partial building is already ready. Last year we started with 300 children; today we have 900.

Vision

My vision is about the students. They should have confidence, good personality traits, good self-esteem. We want to make them grow up to be young men and women of character, of substance. Our vision is to inculcate academic strength, values and character. So the entire programme is governed by this vision. Accordingly, we make sure that faculty also cultivates the same values.

So when a new teacher joins, we organize orientation programme;

they are mentored by a senior teacher; to cultivate the values and create unity of purpose.

Innovations and Strategies

Reading is given a lot of importance in the school. 'We have a junior library and a senior library. Both are automated libraries with around 45000 books and a daily circulation of around 800-1000 books. We try and create an environment of learning and reading. A child of three and a half yrs comes to you with so much of curiosity, so much of inquisitiveness, and all you have to do is nurture that. Hence, we try and develop an atmosphere that attracts and motivates the children. The best thing we ever started was the literary weeks. Each child has to read a book and write reviews. We give different activities to different children. In junior classes the students have posters in the shape of a caterpillar running through the corridors, on which they write one character that really inspires them and the reason for the same. We make it a point that the library stays opened during normal days till whatever time the students want. It also stays open during the vacation; both parents and students come together to read. In classes I & II, grandparents come and bring a book on their grandchild's birthday and read it to the class. That way, the class also gets richer by a book, and the grandparents connect with the children. The students know that if they demand a book, they will get it at the earliest!

For maintaining quality, quality of teachers is the most important criteria. They are recruited only on merit. For a teacher to get into the school, it's a grilling interview by the Subject Experts and the Management. This instills a lot of confidence in the teacher that they are here on their own calibre and strength. Apart from the subject matter, we also assess their delivery, vocabulary, the temperament of the teacher, extent to which they go to help the children, etc., during the interview. Teachers are then oriented through induction programme. They are mentored by senior teachers. School has regular and frequent staff development programme. Everyone hence ends up putting in their 100 per cent efforts. They are ready to stay till after school hours, they come on holidays also without grumbling. Specific library time is allotted to every teacher so that they read and are up-to-date with the current events, strategies, researches, etc., lest they may stagnate. Teachers are specially trained to facilitate group learning so that every child actively participates in the learning tasks and activities. This has become necessary since the classes have become large making it difficult for the teacher to monitor learning of every child.

We make sure that classrooms that are hub of learning are well provided. DAV Public School was the pioneer in introducing smart boards in the classroom, about five years ago. All our classrooms are fitted with e-boards/digital/interactive boards with the requisite software. In fact, quite a number of software has been invented in-house by our teachers, while others have been procured from outside. Unlike the popular notion, teachers have to work more; they have to sieve through the presentations that the software provides and put up the filtered parts that are required in the class. The entire school is networked with two servers; one for classes 6-8 and another for classes 9-12. We have trained our teachers with different classroom strategies also. Teachers are time to time trained in different learning strategies.

We make a lot of strategic intervention. For example, if we want our children to have good oratory skills, then we follow certain strategies. Firstly, we will ensure that classroom instructions are more interactive and participative; organize inter-house competitions aligned to that. We also organize debates and declamations to develop oratory; we choose the themes very carefully so that the students get sensitized to certain important issues and are able to voice their opinions about the same too.

Similarly, if we want average QPI of the school to reach a particular target number, we plan for it. All the children cannot score above 90 or 80. There would always be some children who would have certain weak areas. We mount a strong remedial programme for them after school hours so that they may come up to the expected level.

Another important innovation is mentor-mentee programme. When children have a problem that they cannot share with their friends or parents, they can always find a teacher with whom they can share; and there will always be teachers who can connect with the students better. In this programme, every teacher would have one child whom she will nurture as her own child. So, 250 teachers in the school adopt 200-250 children. This has a tremendous effect.

We have started Wiki classrooms. The basic idea is to help a child at home. If he/she wants to consult a teacher, teacher will provide specific timings on which she will be available on the wiki classrooms. Students send in their queries and the teachers register the problems and help solve real time on the same day. Though it's only the first year, the response is really positive and good. To begin with, we held a workshop on wiki class to train the teachers. So this is how you basically move along with the times.

In another innovative practice, children visit places in order to facilitate better learning. We have been doing this for years. For example, when the history teacher teaches old monuments, she takes the children to places with old monuments. Students go with a questionnaire in hand, ready to be filled so that there is a real time feedback.

Innovations, we try and keep learning from our peers and surroundings; other schools, people, institutes, senior people, professors, orientation programmes, etc. And so we bring all the good and feasible ideas into the school and try to imbibe them. For example, we celebrate different weeks. Like if its year of physics, so we will have physics week and the children would eat, sleep, walk and talk physics, whether its class one or eleventh. And hence all the programmes and activities would be aligned to that.

Lot of training programme go on throughout the year in the school involving as many teachers as possible. Teachers sent to a training programme train the entire faculty on their return to make sure that whatever new has been learnt is shared with all the faculty members. This includes both technological and subject matter updates. Similarly, supervisors are exposed to management development programmes.

Process of Deciding

Process of decision making can be seen from more than one angle. There are several innovative practices in the school that has brought the school to a point of sustainable quality. Question one is: who is the innovator or who introduced these innovative ideas in the school? Second question is who implemented? Associated question is the nature and quality of engagement of the innovator and the implementer? How is the success or failure judged?

Principal is credited for introducing almost all the innovations mentioned in the previous section in the school, except Wiki Class that was an innovative initiative of a teacher. The mentor-mentee innovation was learnt from another DAV school in Odisha. Principal adapted it in this school which is much larger and benefitting much larger number of students. So, Principal herself is the major innovator. Obviously, wherever the innovations relate to classroom practices, teachers are responsible for implementation. She 'discussed the innovative idea with the supervisors, heads of departments and teachers' to take them into confidence. In case of administrative innovations like teacher recruitment and teacher induction and training, principal shares the major responsibility of implementation along with the super-ordinate school management. It is difficult to describe the nature and quality of the engagement between the innovating principal and implementing teachers. Principal is both an employer (in a large measure) and an accepted leader. Her positional authority ensures implementation, and personal power, namely support and encouragement, makes implementation challenging and joyful (not burdensome). Overall decision making stays with the principal.

Management of Resistance

Of course there had been some kind of resistance when you start the school. Our first encounter was the people living in the neighbourhood. Construction does create inconvenience to people, and they resisted. We spoke to the neighbours, and told how much time this would take. We also assured them to reduce the inconvenience as much as possible.

There were issues in administrative management, especially the way one would like to manage the school. The management may not agree; and there were occasions when principal faced some problem. But once she was able to establish the bonafide that her choice of administrative style and strategy was in the interest of the school, there was no big obstacle. In fact, the management became so supportive that she hardly faces any resistance.

Teacher resistance to innovations is normal. This happened when the school decided to introduce smart boards in the school. Teachers were comfortable with their styles and resources. This innovation needed new skills and competencies among the teacher; and training and development of such skills. It took lot of patience in persuading the teachers and their training. Principal had to monitor till teachers got used to and realized the advantage of the innovation. 'You require mentoring as well as monitoring in implementing innovative practices'. The story is similar in almost all cases of academic innovations. The strategy was two fold. Firstly, once an innovation was chosen and decided to be introduced, it was a commitment; and was made known to every potential implementer. Second was the encouragement and support in implementing innovations that provide life to an innovation and protects it from deformity. The entire process was duly monitored.

A few innovations successfully implemented, the system gets used to innovating. 'Keep on giving the staff new challenges, keep on bringing new things to school, teachers remain active learners'. Teaching and learning cannot be monotonous. According to Anita, 'You bring in different classroom learning strategies; everybody has to know how to teach with Graphic organizer worksheets, fish bone structure, include group presentations, peer editing, etc.; then you have e-books, technology, CCE etc. So keep on bringing new things and give them challenges and of course give them a lot of support so that they can overcome such challenges'.

Supervisors and incharges enjoy lot of freedom with responsibility. Principal and supervisors work as a team. They meet every day after school hours. With HODs, meetings are held 4-5 times a year or whenever needed. This frequent consultations and dialogues also help managing resistance.

Leadership Style

That all the ideas get implemented, and the school has stayed at the top of the 600 DAV schools for 10 consecutive years speaks volumes of her leadership skills and qualities. She could not have either achieved this fit and sustain unless she was able to take people along. She tries to take people into confidence while ensuring that every task is accomplished to expected level of quality. Typically, she puts an idea before the teachers, supervisors and others concerned. She persuades in a manner that her followers understand her seriousness of purpose. She neither 'dictates', nor 'leaves it alone' to the people. She tries to convince her colleagues on the value of the innovations, provides all possible support to remove the barriers and develop the necessary skill to implement innovations. She carefully monitors while maintaining a genuine human face of the innovative project.

Only one of the many innovative features was an initiative of a teacher. Thus, school depends on the principal for innovative ideas. Enthusiasm for innovations and change is still to sink among the teachers and staff. It is still to become an organizational culture.

Final Comments

It's a nice place to be; it is like a temple to us, especially when one has devoted her best years in the development of the school. But it is a satisfying experience. Then, there is a sense of belonging to the school which always make us work better and towards the growth and development of our children.

The children spend the most precious years in the school, when they are learning, when they are exploring themselves, and the world. They undergo so many changes in the school years. And how their personality shapes up depends a lot on the schooling.

NOTE

1. Case has been developed based on recorded interview with Principal Anita Makkar by Charu Dhingra.

9
REPOSITIONING AN INSTITUTION
Ramakrishna Mission Vidyamandira, Belur[1]

Although there is no formal ranking, Ramakrishna Mission Vidyamandira is popularly ranked immediately after the Presidency, The St. Xaviers and the Scottish Church Colleges. For Swami Atmapriyananda, the monk principal, there is no reason why Vidyamandira should not be second to none. It is quite strong in mathematics and science departments, but weak in humanities and social sciences. The Swami makes a determined effort to consolidate the strengths, and strengthen the weaker areas. He plunges into new vocational courses, almost sinks with the ship but comes out victorious with spiritual blessings. Inspired by cricket strategy, the Swami emphasizes the right person for the right job, building back-up in every position and team work. He successfully repositions the college in the first orbit.

Accepting the Assignment

Swami Atmapriyananda was a good student of science. He could have opted for engineering, technology or other applied subjects, but he chose physics, theoretical physics, in particular, for specialization. Having graduated with physics (Honours) from Vivekananda Institution in Madras, he completed his postgraduation and doctorate in physics from the Presidency College, Madras under Madras University. According to him, he loved to be in the conceptual world rather than busy himself with solving problems.

It was during Swami Atmapriyananda's study at Ramakrishna Mission Vivekananda College, Madras that he was exposed to Swami Vivekananda's philosophy and thoughts. His intimate contact with Ramakrishna Math, Madras, and the senior monks there, further opened up a world of spiritual thoughts and a luminous vision of a higher Reality that, he felt, could be realized and served. This kindled in him the fire of renunciation (sannyasa) envisioned and activated by Swami Vivekananda along a new channel, where the service of humankind could fuse harmoniously with the realization of the higher Reality or God in the cauldron of universal love and service. Finally, he got inducted into the Ramakrishna Mission as a brahmacharin (spiritual novice) and took to monkhood in 1978.

He began his academic career as a teacher of Physics in Loyola College, Madras. He joined Ramakrishna Mission Vidya Mandir, Belur, in 1978, as a lecturer. He was designated vice principal in 1988 and as principal in 1992. Thus, Swami Atmapriyananda has been associated with the Institution for nearly 25 years. As a monk of the Mission, he was given this assignment, which was not his choice. The Mission assigns responsibilities to the monks, depending upon their potentialities and educational background. It was the choice of the Mission.

He, however, had his own argument in favour of teaching as a career. According to him, 'teaching enables us to influence young minds. Of course, not any type of teaching. Teaching can influence young minds when the purpose of teaching is seen to enthuse, motivate and develop love for the subjects rather than making the students knowledgeable about a subject. Students should be able to construct their learning once they love a subject'. For Swami Atmapriyananda, 'teaching has to be a passion. It is not enough to make teaching a mission or a profession. For, passion has an emotional component, and that is important. It is the emotionality attached to a cause, the way the suicide squads dedicate their lives with full knowledge of self-annihilation for a cause. Teaching must have that emotional component'.

Mission

Swami Atmapriyananda decidedly disagrees with the concept of missions for an institution in advance. According to him, "the mission of an institution cannot be placed in the womb of the future". The mission must evolve over a period of time. 'What is important is to take care of the present so that good future can evolve'.

There were, however, enough indications that Swami Atmapriyananda nurtured dreams about the Vidyamandira, though these were not articulated in documents. His dreams or visions were not static. They were dynamic. They evolved with time.

Vidyamandira is located adjacent to Belur Math—headquarter of Ramakrishna Mission. It is one of the best colleges affiliated to Calcutta University. The institution enjoys a distinct reputation for high (moral) quality for its value orientation. It is a residential college for boys. One of his major dreams was to further improve the performance of students to be competitive with the best(s) in the University. The new mission was to reposition Vidyamandira along with Presidency College, St. Xaviers, etc., that enjoyed the reputation of the 'best' in the University. There were several other supportive missions. One such mission was to reconstruct the mindset of teaching and non-teaching staff, and students to share the dream and believe that they could be the best. For, unless the dream is shared, chances of its translation will be at risk.

Within the philosophic framework of the Ramakrishna Mission, one of the other missions of Swami Atmapriyananda was also to cope with time and make the college as modern as possible in the courses and the curricula.

Although Swami Atmapriyananda made some efforts to take people along in deciding the missions, almost all the missions were his own. The visible and subtle resistances indicate that 'people' in the organizations were, on the one hand, fairly comfortable and satisfied with their performance; and on the other, they found it difficult to share Swami Atmapriyananda's mission of either repositioning the college or introducing new courses, particularly vocational courses. Swami Atmapriyananda had to prove the feasibility of his missions. Thus, in a way, he took people to share his vision through demonstration.

Action Strategies

Major emphasis on achieving excellence in performance of students and repositioning the institute into a new orbit were designed to be achieved through several activities intended to improve the performance of the teachers and the non-teaching staff of the institution. The emphases were on the right people in the right job, development of skill-based back-up, team work, etc. During a discussion with me, the Swami used cricket as a metaphor to illustrate his points. 'What is important for the team is to win. For a team to win, every department like bowling, fielding, wicket keeping and catching have to be the best. An institution needs people with different types of skills and competencies. Like in cricket, a person fielding in the first slip must have good reflexes whereas a person in the outfield must be a great sprinter. A great first slip player may be unsuitable for the outfield, and a sprinting outfield player will be a batsman's delight if brought to the first slip. A team cannot depend upon just one great first slip fielder. It needs back-up in the team to win. A team needs players at second and third slips as well to back-up the first slip'. This analogy is totally valid for managing and taking Vidyamandira to the new height.

There were several identifiable activities. One of the major activities was job re-designing primarily to get people out of the fixed view about the structure and roles in the job. For example, Vidyamandira has a capable, competent and dependable accountant. However, Vidyamandira was completely dependent on him. Hence, there was a crisis whenever the accountant was on leave. This accountant was committed, hardworking and knowledgeable. He had developed, over the years, a deep love for the institution's ideology—mainly through continuous pep talks and informal conversations with the principal whom he had to meet several times a day. He had come to feel that he was not a mere 'employee', paid for the job assigned to him; rather, he felt himself to be a participant in the great mission of imparting 'man-making', 'character-building' education that Swami Vivekananda envisioned. By and by, when this accountant became proficient in many things relating to educational administration and was willing to rush and serve wherever there was a need or a crisis, the Swami noticed that some of the more mechanical jobs that this accountant was doing could be delegated to someone else with a lesser capacity, so that not only this helped the overworked and overburdened, committed person to get some relief, but a second line of defence could be built up with this person at the helm. This had two advantages: one, the others who thought themselves less capable and therefore, less needed now felt a sense of participation in being called upon to be in the team eleven; and two—this is more important—they were influenced and inspired by the dedication and passion of the accountant under whom they were put. Over a period of time, this had a cascading effect and led to, what one might call, a telescoping of faculties and talents, rather than an hierarchy. According to the Swami, 'The team slowly got more closely interwoven, with everybody thus, not only in contributing something, but also feeling that his contribution is also responsible for the team's victory'.

Let us take another instance. A problem arose in the management of the hostel. The hostel is run with strict discipline. One of the students found it difficult to cope with the discipline, though he did not disturb others or miss out his studies. For example, when he was supposed to study, he slept or played; when he was supposed to sleep or relax, he was deeply engaged in reading and writing. Yet, he was a good student. The warden recommended the student's removal from the hostel; since Vidyamandira is a residential institution, it would automatically mean his removal from the college. The warden's contention was that the student was undisciplined, and this set a wrong example for others. When the incidence was brought to the notice of the principal, he had a prolonged discussion with the warden, who insisted that the boy must be removed. He claimed finality of his authority on the issue as in-charge of the hostel. His basic argument was that the student violated the discipline and was setting a bad example for others, who might raise the issue of discriminative practice of protecting an undisciplined student, when others were being asked to follow discipline. The principal counselled and coached the warden to adopt a persuasive approach to the student because he was a good student, although he did not conform to the time prescribed by the hostel. Swami Atmapriyananda also had a discussion with the student. After a prolonged discussion, he asked the student what he would have done if he were the warden. The problem was resolved. This was one of the many examples how the principal resolved human problems through a variety of cognitive reorganizations.

Another important consideration of the principal was: the organizational efficiency depends upon putting the right people on the right job. However, this need not necessarily be true that the right people are on the right job in the Vidyamandira. The institution is run primarily by conventions. For example, some teachers have been teaching a particular subject or part of the subject for years and decades together. Whatever be the quality of teaching—good, average or poor—it gets repeated over the years. Whenever a new member of the staff joins, he/she is given the subject that was taught by the person who might have retired or in case one of the existing faculty members wants a change. Quality instruction, thus, is just a matter of chance. But the situation can be substantially altered, if allotment of teaching subjects is done according to competence and interest of the faculty members. Swami Atmapriyananda illustrated the issue of job relocation for achieving greater efficiency in the Department of Philosophy.

The principal was a teacher of physics. He studied philosophy extensively as part of his education in the Ramakrishna Mission Order. He participated in the departmental meetings of the Department of Philosophy on allocation of papers to teachers. The head of the department used to teach part of the Indian philosophy and logic. The principal proposed that the newly recruited young teacher be given the teaching of logic. The principal, as he had seen the new teacher during the selection interview, believed that he would do a good job of teaching logic. The head of the department argued that he has been teaching logic for so many years, and it requires high order of skills. The new teacher 'should be able to teach Indian philosophy'. Swami Atmapriyananda persuaded the head of the department to continue to teach Indian philosophy and share logic with the new incumbent. The head of the department agreed to share the subject with the new incumbent. According to the assessment of Swami Atmapriyananda, this brought in a significant improvement in the teaching of philosophy in the institution. There are many similar instances in various areas of the college management.

Traditionally, Vidyamandira has strong departments in sciences and mathematics. The departments of Sanskrit, Political Science, History, etc., were comparatively weaker. One of the important interventions was not only identifying the weaker departments, but also deciding to make positive interventions to improve the quality of instruction in the departments. At the first instance, the principal's efforts were to identify the basic reasons for the weaknesses of the departments. According to his assessment, the students in these departments were comparatively weaker than the students in the departments of science and mathematics. This may also be true about the teachers of science and mathematics, vis-a-vis teachers of languages and social science departments. To upgrade the departments of social sciences and humanities, Swami Atmapriyananda spent time with each department in the departmental meetings; he also involved himself in the selection of students in these departments. His involvement not only facilitated selection of better students but also gave a different perspective to the departments about their relative importance due to principal's personal participation. Over the years, the performance of the students in these departments also significantly improved. This proves the point that 'supporting and improving' weaker departments brings overall improvement in the college.

While the Vidyamandira was consistently and continuously making efforts in achieving excellence, Swami Atmapriyananda had serious reservations, even rejection, about the concept of competitive excellence. He was emphatic on building cohesion as the foundation of institution building rather than competitive excellence. Cohesion can be built by looking at others' point of view. The cohesion should also allow competition within and with self for optimization of the dormant potential in every individual in the institution. The emphasis on the right people for the right job and job re-designing aimed primarily at optimization of human potential.

One major innovation for which Vidyamandira was nominated to me as a case was its excellent work in vocational education under the UGC scheme of 'vocationalization of education at the first degree level'. Calcutta University decided to take up the scheme in a big way. The West Bengal College and University Teachers' Association (WBCUTA) and its general secretary, Sri Anil Bhattacharya, played a key role. Vidyamandira also applied to UGC for starting three courses under the scheme. With the UGC sanction, B.Sc. in Computer Applications and B.Sc. in Industrial Chemistry were started in 1994. There were, however, hiccups galore during the initial stages. There were no full-time teachers available; qualified instructors and teachers, willing to teach part-time, were not easy to procure. The Vocational' tag attached to the course raised doubts in the minds of the prospective students about the status of the course. Since Calcutta University teaches honours courses at the degree level, the question of whether these vocational courses would have the status of the honours courses came up repeatedly. There were several other questions. What are the prospects of this new course? Where does this lead to? Where are the competent teachers? Will there be a vertical mobility for students passing out of these courses? With no satisfactory answers to any or all of these, the wisdom of the principal, who started these vocational courses, was called to question. The whole scenario was one of depression and scepticism: the students were depressed and demoralized; the teachers were critical, with the sympathizers among them watching with a deep sigh; the principal was criticized for pushing the college, reputed for its high standing in purely academic and theoretical subjects, to a path that threatened to alter the very character of the institution. The reputation and the image of the institution, built through decades of hard work, appeared to be at stake. The principal seemed isolated and the fight did not appear easy.

Swami Vivekananda's words of exhortations, according to Atmapriyananda, charged him with a new power. Rather than giving up, the Swami decided to find new ways to solve the problem for maintaining the image and reputation of the institution. The massive resurgence of the programme that followed, according to Swami Atmapriyananda, was due to the power of prayer. The principal addressed a personal letter to the General Manager (GM) of Andrew Yule Company, an MNC, now renamed, that was opening a new sector on Information Technology in Kolkata; he sought placement of two boys of Vidyamandira. The GM, while interviewing the students, was deeply impressed, primarily due to their behavioural quality. Their knowledge of IT was good enough for induction into Andrew Yule. Swami Atmapriyananda had briefed the students about the kind of interview they might face—more questions and discussions on Indian culture, spiritual heritage, higher human values, etc., than dry technical questions on computers could be asked. Coming out from an institution created to actualize the 'man-making' educational vision of Swami Vivekananda, they were most suited for an organization just starting on a new venture that required qualities like teamwork, dedication, integrity and obedience to the leader, etc., above all else. The GM found out that there were nine students in the class and asked the principal to send all the nine for the interview. Surprisingly, he offered immediate placement to all the nine, incurring the displeasure, if not wrath, of many of his colleagues who said it was perhaps not proper that nine freshers from a single institution be selected at one go at the very beginning of the new IT venture. The GM's answer was that he would not have singled out any of the institutions, if it was not the Ramakrishna Mission.

In a couple of years, the company sent a few of their young recruitees (ex-Vidyamadira) to man their installations abroad, particularly in UK. The depression that had overtaken these boys and the cloud of gloom that had descended upon the institution, as a whole, now changed into sheer ecstatic delight. Swami Atmapriyananda spared no opportunity in exhorting them to think of their younger brothers now studying the same course at Vidyamandira and to contribute to their alma mater in terms of advice, experience, resources, etc. The net result is now obvious. Today, the Computer Applications Course in Vidyamandira is having a tremendous demand because of placement opportunities not only within West Bengal and other parts of India, but also all over the world.

The Swami experienced a 'mysterious blessing' for his efforts. Brahmachari Shreesh (a novice-monk of Ramakrishna Order) was posted to Vidyamandira by the Ramakrishna Mission authorities at the Belur Math Headquarters. He was a product of Indian Institute of Technology (IIT), Kanpur, one of the finest institutes in India in Information Technology. Brahmachari Shreesh was a brilliant student. He finished his doctoral programme there. Shreesh joined the Ramakrishna Mission as a monk at the Belur Math and after a few months was posted at Vidyamandira by a sudden turn of circumstances. He took full charge of the Computer Applications Course and the computer laboratory, teaching both theoretical and practical classes with great efficiency. He thoroughly revised the ten-year old syllabus, raising its standard to international levels, downloading these syllabi from the Internet. Students passing out, though not very brilliant, now get raised to such a level of appreciation for the institution that it draws the admiration of all the companies that eagerly recruit them.

In the process, Vidyamandira learnt the new skill of quality management. Since there was a dearth of skilled teachers of computers and IT, as well as Industrial Chemistry, senior students were involved in coaching the junior students. On the one hand, this peer-teaching filled the important gap of teaching staff; on the other hand, it resulted in excellence in learning of the outgoing students. The peer-teaching was used for tutorials, remedial instructions, but, more importantly, for enrichment learning for the brighter students.

Vidyamandira, Swami Atmapriyananda contended, takes full advantage of the proximity of Belur Math, visited by scholars from all over India and the world. Swami Atmapriyananda invites regularly experts from different institutions within West Bengal as well as outside. Although initially such expert invitations were for presenting a seminar or a lecture, Swami Atmapriyananda extended this event to actual classroom teaching. One example was asking Prof. H S Mani, a scholar in Theoretical Particle Physics and a former professor at IIT, Kanpur, to take a series of classes, which he did. There are many instances where such outstanding experts from Indian Institute of Cultivation and Science, Indian Institute of Science, etc., took regular classes in the college.

Another important strategy of building excellence and repositioning the college was encouraging the students to look for international opportunities for post-graduation and other research. Students from Vidyamandira usually seek admission to the postgraduate departments in Calcutta University. Swami Atmapriyananda started encouraging them to seek similar opportunities in the universities of USA, the UK and other countries. Students were hesitant—'nobody has done so'; 'they may not succeed in getting the admission in a foreign university'. The encouragement of the principal led many students now seeking admission and succeeding in the US universities. A new precedence was thus created encouraging other students to try further.

Swami Atmapriyananda persuaded in enlarging such visions into more areas, primarily to create a mindset for repositioning the Vidyamandira. An interesting event was invitation to Prof. Kaushik Basu, an eminent Economist of international acclaim from Cornell University. He was invited to deliver a lecture on Game Theory, on which he was an outstanding expert. Swami Atmapriyananda asked his colleagues to invite all the professors as well as students of Presidency

College, St. Xavier's College and other such renowned colleges of Calcutta for Dr. Basu's lecture. There was a big elite audience. The event boosted the morale of students and teachers of Vidyamandira.

During the last couple of years, particularly since 1996, students of Ramakrishna Mission Vidyamandira have been occupying a large number of top slots in the university examinations, challenging the students from other reputed colleges like Presidency, St. Xavier's, etc.

Managing Resistance

The primary source of resistance to any efforts in improvement of a college, particularly in the teaching-learning process is the additional work and the work load of the teachers. Private tuition is plenty in West Bengal; hence, there is vested interest in managing teaching-learning process in a particular fashion in the college that generates a private tuition market. This is anti-thesis to Swami Atmapriyananda's 'teaching as a passion' position. The exposure of the students to national and international experts also generated resistance because it generates comparison of scholars of different standings with those in the college. Yet, this led to striving for excellence among the teachers and among the students. Department of Mathematics is a case in point. Private tuition business has been totally eliminated from the minds of the students and their parents. Not that the students did not face problems with understanding some of the lectures by some teachers. Supplementary and remedial teaching by scholars and sometimes 'peers' were arranged to solve these problems. Interestingly, over the years, the Department of Mathematics has been producing first-class-first rank students at the university examinations. That has been the envy of all the top ranking colleges in the state. They were amazed to learn that it is due to the elimination of the private tuition mindset; private tuition spoilt the creativity of the students and made them mediocre. But then the long-drawn struggle on this issue over decades in the face of resistance is a success saga of which Vidyamandira is proud.

The most visible and powerful resistance was regarding introduction of vocational courses not only from the teachers, but also from the fellow monks. As mentioned earlier, the resistance was replaced within a year with a new found enthusiasm when Swami Atmapriyananda succeeded in the placement of the students. That breakthrough has given a new form of confidence everywhere.

Leadership Style

Swami Atmapriyananda was candid to admit that he hardly studied modern management and leadership. His basic inspiration was Swami Vivekananda. According to him, the first important component of his leadership style is respect for human dignity. Deriving inspiration from Swami Vivekananda's "Service to people is Service to God", he recognizes every individual, at whatever level they work, as God's own incarnation. His second important style was drawing out the best in everyone—Swami Vivekananda's concept of education as manifestation of the perfection already in man. His basic strategy of drawing out the best in everyone is depicted by the right people in the right job, job re-designing and re-orientation of the people through coaching, counselling, pace setting, etc.

Another important component of his leadership is the recognition, a clear acknowledgment that the more creative a person is, the more difficult it is to control him/her; whereas a person who works mechanically may be easily controlled. A creative person is a non-conformist with no fixed routine; he/she is very sensitive in matters of inter-personal behaviour, lives in a world of ideas rather than in the familiar world of gross objects. To be able to control him, the 'leader should first give up the very notion of trying to control' The leader needs to possess 'infinite patience, perseverance and, above all, love'.

Although insisting on production emphasis, Swami Atmapriyananda immediately adds that there is need to check the problems as well. He discusses the issues with so many people who might be directly or indirectly connected with them—and this, in an informal fashion without the person concerned being aware that a certain issue is being discussed. This is primarily to collect ideas, no matter what the source is and putting these ideas together, one could try to see the emergence of a concrete picture. This style is typical of a democratic leader in a contemporary organization.

Swami Atmapriyananda involves himself with the individual staff members at every level, including the personal level to help solve their problems. While he insists on getting involved, he makes it a point that such involvement should not be a 'strategic action'. The involvement must be genuine at emotional level rather than at cognitive level.

Success and Failure

Success and failure seem to be reasonably visible in Vidyamandira. It is able to improve the excellence in performance. It was established as one of the best colleges. The institution has excelled further and positioned itself with the top elite institutions. That the students of this institution occupied the top six positions in one subject and similar positions in other subjects is an indication of its achieving the objective of excellence. Similarly, despite resistance and demoralization at different points of time, the introduction of vocational courses by Swami Atmapriyananda in the Vidyamandira is an indication of its success. One of the major missions of Swami Atmapriyananda was to develop 'passion for teaching and passion for study'. It is difficult to measure the success of this mission, unless it is derived from indirect sources like performance of students in different subjects. Vidyamandira has been recognized as one of the best colleges in the country by the University Grants Commission. It is regularly invited to important forums at different places in the country.

It has, however, failed to get the autonomous status. It awaits clearance of the university and the state government. Secondly, Vidyamandira wanted to run a few postgraduate courses. Although postgraduate classes are generally conducted by the university itself, there are exceptions like Presidency College that offers postgraduate programmes. In the re-positioning of the college, this is an important landmark which it is yet to achieve. The third important failure is the lack of excellence and re-positioning of the humanities and some of the subjects in social sciences. As the university results indicate, Vidyamandira has excelled in science and mathematics, but not in humanities and social sciences.

Learning

There are several important lessons to be learnt from the experiences of institution building by Swami Atmapriyananda. The first and foremost is getting involved with all in the organization in their personal well-being, to be with them in their happiness and sorrows with an open heart, a deep involvement not at strategic level but at emotional level. This genuineness will create an environment where people will look up to the leader'.

The second important learning is absolute transparency deeply rooted in institution building, so that people do not suspect or look for a hidden agenda. Failure in this aspect seriously erodes the credibility of the leader and once credibility is lost, the institution collapses like a pack of cards. It takes years, if not decades, to build up this credibility and the one and the only means of achieving this credibility is through absolute transparency of approach.

The third learning is human management. In any institution, there are a handful of good and sincere workers; there are some shirkers; and some fence sitters on the watch out for the way the wind blows. In order to manage an institution, people who do good and sincere work are usually given more and more work. On the one hand, they become pressurized and hard-pressed, and on the other hand, they unconsciously form a coterie. Atmapriyananda's learning was to 'involve everyone rather than a few who produce and form the coterie', giving, at the same time, due and proportionate regard to the contribution of each. A weak leader, however good and well meaning, usually gets work done by the sincere and hardworking persons, but pampers the shirkers and fence sitters, out of fear of criticism that he is favouring only those who perform and work for him, with the result, that the hardworking ones gradually get demotivated and wish they could also shirk work. The Swami was quite clear about this. He followed the principle of "no favour and no fear". But then, the shirkers need to be motivated rather than sidelined or subtly punished in the form of disfavours, while, at the same time, the performers and sincere workers ought to be kept under leash, lest they should arrogate to themselves a special and exclusive role in the achievement of excellence by the institution. These two groups, with diversity of temperaments, were cemented together by the power of love by the mature leader, Swami Atmapriyananda. The Swami's learning, in this respect, was not just to try, but achieve some positive results.

NOTE

1. Between then (2004) and now (2005), Ramakrishna Mission has been repositioned. It is now a deemed university, declared in the meeting of education Ministers of States in Bangalore in 2005. Swami Atmapriyananda is the first vice-chancellor.

10

TRANSFUSING FRESH LIFE

Mrinalini Devi Mahavidyalay

The college was in a chaos, when the new principal joined. Teachers spent minimum amount of time in the college as they were busy in private tuitions. Student leaders' primary concern was student union elections; for the rest, the pressing engagements were socializing, dating, etc. The college had a poor infrastructure with ill-equipped laboratories and a library with a scanty collection of books. Dr. Ranajit Basu's is the story of reconstruction where teachers now spend more than five hours every day in the college, students attend classes, student union elections do not bring in any more fights; teachers and students are engaged in serious academic dialogue through college seminars, the performances of students have significantly scaled new heights; etc. In the short span of a few years, the principal mobilized a large amount of money from the UGC, the state government, the local community and the political leaders; achieved a qualitative shift in the infrastructure and the programmes. With a visible positive shift in the organizational culture, the college is now poised for a new leap.

Early Development

Dr. Ranajit Basu, a qualified english scholar and teacher, and principal of Mrinalini Devi Mahavidyalay was born in Rangpur, now in Bangladesh. His father, a postgraduate in history, was the headmaster of a high school. The dominating influence on Ranajit was of his uncle (father's elder brother), who was an advocate. Almost everyone in the family was a graduate. Ranajit grew up in a family that maintained high moral standards. The members of the family participated in social action programmes; there was a leftist orientation. One of his uncles was a cardholder of the Communist Party of India.

College and the Assignment

The college was in a bad shape. The college timetable was divided into two halves. One batch of teachers came in the forenoon, took classes till 1 p.m. and left for their residences. Another batch of teachers would come in the afternoon and take classes. This arrangement was designed and adopted to facilitate private tuition which was very common among the teachers in the college. Students did not show interest in attending classes. A few were interested in getting through the election of office bearers in the students union. Anything other than that was not of much interest. Very few students attended classes. It suited the teachers as well. Students attended paid tuition classes at teachers' homes.

The college was nicknamed 'vrindavana',[1] place for dating among boys and girls. The college provided the necessary space for dating. The college was largely run by the office staff who dealt with the local finances raised through student fees, the college fund and the grants received from the state government. Teachers were not interested in the affairs of the college, as much as the students who were busy, either dating or practising politics.

It is in such a situation that Dr. Basu applied for the post of principal. According to his statement, he saw an enormous challenge in the assignment. He could 'have tried for a better and well-established college'. But he loved 'challenge and preferred this college, because the job was extremely challenging', particularly since the college was in fact not functioning. He mentioned that he had a knack to administer and based his assumption on another incidence. He attempted Union Public Service Commission exam. He was selected for the Indian Police Service, one of the allied services, but could not clear the police verification. He believed that it was because of his leftist background. The selection to the IPS, an elite service gave him the confidence to administer and manage. This encouraged him to accept this assignment.

Missions

Since it was not functioning properly, the college was affiliated to Calcutta University, his first and foremost mission was to bring discipline back to the college, where teachers held their classes and stayed in the college for a reasonable period of time, where the students attended the classes. In other words, his mission was to ensure that the college carried out the charted academic activities.

Consequent to bringing back the discipline in the college and ensuring normal functioning, his next important agenda was improved performance of the students in the university examinations.

According to his assessment, the college had very little infrastructure that could facilitate and encourage a good teaching-learning process. So, one of his agendas was to improve the infrastructure. Dr. Basu was a loner in conceptualizing and articulating the missions, without much support from the college, at least in the beginning. Neither were teachers interested in staying in the college for longer hours, because it affected their private tuitions and hence, their earnings, nor were the students interested in their studies. When neither of them was interested in teaching-learning, they did not show any concern or interest in the development of infrastructure and other facilities in the college.

The principal has referred to the support received from Prof. Ranen Poddar, former vice-chancellor of Calcutta University, who became the chairman of the Governing Body of the college. 'Prof. Poddar inspired and provided strong support' to Ranajit's mission of institution building. However, as he moved on and indicated his firm resolves to effect changes in the college, he received support; the missions were accepted by the students, the teachers and the administrative staff.

Strategic Actions

In the first instance, he wanted to make the teachers stay back in the college for longer hours. One of his strategies was to involve the academic committee in reconstructing the timetable, so that the classes of the teachers were not compacted within half a day; instead, they were to be spread over the entire working day with leisure periods in between. That would make the teachers stay for longer hours in the college. A new norm was developed: the teachers had to stay in the college for five hours every day of the week. This was seriously resented and resisted by the teachers. The teachers enjoyed the benefit of staying in the college for a short period, which yielded ample time for private tuitions. Long hours in the college would adversely affect their tuition hours. Also, students had to stay in the college for longer hours to attend the classes that would now be spread over the whole day. Attendance was necessary to be eligible for appearing in the university examination. Things started improving though with reluctant cooperation. Teachers grudgingly stayed back.

When the teachers started staying back in the college, the principal made an effort to improve the library facilities, so that teachers could engage their leisure hours for academic preparation and enrichment.

The Principal mobilized grants from the University Grants Commission; he received about eight lakh rupees for the library for books and journals. The college library has now more than 30,000 books, which, for a college of this size is fairly large. The principal believes that reading habits of the teachers have improved because of staying for longer hours in the college. 'We initiated academic seminars in the college where students and teachers participated', says the principal. Teachers were involved in tutorials and counselling of students. Although the tutorial was an official practice, violation was the rule hitherto. It was brought back. An important new addition was the teacher's counselling of a small group of students. The teachers not only helped the students in improving their skills in solving their academic problems and their performance but also in solving their personal problems. This personal help to students improved the mutual relationship between teachers and students. The college did not have a single qualified or professionally trained counsellor. Personal counselling is, however, largely based on common sense and experience of the teachers.

As the teachers' participation improved and their competence also improved through peer group interaction, the principal tried to mobilize the students through the students union leaders to participate better in the classes. Since the teachers were not available for private tuition, the students, despite their initial resistance, started participating in the classes almost out of compulsion. Subsequently, the students were also involved in the seminars. The principal encouraged them not only to be listeners, but also to be active, to ask questions, to make comments on the teacher's presentation. The maturity of the process of this interactive seminar is indicated by the students presenting papers in the seminars. Steadily, with the improvement of the teachers and the involvement of the students, the college was brought to a situation, where a minimum level of acceptable academic operations was possible.

This obviously led to a significant improvement in the results at the university examinations. The principal claimed that more than 90 per cent students succeeded in the university examinations which was at a miserably low level a couple of years ago. He also mentioned that majority of the students in honours courses in various humanities and social science subjects now got more than 55 per cent marks. One of his students in English honours, 'missed first class just by seven marks'. Thus, over a period of time, there was a significant improvement in academic programmes in all the departments.

His second important effort was mobilizing resources and building infrastructure. He narrated one of the incidents of infrastructure development of the college before he joined. The college got a grant of Rs. 1 lakh for building construction. As per normal rules and practices, the amount was handed over to the Public Works Department (PWD) of the government for construction. The PWD constructed four walls and half of the roof, and left the construction halfway, under the pretext that 'the money was over'. The principal mobilized a grant of rupees Rs.4 lakh from the state government for civil works. He made a new experiment. He consulted a young engineer in the PWD who had joined recently. He narrated the experience of the college with regard to the previous grant. The young engineer advised him that it was of no use commissioning PWD for small-grant projects. He would have the same experience. The college would not be able to derive the full benefits of the grant. The young engineer advised him that the college could take up the construction itself. The principal consulted an architect agency for architectural design and implementation for a token amount of about five per cent of the construction cost. The college involved a local retired engineer who offered his services free for supervising the construction. The principal and one of the members of the managing committee, moved to the brick kiln and negotiated the price for the college. He was able to buy the bricks at a reduced rate. Similarly, he negotiated with the cement and other companies. The success is indicated by the construction of six all-weather classrooms and completion of the previous unfinished classroom with the small grant of Rs.4 lakhs.

With this success, he moved further to mobilize funds. He mobilised about Rs. 10 lakhs, five lakhs each from the fund of the member of parliament and from the district panchayat. These grants were used to construct hostel, improvement of the classroom facilities, and an auditorium. He was able to mobilize grants from the University Grants Commission for sports and games facilities; and a departmental grant of Rs.3 lakhs for construction of a gymnasium and other sports facilities.

Besides these grants, he mobilized contributions to the college fund. Besides the tuition fees that could not be used for purposes other than teachers' salary, other kinds of developmental funds were raised amounting to about Rs. 15 lakhs. Thus, within five years, he mobilized Rs.37 lakhs for the college. More importantly, these funds were not handed over conventionally to the PWD. Instead, the local members of the community, members of the managing committee, the principal and some of the teachers joined hands in utilizing the money, as best as they could. The worth of the money was much more now.

The third important area of innovation in the college was the beginning of new courses. The college already had a number of honours programmes in the humanities and social sciences, but it did not have a science department. The principal initiated a large number of science courses, though not honours programmes. Similarly, he introduced the compulsory programme of computers for every student. This programme was not free; it charged a token amount of fees—Rs. 67 a month per student. The entire contract was given to West Bengal Electronics Ltd., a government of West Bengal undertaking, which conducts a complete programme for the students. Fifty percent of the total collection is handed over to them as their charges. The college retains 50 per cent of the fees for further development. Besides this, the college has a vocational programme on Advertising, Sales Promotion and Sales Management. It introduced the programme of Bachelor of Business Administration, as a self-financing programme, charging Rs. 14,000 per semester. The number of participants was low, hardly ten. Because of the economic conditions of the local people, this price is considered to be high.

On the issue of staff development, the principal claimed that almost all the teachers were highly qualified. He, however, encouraged them to participate in programmes in the academic staff colleges, and in seminars, conferences, etc.

Designing of these innovative activities did not seem to be based on any pre-planning. They were primarily based on the need for contingency management. Most of these ideas and initiatives came from the principal, though at different stages, he consulted and involved the teachers.

Management of Resistance

By asking the teachers to spend at least five hours in the college, Ranajit invaded the private space and the vested interest, and faced stiff resistance from teachers. In the first instance, the teachers refused to obey his orders and told him that they would obey only the instructions of the West Bengal College and University Teachers' Association (WBCUTA) to which they were affiliated. The principal confronted them on the ground that WBCUTA was an association of teachers; whereas the paymasters are either the government or the university. It is important that 'they follow the instructions of the university'. It took quite some time for Ranajit to pursue the teachers. Long after he actually succeeded in this venture, WBCUTA issued a circular to all colleges asking its members to stay in the college for five hours a day, which was not being followed in many colleges. Students also resisted because they were enjoying much more opportunity for unionization, dating, etc. According to the principal, it was through his persuasiveness that it was possible to improve the situation. Gradually, the resistance reduced.

Another new practice in academic management was the principal's rounds, three times during the day—in the morning, around noon, and in the afternoon—to check whether classes were engaged according to the time table. He would compare and cross-check his observations with the teachers, if the classes were not engaged. An interesting example was the case of the Teachers' Representative to WBCUTA. He was found absent from his classes on several occasions.

The principal confronted him and asked him about his absence. The teacher's representative counter-questioned the principal about the latter's authority to monitor him. The principal insisted that he had been asking every teacher to engage his/her classes. Since he was the teachers' representative, it was all the more important that he engaged all his classes, lest others should emulate his wrong example. The new teachers might feel that the rule was only for the new and not for the old and the 'powerful' teachers. The principal must prove his impartiality. It worked.

In tune with the local cultural traditions, Ranajit carefully demonstrated his respect for teachers who were senior to him. When he joined the college as principal, he was relatively young. There were many in the staff who were senior enough to be his teachers. The principal made it a practice not to call any senior teacher to his office for discussion. Whenever needed, he would walk upto that teacher for discussion. This practice and behaviour of Ranajit was well appreciated by senior teachers. Teachers appreciated his humility and courteousness. This also helped in reducing resistance.

There were other instances of resistance. When the construction work was not given to PWD, but was taken over internally by the college, the office staff resisted and criticized. They advised and warned the principal of the risk in undertaking the work themselves. The under-current was that there was some kind of sharing of the construction costs between the office staff and the contracting agency. This vested interest was also kept alive by involving the community leaders. But as mentioned earlier, Ranajit took the risk. With the support of the chairman of the Managing Committee, he involved architects, retired engineers and some of the staff members in executing the construction.

The other kind of resistance came from the students' union, particularly from the competing groups backed by rival political parties. During the union elections, one of the contesting groups destroyed the furniture. They had a suspicion that there was some kind of complicity between the principal and the rival party that won the election. But, at a later stage, when they realized their mistake, they apologized. Ever since then, the student agitation has not visited the college again.

Leadership Style

Ranajit's leadership style was characterized by 'persuasiveness', rather assertiveness coupled with persuasiveness. He was emphatic that he did not impose things on others. He preferred to pursue with patience. He claimed to have a democratic style characterized by consultative decision-making. His actions and successes indicate a different story. For example, against the wish of almost all teachers, he decided to extend the actual working hours of the teachers to five hours. Indeed, he used power coercive strategies, though veiled, to begin with. And that was necessary. His democratic style was revealed later by his consultation with his colleagues, student union leaders, local community leaders. When a decision was taken, he pursued it to the end, even if it was resisted. His persuasiveness gave him an image in the college that he could be cowed down; he meant business and would see through things. He mentioned an incident. Students had a sit-in strike in his office for more than eight hours, without allowing him to drink water or go to toilet. He didn't, however, budge or surrender to the students the message was loud and clear that he could not be cowed down; students had to listen to him and later they withdrew the agitation. He overcame all such resistances over a period of time.

Success and Failure

Ranajit succeeded in bringing back the college into the mainstream by improving the discipline. Teachers started taking classes; they stayed back between the classes for five hours; they used the library frequently. The students attended the classes; they participated actively in the seminars. The results of the college in the university examinations improved substantially. From that angle, he considers his mission to be successful.

He has been successful in some major improvements in the infrastructure, classrooms, library, sports facilities including gymnasium, etc.

When it came to the question of failure, his main contention was that he wanted to attract good students, which would have significantly altered the quality of performance of the students in university examinations. It was not possible. The majority of the students preferred to go to Calcutta, even if they did not seek admission to colleges like Presidency or St. Xaviers or St. Pauls or Scottish Church. They would seek admission to Vidyasagar or Surendranath College that are not necessarily good colleges, but because they are located in Calcutta'. He considers this to be his major failure.

Similarly, he considered himself as having failed in inspiring the teachers for academic excellence and contribution to the college development. He narrated an incident. In this college, he made it a practice that no student would be deprived of writing the exam because of financial constraints. Whenever a student was in difficulty, he would help him from the college funds, or put his own money to alleviate the situation. Three or four teachers would join him. But he was not been able to expand this mission to many more teachers. On the contrary, with the retirement of a few of such helpful teachers, the number of teachers who helped the cause was reduced further.

NOTE

1. The holy place popularly known for the love story of Lord Krishna and Radha.

11
GRAMMAR BOOK STYLE
SMT. PARVATIBAI CHOWGULE COLLEGE

Chowgule College in Margao, Goa was in doldrums when the new principal took over. Here is the story of its resurrection. The college was characterised by severely hampered interpersonal relationships between teachers and management, different groups of teachers, teachers and students and so on. Every action was scanned with suspicion. Dr. Shirgurkar[1] made a determined bid to bring back the college through a series of participative approaches in decision-making and decision implementation in the college. Shelving his personal vision, the principal adopted a near perfect grammar book approach; experimenting Peter Senge on field. He engaged all his colleagues, students, parents and members of the managing committee in collectively defining the mission of the college. He involved everyone who had a stake in the college in designing and implementing activities to translate their mission into action. The principal proves his point that participative management works magnificently in institution building.

Early Development

V R Shirgurkar (1942) was born in a Brahmin family in a village of Karnataka. His grandfather was his first tutor, who tutored at home till his third standard; later, he joined the village school. His father died when Shirgurkar was 17. His grandfather encouraged him to work hard and take the responsibility of his family of four brothers, a sister and mother. "That made me a grown-up person at a young age and helped in completing the studies", he said. Shirgurkar graduated at the age of 19 and got his postgraduate degree at 21.

Shirgurkar belonged to a farming family. All the brothers used to work on their farm along with other labourers. His father insisted that they work along with the hired labour. Even though there were servants at home, children had to wash their clothes and do their household work. His school was 16 kilometres away from the village; he used to pedal 32 kilometres every day on an old bicycle.

His father and grandfather were considered 'God-send' by the villagers. Every person in the village respected and treated them with great honour. Shirgurkar and his siblings observed these—helping the poor, sacrificing for others, sharing with relatives and villagers, fighting for justice, showing respect for the aged people, respecting and tolerating other religions, and so on. The family lived a simple austere life. Children had only two pairs of clothes; in rainy season, shirts had to be dried up in the heat of the earthen oven in the morning before going to school. They learnt to be 'happy with what God has given'. These lessons were very important. This family tradition and upbringing laid the foundation of Shirgurkar to be.

The Assignment

When Shirgurkar took over the college, the results in the university examinations were very poor. Students were undisciplined. There were fights among students' groups on the campus almost every day. Teachers were afraid of them. No teacher had the courage to confront the students. The teachers themselves were divided into warring factions. Teachers had gone on strike before he joined. Relations between teachers and management were very strained. There was no dialogue between them. Management had not paid the teaching staff salary for 51 days. The matter was in court. Teachers had approached the vice-chancellor of Bombay University to change the management. The earlier principal could not function at all. He had to go underground for a few days due to students' agitation and had to leave the college and Goa abruptly. The quality of education on the campus had suffered for at least five years before 1985. Students from Margao would not join this college. They would prefer a college in Panaji, Goa. A friend of Shirgurkar even advised him not to join the college as 'it was beyond control'.

Before joining the college, Shirgurkar lived a comfortable and prestigious life in Pune. He was a Life Member of Shikshana Prasaraka Mandali, a renowned educational institution, running more than 30 educational institutions in Maharashtra. Shirgurkar was working as the head of the postgraduate department of Economics and Rector of gents hostel in the Sri Parashurambhau College, Pune; he was visitor of a deaf and dumb school run by the same management and chairman of a cooperative bank started by a few college teachers in Pune. He had a spacious bungalow on the campus to live in and his wife was also employed in a high school.

Both of them resigned their jobs and took up this new challenge—an opportunity to test their mettle when their (two) children were very young. His wife had no job immediately at Margao, Goa.

The new management had identified Shirgurkar through their sources from Bombay University. In course of time, the management gave him full freedom to handle the situation. Perhaps they had no other choice. It took him almost two years to show first signs of improvement, after which he started getting good response form the students, parents, teaching and non-teaching staff and the local community. Shirgurkar saw scope for doing new things and started painting colourful horizons for the college.

Mission for the College

Shirgurkar's initial mission was to resurrect the college from its non-functional stage to a working condition; then, to transform to make it the best college in the state of Goa and place it at the national level as one of the best colleges, at a later stage.

The University Grants Commission had identified Smt. Parvatibai Chowgule College, Margao, Goa, for special grants under its new scheme for colleges having potential for growth. Under this programme, the college might get an additional grant up to Rs.50 lakhs and get a place in the list of a few top colleges in the country. The college was assessed and accredited by NAAC in 1998 with four stars, when accreditation was voluntary in the country. Shirgurkar had a moral reason for getting his college assessed. In his own words, "The National Assessment and Accreditation Council had identified my name to be on the peer-teams in 1997 only, when I was a member of the General Council of NAAC. I had gone on a few visits to assess and accredit some colleges in 1997. While visiting colleges as a peer-team member, I felt that I had no moral right to assess other colleges, unless I got my own college assessed and accredited by NAAC. And I decided to volunteer to get the Chowgule College assessed and accredited".

Shirgurkar seems to have been significantly influenced in formulating his vision by several books. He made a special mention of 'Seven Habits' by Stephen Covey, 'The Fifth Discipline' and 'A Fifth Discipline Resource—Schools That Learn' by Peter Senge, 'Quality is Free—The Art of Making Quality Certain' by Phillip B Crosby, and The Critical Chain, The Goal by Goldratt. He was equally influenced by his cousin, who runs a production unit in machine tools, at Bangalore; they discussed quality initiatives in the corporate sector that motivated Shirgurkar to bring suitable changes in the process of education in the college. The theme of their discussion covered how quality in production and in service sector like education could be continuously improved, what efforts would be required at the level of the leader, etc.

The selection of the college by the Ford Foundation for participation in the Campus Diversity Initiative programme brought in an extra amount of Rs. 15 lakhs without any strings. This fund could be used for any initiative relevant to the basic theme. With this fund, a large number of workshops for faculty were organised in three years from 1995-98.

Shirgurkar brought in a new dimension of factors hitherto unknown, influencing him in formulating his mission. According to him, "I got help and direction in whatever I wished to do on the campus without any difficulty and on time. Apparently impossible things happened on the campus, which cannot be explained on the basis of logical reasoning. I attribute this to the Divine Support to me in my efforts to transform the institution without expecting anything for my personal benefits." For him, this was a very important factor in his work in the society and in personal life as well.

Action Strategies

The first major innovative effort was building a mission statement for the college in 1997. Following the grammar book approach of Peter Senge, all the teaching and non-teaching staff along with the members of the college students' council and gymkhana council were involved in the process of building a vision/mission for the college. "I myself could have written it without any difficulty. But then, it would have been my vision/mission imposed on the faculty and other staff. It might have worked," said Shirgurkar. The major agenda was complete involvement of all the stakeholders in the college to admit a commitment that they would strive hard to bring that mission into reality. Professional experts were consulted as facilitators. In all, 177 persons including teaching and non-teaching staff, some students and some persons from the college-management worked for three days from morning nine to five in the evening to bring out the mission statement of the college. There were several brainstorming sessions generating ideas about what the college could do, what should be the priorities, what were the expectations of the parents and the society at large, role of parents, teachers, non-teaching staff, the principal and the management, in finding out in what direction would the future education move on the campus. Numerous ideas were generated and a large number of suggestions were put forward. There were heated arguments, voting and what not. Every participant was totally involved in the exercise till it was finalised and everybody signed the document of the mission statement. For Shirgurkar, it was a thrilling experience. Ford Foundation grants were utilized for this activity.

The mission statement was:

'We, at Chowgule College, are committed to Excellence in Education, Empowering Personalities and Developing Responsible Members of Society'.

The task had just moved in the right direction. It was recognised that only displaying mission statement at different places in the college would not ensure the results. To make it operational and result-oriented, a two-day workshop was again organised to write the mission manual—a sort of an action plan giving responsibilities to the staff, principal, management and even students. Monitoring mechanism was also chalked out. Printed copies of the action plan were made available to every faculty member and the management.

At the end of two years, the faculty sat together in a day-long dialogue to introspect and find out what portion of the mission manual was actually brought into practice. How many goals were actually reached? In the light of the discussion, the action plan was re-drafted to make it more realistic and bring it within the reach. There was a collective support from the staff; the exercise was successful.

Right from the first day, shirgurkar made an effort to involve the faculty in decision-making. He held the first staff meeting, immediately after taking charge of the college. Shirgurkar was not sure as to how to handle the situation, if it went beyond his control, as the teachers were agitated and had gone on strike earlier to protest against some decisions taken by the management. As expected, the meeting took an unpleasant turn and teachers started arguing 'with me', putting their complaints, demanding certain facilities on the campus and so on. Shirgurkar 'too got irritated, but soon regained control over the situation and requested every faculty member to give in writing at least five suggestions in the next week for improving the college'. Every teacher submitted suggestions. Shirgurkar called those teachers who were making arguments in the first meeting and handed them all the suggestions received and requested them to classify them issue-wise. They readily complied. Then, Shirgurkar called the next staff meeting-cum workshop, made some six/seven groups of teachers and handed them all the suggestions received on each issue. Shirgurkar told them to prepare an action plan on the basis of the suggestions. All the groups prepared the action plan. Most of it was acceptable. Immediately, Shirgurkar announced those action plans that could be implemented with immediate effect. Again, the implementation part was to be taken care of by the committees of teachers. The whole exercise was very effective. The college atmosphere started improving substantially. Shirgurkar made an impressive list of his strategies:

- Gave freedom and responsibilities to staff and students.
- Appreciated their efforts when they succeeded.
- When they could not succeed, they were not blamed; corrected them through open discussions.
- When they mishandled situations and there were serious problems, the principal took the responsibility of answering the management, the parents and students without holding the staff responsible for them. Simultaneously, there were open discussions, diagnosis of the problems and alternative solutions.
- Faculty members were empowered to take decisions.

There were 28 committees in the college. Though they were functioning over the years, no policy on the committees was written down. It was decided to write a manual on the college committees defining their structure, nomination of members on them, their tenure, functions, jurisdiction, etc. The work was done through a faculty workshop. The principal exhorted that there should be provisions in the manual that the decisions of committees would be binding on the principal and he would accept them. The purpose was to empower them to take decisions in the committees with great responsibility, taking implications of their implementation into consideration. The faculty appreciated that. Not all committees took such powers to themselves, but the message was effective. Shirgurkar is now consulted by many colleges in the country, in preparing similar documents in their colleges.

Some Innovations

Chowgule College introduced Course Registers. Every teacher wrote teaching plans, and their execution in the course registers. Similarly, they wrote comments on the basis of day-to-day classroom teaching that would be useful in revising the syllabi of the subjects they taught. These suggestions were discussed in the term-end departmental meetings for making recommendations to the university to revise the courses. The course registers were thus used as an important instrument for developing a mechanism to suggest changes in the courses, for developing question banks, for listing topic-wise relevant readings, for listing all the activities in which teachers participated during the year. It was also used by the teachers for writing self appraisal reports at the end of the year. Every teacher was expected to carry with him/her course registers when they wanted to meet the principal in connection with day-to-day work to ensure that the registers were written every day.

Another innovation was evaluation of the teachers by students introduced in 1996. The faculty had to be taken into full confidence to introduce and implement this innovation. A questionnaire was prepared by the principal to collect feedback from students.

Teachers were initially skeptical about the exercise. The questionnaire was circulated among the teachers and their comments were invited. These comments were discussed extensively in a staff meeting; and the teachers finally accepted the instrument. Before implementing the same, teachers were assured by the principal that the feedback would not be used against them in the first three years and the objective was to improve the overall teaching-learning process in the college. Everybody accepted.

Micro scale testing in chemistry was first introduced in Chowgule College. Workshops for teachers in chemistry from all the colleges in Goa were organised by Chowgule College. Based on the feedback, the proposal to introduce the same in the university syllabi was sent to the university and it got approved for all the colleges in the state of Goa. New courses in environmental chemistry, pharmaceutical chemistry were designed by the faculty of the college and sent to the university for approval. Similarly, the college introduced a PGDCA as early as 1985 and kept it open for Arts and Commerce students as well, though the trend in the country was to keep such courses open to only science graduates.

College Night, an event which was organised by the students every year since 1962 onwards without a break and which used to bring disgrace to the college due to indiscipline and quarrels on the campus was stopped through continuous dialogue with students. Panorama, an inter-collegiate youth festival, which used to be vulgar, was made vulgarity-free through a series of discussions with students' representatives of the college and other colleges in Goa.

Students and faculty members were motivated to stop using vehicles on one day in a week, during the earlier Iraq war to show concern for the need to save fuel. Similarly, there was a Raddi (old newspapers) collection drive with the help of students and faculty to purchase an ambulance for the citizens of Margao in collaboration with Lions Club. People were involved in raising funds for poor students; no student from south Goa who contacted the college for financial help remained deprived of education for lack of money.

Other innovations were:

- Landscaping by involving teachers and students.
- Workshops on curriculum development for faculty members, including those from other colleges from Goa.
- Programmes for NTSE guidance, IIT JEE- guidance, IAS guidance, and overall student development.

- Placement and counselling cells were set up in the college. Link between education and industry was developed extensively.
- Buildings for the department of computer science and library were constructed.

All the stakeholders were involved, while introducing new ideas and implementing them.

Taking People Along

Shirgurkar was decidedly successful in taking people along; he gave importance to staff, students and parents; listened to them very patiently (impact of Senge and Covey); encouraged and appreciated their contribution, though small; entrusted responsibilities; gave freedom to take decisions; honoured their decisions. At times, the decisions might not have been the best in that situation, but, if those did not have a significant long-term impact, Shirgurkar honoured the decisions. However, if such decisions had the potentiality of affecting the general policy of the college discipline on the campus and development of the college in the long run, he did not hesitate to change by taking the concerned people into confidence.

Leadership Style

Shirgurkar believes that his leadership action and style was shaped by the prevailing situation in the college when he took over. The earlier principal was isolated. Rapport between the principal and the management, on the one hand, and the staff and the students, on the other, was very weak. There was no trust between these groups at all. Suspicion coloured all communications. In this situation, involving the staff in decision-making alone would have worked. And it worked in Chowgule College.

Shirgurkar contends that ideas were scarce, but not funds. Peoples' participation opens up new vistas, new areas, new ideas which are required, if the institution has to grow. He strongly believed that each one working on the campus could contribute in terms of new ideas. Accordingly, he followed almost a grammar book approach of democratic leadership. He supported the staff whenever required; gave them directions when necessary; and worked along with them on important projects. He has great faith in peoples' constructive approach and their capacity to contribute. Shirgurkar believes that the intuition played an important role in his leadership and decision-making process.

Learning

For Shirgurkar, Principalship at Chowgule College was, in the real sense, an on-the-job learning. He believes that a lot of changes can be brought about in education. If at all, there is any chance to bring about desirable changes in society, it will be possible to do so only through the educational institutions in the country. He would have been able to do better, had he been trained as an educational manager.

"Given a chance, I shall initiate the second round of reforms in the college to complete die unfinished tasks", said Shirgurkar. There is always room at the top. The mission now would be to get autonomy and develop the college as a role model, not only for the colleges in the country but even in other countries. It is possible to achieve this without losing its own identity. Without copying what the colleges in the western countries are doing, the principal strongly believes, that it is possible to create something very new, very appropriate to cater to the needs of society all over. "The concept of free progress education, given by Sri Aurobindo, can give us the direction. We can suitably fill in the gaps".

The process and the style followed by the principal would continue with some modifications to suit the changing times. "The process of conducting education on the campus is in itself a dynamic one. The ground is ready to start systemic thinking about what we do in a college and how we empower the staff'.

NOTE

1. Dr. V R Shirgurkar, Principal responded to a set of questions. I could not personally interview him. This case has been built up solely on his response. I acknowledge Dr. Shirgurkar's contribution with gratitude.

12
TOWARDS CAMPUS DIVERSITY
JAI HIND COLLEGE[1]

Jai Hind College is a new institution, with young faculty, located in the tribal area of Maharashtra. The major mission of the college was to provide quality education to the otherwise deprived tribal community through a series of innovative actions guided by campus diversity programme. Breaking away from the conventions, the emphasis was on all round development of students through sports, cultural activities, etc., and teacher development in communication, leadership, research, counselling, etc. With the help of the students, teachers and the community, the college set a new standard in college education, which included financial support to the weak students, so that no student was deprived of education because of financial constraints. The campus diversity programme, supported by a grant from the Ford Foundation through an NGO in India, was used as a lever in institution building.

Early Development

K.B. Patil was born in a small village at the foothills of the Ajanta range in Jalgaon district. His father was the headman of the village. From him, Patil imbibed the reading habit. Right from his early life, he enjoyed reading Sane Guruji, V.S. Khandekar and P.L. Ueshpande. His father's simplicity and urge to help others, in spite of personal hardships and his mother's 'volatile temperament', helped Patil form an early judgment of a situation. He began to realize that 'I should avoid certain kinds of behaviour and confrontations'.

Pandit Govind Garud was a teacher, a close friend of Patil's father and a frequent visitor to their home. Pandit Garud was affectionately and respectfully called "Aba Master" by the villagers. Aba Master was a man of strong principles; he never compromised in his life. He was helpful to others; he faced suspension twice, but never gave up his principles. Aba Master had a moral authority in the village. His self-respect, selflessness and self-discipline left a deep impression on Patil.

Patil believes that books had a major influence and impact on the development of his sensibilities and value system. Right from his school days, he was very good at studies which helped him build self-confidence; it also helped him enjoy a leading position on many occasions. Patil grew up in an environment of expectation to be a good student and a good human being. For him, he 'did not have any alternative but to be good'.

Challenge

After returning from Canada, Patil had a hard time getting a proper job. In spite of the good academic record and fairly good research work, he could not pursue research in mathematics. He was depressed as he could not do much, despite his potential. It was at this juncture that he received the offer of principal's position in Jai Hind College, Dhule. Without much choice, he accepted the assignment. He did not apply for the job. He was recommended by Shri N K Patil, former principal of the college who happened to know him since his student days.

'The tradition of Jai Hind Educational Trust, the complete academic outlook of the management, the dedication and devotion of the chairman gave him the confidence that his value system matched with that of the institution'. Patil was at ease; he felt that he could do something constructive and positive to this college.

Mission

Jai Hind Educational Trust had a reputation for academic excellence. The ideals of hard work, integrity, discipline and self-reliance were deeply sown into the tradition of Jai Hind College by the founder chairman Nanasaheb Z B Patil. He too, moved on the same path, gathering strength from his own convictions, values and faith in humanity. He believed that the students could be mobilised and channelised to develop as nation builders. 'It was my belief that education was to be made more meaningful through the students' potential and latent energies, utilized in creative pursuits. Teachers were to be role-models, extending themselves towards excellence and access even outside the classroom', professed patil.

Our mission was to provide opportunities of higher education to the socially underprivileged, and economically marginalized weaker sections of society. This led Jai Hind College to concentrate on students from the poorer sections of the society, the tribal students and the girl students. There were several development schemes and financial aids like 'earn while you learn, book-bank, counselling, remedial coaching, teacher student-guardian committee, women's empowerment programmes and such other methods to reach out to the deprived students. This enhanced their self confidence and led to their inclusion in the mainstream of the campus life. These motivations 'led us to frame the mission statement of our college':

"We aspire to mobilise student strength for the sustenance of a healthy democracy and betterment of humanity by including leadership, creativity, aesthetic values, scientific temperament, citizenship and a rational eco-friendly approach through academic excellence".

Action Strategies

When Patil joined Jai Hind College as principal, the college was just nine years old. The faculty was very young, the average age being less than 30 years. Many of the faculty members were very active, enthusiastic and hardworking. Since Jai Hind was already known for its academic excellence, it was decided to concentrate on sports, cultural activities and such other activities necessary for all round personality development of students.

The focus of faculty development was on motivation and encouragement. The faculty members were encouraged to submit research projects and undertake research for their Ph.D. Patil took a special initiative to get the college registered under section 12(8) of UGC Act. This status and that of permanent affiliation helped the faculty to attend national and international conferences, seminars and workshops not only in their own fields, but also in diverse areas like

Leadership Skills, Development Communication Skills, Computer Awareness, etc.

For students' development, besides excellence in academics, the concentration was on access to the underprivileged and socially marginalized students. Dhule, where the college is located, being predominantly a tribal area and an economically backward district, he says, "we realized the importance of access to the tribal students. We ensured that marginalized students would not remain shy and inhibited. Such students were to be brought into the mainstream of life in the campus by way of admissions as well as involvement in all academic events."

There were weekly meetings of tribal students, special personality development workshops, economic help through alumni, staff and different NGOs located in India and abroad. Sports activities helped build up a healthy campus climate. At present, Jai Hind is at the top in sports in the university. Two Jai Hind students represented India at international sports and games meet.

The Campus Diversity Initiative (funded by Ford Foundation) was one of the major innovative projects introduced in Jai Hind College and the North Maharashtra University, Jalgaon. The project was implemented in two phases for six years. The project aimed at bringing about an understanding, appreciation and a healthy tolerance of all issues related to diversity. Diversity was to be made a strength of the society. The main thrust was in tune with the mission of faculty motivation to strive towards excellence as well as students' all round development through different activities. Some programmes conducted under CDI were Inter-religion Studies, Science and Culture, National Heritage, Women's Identity. Unconventional methodologies like seminars, presentations, workshops, screening of movies, visits to different places of worship, social surveys, etc., were adopted.

There were a few academic improvement programmes like Study Centres, Coaching Classes for Educationally Disadvantaged, Counselling, Workshops on Study Skills, Life Skills, Personality Development, Leadership Management both for the students and the faculty.

Jai Hind College organized a series of National Conferences on Concepts and Implications of Diversity, Religion as a Bridge to

Humanity, Empowerment of Women for National Development, Tribal Culture, etc. The college started a special section on Gandhian Thought and Vinoba Bhave's literature in the library, coupled with National Integration Camps, Cultural Exchange Programmes by networking with 13 CDI centres all over India.

Several other innovations include expanded sports activities, establishing Student-Teacher-Guardian Committee, Short-term courses in Screen Printing, DTP, Photography, Computer Awareness, Art of Living, Yoga, etc. In collaboration with Brilliant Tutorials, Chennai, the college started a course on Computers for students and the staff.

The college took special initiatives in developing interface with international agencies and NGOs and non-resident Indians. It introduced Foundation for Excellence Scholarship for deserving students through a US based NGO, Ford Foundation sponsored project titled "Pathways Project" of Foundation for Academic Excellence and Access, New Delhi, under which 21 students have received scholarships and a fund of Rs. 15 lakhs as endowment. The college contacted the NRIs abroad for library donations, scholarships, tribal development programmes, etc., and has initiated a special fund to help socially marginalized and educationally under-privileged students.

These innovations were designed through discussions, brain storming sessions with faculty and experts from various fields.

Managing Resistance

From the beginning of his career, Patil 'never had any problem of taking people along'. As mentioned earlier, when Patil joined the college, he came into contact with a group of 10 teachers who were hardworking, sincere and committed to their work. Patil placed trust in their abilities and judgment; he built a close rapport by delegating power and through participatory decision-making. More people joined this core group. Maintaining transparency in all his relationships, Patil depended more on his personal power, rather than on his positional power or authority to influence people. "My easy accessibility and empathy for the students have also helped me to overcome resistance". While taking people along, Patil respects 'their self-esteem'.

Not that everything was smooth and nice. Immediately after he joined the college, a few people in the college tried to influence him in a variety of ways. He listened to them without being influenced and altering his belief in the basic goodness of people. This helped him immensely to take people along.

When Patil joined the College in 1991, Jai Hind College already enjoyed the reputation of promoting academic excellence and quality education. The strong foundation given to the college by the chairman, the former principals, and a team of committed teachers helped Patil bring about innovative changes like the Campus Diversity Initiative. The majority of the teachers was passive onlookers initially. When they realized the sincerity of his efforts, they joined and went along with the principal.

He met a major challenge when there was a change in the management in 1996. At every step, his values clashed with the new director. There were several confrontations and a lot of resistance. For five years, with the help of his colleagues, he had to try hard to maintain the traditions of Jai Hind. 'This was an arduous task that caused a lot of mental and physical turmoil'.

He says, 'I overcame resistance through my openness, transparency, confidence-building, trust, discussions and impartiality, with the support from my colleagues and students.'

Leadership Style

As mentioned earlier, Patil's father had left an indelible impression on him. His father's selfless service taught him not to expect anything from others while doing something for them. His teacher in the college, Prof. Sardesai, was a strict disciplinarian; though a very kind hearted and an understanding human being. Prof. Kharul was yet another source of influence on him, who taught Patil, 'I could influence people through my personal power without using authority or even raising my voice.' He could pursue his point and convince people which was a great advantage in administration. Principal N K Patil, his teacher, mentor and guide strongly influenced his trust in people to accept them with their strengths and weaknesses. From these teachers, he learnt that he could handle any situation better by remaining calm in the face of any difficulty.

His second source of influence was his subject of study. Mathematics enforced preciseness, analytical thinking, a discipline of mind and a balance of temperament. The four years of research in Canada broadened his perspective and gave him a vision about education in India. In Canada, he was exposed to an entirely different way of functioning. He imbibed work ethics and the value of time management. He practised time management and worked hard to complete assignments in self-stipulated time. Patil thinks that he has developed a strong belief in the positive side of people, things and situations.

Learning

Patil has listed several lessons learnt during his service as principal of Jai Hind College. Some of the important ones are:

- The traditions of quality education of an institution have to be vigilantly watched and maintained by the people who work there.
- Personal power is more effective than positional power.
- People work more efficiently if they are trusted.
- A personal approach in building up team effort is important.
- One has to be a role-model and combine precept with practice.
- Financial and academic matters have to be transparent and clean for effective functioning.
- Self-discipline.
- Empathy with the students and a commitment to the work at hand.
- Accept responsibility for any mistake, without blaming others.
- A strong image built up socially and academically helps in administration.

To fulfil a dream of developing an institution, academic as well as financial autonomy is essential.

For Patil, working in Jai Hind College has been a pleasant and enriching experience. But, if he were to work again to build another institution, he would adopt some changes in his style of functioning. To work efficiently towards a mission, a conducive atmosphere in the nature of academic and financial autonomy is an imperative to fulfil the dream of an excellent educational institution.

After twelve years as principal, he could have done better in moulding the administrative staff of the college by asserting his positional power. His natural reluctance to use authority as a principal may have inhibited some members of the teaching faculty and administrative staff and kept them aloof from the day-to-day functioning.

Patil candidly confesses that he works better with people who fit into his value-system and who show some drive and motivation. He seems to feel helpless in involving all the members of the staff in college development. His image and moral standing may have also led to this gap.

Looking back, he would have preferred to have better competence in managing financial accounts; also a certain variety of writing skills would have definitely enhanced his administrative capacity.

In the past, he says, "I have always worked intuitively, and taken one step at a time". He believes that with training, he could have learnt to handle multiple jobs more competently. He could have worked in a more organized and planned manner. And, he could have been more effective.

NOTE

1. Contribution by principal K B Patil came in the form of a response to my questions. I could not personally interview principal Patil. This case has been built up solely on his response. I acknowledge Prof. Patil's contribution.

13

LIFE SAVING

Centre of Advanced Studies in Education

The Department of Education in the MS University of Baroda was upgraded as Centre of Advanced Studies in Education (CASE) in 1964, initially for five years, to be reviewed by the University Grants Commission. It was the only such centre in education in the country then. According to the review committee in 1969, the CASE had not achieved its objectives. It recommended continuation subject to the condition that the university invites a professional who can really lead an Advanced Centre. Professor Madhubhai B Buch was invited by the University. In five years, CASE achieved significant reputation in the national and international community of educators. His armory had emphasis on putting bright young students from all over India together in an academically charged atmosphere, with production emphasis, empathy and personal concern for young research scholars, and creation of a cosmopolitan culture. The result was the evolution of an alternative structure of young scholars bringing laurels to the Centre when the permanent members of the faculty continued with their mundane work in a mundane manner. Thus, it offers the story of an out-of-crisis march, with sustainability under a scanner.

Accepting the Assignment

Under the scheme of the University Grants Commission, the Department of Education in the MS University of Baroda was upgraded to the status of Centre of Advanced Studies in Education, the only one of its kind in the whole country. The primary objective was to develop the Centre into an excellent research institution that could provide leadership to the

University Departments of Education in the country as a whole. The Department of Education and the Faculty of Education and Psychology at Baroda had a few stalwarts like Prof. T K N Menon and Prof. S N Mukherjee to lead. The upgradation of the Department to the status of CASE was initially for five years; the continuation was to depend upon the result of the evaluation by a committee appointed by the University Grants Commission. The UGC Evaluation Committee, appointed in 1968-69, was not convinced that the objectives, for which the Centre was established, were being fulfilled. The Committee also recognized that the Centre did not have the right kind of leadership. Accordingly, it recommended a conditional extension; CASE could be given a fresh lease of life for another five years, subject to the condition that the university would bring in an eminent person to head the Centre. Such review outcomes led to the reversal of several advanced study centres in other subjects to their original position. The MS University at this stage, brought in Dr. Madhubhai B Buch, a former student and teacher of the University, then in the NCERT, to head the CASE.

One of the articulated principles, rather philosophy of Madhubhai was that every crisis is pregnant with opportunity. The 'successful people jump on to the crisis, when the majority runs away, because achievers see opportunities hidden in the crisis'. Madhubhai saw the opportunity of institution building in the new assignment, which was, otherwise, financially and materially not attractive.

Madhubhai had made his presence felt in the national scenario. He accomplished a difficult and complex task of national dimension and importance. The All India Educational Survey, which was the responsibility of the Survey and Evaluation Department of NCERT, was an extremely difficult task, since it needed collaboration with every state government. After several abortive efforts, Madhubhai took it over and led it to a point of success indicating his enormous skill and competence in pioneering difficult tasks. The authorities of the MS University of Baroda preferred him to lead the Centre of Advanced Studies for several reasons. One, is his success in conceptualizing and managing massive complex national projects, his skills of collaboration, and his familiarity with the ground conditions as an old student of the university, and later as a teacher. Along with his conceptual skills, he was rich with the understanding of the university's culture and dynamics.

To his distinction, Madhubhai was invited by the university authorities to head the CASE. He was not an applicant. Being familiar with the recommendations of the UGC committee, he obviously knew the crisis. Nonetheless, according to his upbringing, convictions and the style, he did see opportunities. He took no time in deciding to accept the assignment and moved over to Baroda. On many occasions, he articulated that it was a great challenge to build an institution in education that can lead the whole country in research in education. On a personal note, when he compared his role in the NCERT with that in the Centre of Advanced Studies in Education, he did find a greater opportunity of self-actualization of his creative energy in CASE, compared to NCERT, where he was 'one of the many professors'.

Mission for CASE

Madhubhai did not have an articulated mission for the Centre. He did not follow the normal rules of institution building of a set of articulated missions, share with others and work towards that. Madhubhai's missions can be derived from his actions. He added many new dimensions on his way to the institution building. A few clearly visible missions can be identified.

His important mission was building leaders in education and educational research. That Madhubhai concentrated the largest amount of his energy on capacity building of the young researchers drawn from all over the country, is the indication of his emphasis on building leadership. India Today', a popular magazine, interviewed him about his contribution to Indian educational research. Madhubhai's forthright response was: his contribution was researchers and not necessarily educational research. Apparently baffling, this response has a very significant meaning. During personal discussions, he was emphatic that he could personally contribute in five to six years, a few high-quality research studies. But, if he concentrated on building researchers, in five to six years, he would be able to build 30 to 40 researchers who, in turn, would contribute to Indian educational research for the next 20 to 30 years. Hence, one of his missions was building educational researchers for the country. Further, he was assigned the responsibility of building an institution, and not necessarily conduct research himself. To that extent, his role was more than that of a professor.

His perceivable second mission was initiating planned research in selected areas of critical importance. His choice fell on 'teaching and teacher behaviour', the core of the educational processes at all levels of education, programmed learning, the newly emerging science of individualized instruction, and innovation and change that would ensure adoption of innovation for bringing about systemic changes. Although the focus of advanced research was on these three areas, he did not restrict other research areas and problems to be dealt with by the faculty members. Importantly, the mission was beyond the identified areas; it was on the new concept of planned research, in contradistinction to the sporadic research that was the culture not only in CASE, but also in all such departments of Indian universities.

The third important mission was to raise the level of the institution to an all India level and look beyond at international presence. He developed a distinguishing feature of networking CASE with other institutions of similar nature. On the one hand, he chose his research scholars carefully to represent an all India character in sharp contrast to the previous situation, where majority of the scholars were from the local areas and the state. Simultaneously, he also invited scholars from different parts of the country to participate in the scholarly activities of the CASE, threw open its library and other facilities. Steadily, this network was extended to international institutions, resulting in visits of international scholars to CASE as well as scholars from the Centre visiting abroad.

The major mission of building the CASE as the national lead organisation and of the international standard was derived out of the stated purpose of objectives for which the Centre was set up by the University Grants Commission.

The second mission of planned research as an alternative to the sporadic research has primarily been on the basis of his consultation with the professionals in various other universities and national institutions like NCERT. Also, his continuous interaction with the international professionals facilitated in crystallizing the mission of planned research, particularly, in selecting the areas that were of contemporary interest. As can be seen, the time lag between the beginning of the programmed learning movement in the world in 1962, and that in CASE, is only about seven years. This is equally true about the research on teaching and teacher behaviour which was pioneered by Ned A Flanders in 1962. Management of change and innovation is the perennial question in organizational management.

The third and most important mission, capability building and developing leaders in education and educational research, was derived largely out of his personal convictions and background. Before coming into the profession of education, Madhubhai was a trade union activist leading the railway employees union; he had concern for people and he recognized the necessity of leadership. One important possibility of his concentration on building leaders in CASE is derived out of his experience in NCERT that had a number of excellent scholars as professors, wanting in skills of organization and management of complex projects.

Translating the Vision

International and Indian research literature on management of institutional change indicate, almost without contradiction, the significant variance explained by the behavioural attributes including 'source credibility' of the head of the institution. In confirmation, it would not be an overstatement to assign the largest single premium for ushering in a new research climate in CASE to its new leader in Madhubhai. This is evident from the sudden spurt in the research output from 1969 onwards; and a slow and steady decline in the 1980s, originating the process of deceleration somewhere in late 1970s. Let us examine some of the strategies adopted to generate the research climate.

Alternative Structures

Madhubhai inherited about 25 members of the faculty, many of whom were his seniors and even teachers. The faculty members were accustomed to training teachers although not necessarily, in a conventional manner, comparable to a large majority of similar other institutions. Their orientation to research, however, was marginal and largely conventional. Given the challenge of leading CASE, emerging as the centre for advanced study, within five years, it was non-viable and risky to build a research climate and quality through reorientation of the existing members of the faculty. The strategy was to create an alternative structure—a fresh research group with bright and young minds—rather than trying to rebuild the existing faculty and changing them over from training to research orientation.

The major emphasis on research activity and output was hence, diverted to the doctoral programmes by the full-time scholars brought from all over India, supplemented by a large number of part-time students, enrolled from different parts of the country. The doctoral students often had a stake both for quality and completion of the projects in time. For, completing Ph.D., with reasonable quality was a positive instrument for the job market. Quite a few fellowships were available at the disposal of the CASE—Junior Research Fellowships (JRF), Senior Research Fellowships (SRF) and Teacher Fellowships (TF). The total number of full-time research scholars of various categories was almost equal to, or sometimes more than the regular teachers in the department. This alternative structure-building through young scholars was comprehensively strengthened by recruitment of faculty members with strong research background against four vacancies available. CASE filled up the three positions of readers and a professor, drawing from University of Punjab, NCERT and SP University. The newly inducted professionals brought in a national character and comparatively a higher level of competence.

Process Building

The alternative structure was rather informal, built around certain basic processes. As a matter of strategy and in total agreement with the laid down goals of the Centre, the junior fellowships, senior fellowships and teacher fellowships were utilized to draw talents from various universities in the country. At a given time, there were not only the first class postgraduates, but also the toppers from the universities of Bangalore, Banaras, Calcutta, Kerala, Mysore, etc., together. Once such bright minds were put together and motivated, they generated a natural learning environment that nurtured and favoured human resource development among the researchers.

Besides this natural interaction, formal opportunities were also created. The weekly seminars on research and research methods were academically exciting forums where researchers presented their detailed research proposals, review articles, research studies as well as papers on research methods. Each such session was long, extensively debated, at times, followed by individualized feedback by Madhubhai on their personal performances. Quite often, this interaction rolled over to informal settings with equally involved argument, debate and discussion during the tea club of the scholars on research hypothesis or research design or application of statistics in educational and social research.

This lively learning environment was further supported by the opportunities created by the Centre for interaction with outside experts. It was common for the Centre to invite experts from various institutions in the country and/or to get hold of the visiting foreign experts to present seminars in CASE. These were quite frequent. These interactive processes, both formal and informal, created an environment of reading, interacting, conducting critical analysis and thinking, and writing research papers, which are the basic qualities of the researcher and the basic components of research climate.

At the instance of Madhubhai, MS University of Baroda was the first university to introduce interdisciplinary research in education, whereby any individual with a postgraduate degree in any subject and proven interest in education could pursue doctoral research in education. Indeed, there are many doctorates in education from the MS University of Baroda who were originally students of psychology, sociology, literature, economics, engineering and a host of other subjects. Besides this basic question of freedom from the qualifications, it provided a new interactive forum to create an interdisciplinary approach in thinking, which is very critical for high quality research in education, since education itself is an interdisciplinary subject.

Cosmopoliteness

Along with the research students brought from all over the country, there were also quite a few scholars from Thailand, Bangladesh, etc. The careful avoidance of regionalism, parochialism and inbreeding in selection and recruitment made CASE a rendezvous of researchers from east and west, and south and north. The 'living together' and 'growing together' with ample opportunities of interacting with outside experts made the Centre a cosmopolite island.

Another important, though apparently a small practice, influenced the young minds significantly. Whenever an expert of national stature came for the national lecture series in CASE, one of the young research scholars was attached during his/her stay at Baroda, particularly, during their leisure hours, compared to the practices in other universities of attaching either a senior university official, protocol officer, or a senior member of the faculty. For example, then as a junior research fellow, I had the privilege of hosting Prof. Rais Ahmed, then director of NCERT for two days, during his visit to CASE. Unless I met him for hours over morning and evening walks, lunch and dinner and all other spare hours, I would never know that a physicist of his stature was so deeply read in psychology, leave alone his enormous insight into human mind. His scholarship, modesty, encouragement and appreciation reverberated long after we were physically disconnected. This attachment programme was not only enriching, but also inspiring. It created 'learned optimism' and ambition among the young scholars.

This was a very calculated approach, as it provided the opportunity to the young research workers to interact for long hours with men and women of eminence and thus get exposed to the whole concept of 'higher beings' in education. On the one hand, this reduced the hesitation of the young researchers to communicate and discuss with 'people at the top'; on the other hand, this also provided the opportunity for understanding the large gap between the intellectual height of the nationally eminent professors and scholars and the young research workers at the Centre.

Production Emphasis and Recognition

A large majority of the research workers consider the period of working in CASE "as living in CASE". In fact, quite often life began much before 8 a.m., and one hardly ever knew when it ended. Living in the Centre was never an easy task, especially for those who preferred easier alternatives to life. Madhubhai had a high production emphasis. May be, under compulsion of doing and proving everything in five years, or because of the 'style of the man', CASE got used to accepting or creating a large amount of tasks for itself within a time target, that often appeared unreasonable, but it strived to achieve. During the period between 1969 and 1976, not only were a large number of students enrolled for Ph.D., but also everyone was under pressure to complete the doctoral work within two or three years. Further, hardly was any research fellow really on full-time only for his/her Ph.D. work. During this very period, everyone contributed to various other institutional projects including the massive project—Survey of

Research in Education. This production emphasis, coupled with insistence on quality, saw through not only a large amount of research output, but also an understanding amongst the research scholars about their own and also their hidden capabilities. This helped them in developing confidence and enlarging their capabilities.

Production emphasis was complemented with recognition accorded to the young research workers. Madhubhai emphasized professional publications. Quite often, the senior faculty including Madhubhai would assign young researchers writing assignments like review papers, case studies, etc. They would guide at every step of the assignment. Once the draft was submitted, the senior faculty would carry out extensive and intensive editing, put the name of the researcher onto the document as co-author as a record and recognition of his/her involvement and contribution. Madhubhai led this practice himself. There were instances when a JRF and a professor sat through hours drafting a paper. This happened to many documents and assignments originating from international organisations, like UNESCO. The apparent production emphasis coupled with professional support and recognition helped building mutual trust, work teams, affiliations and ethics in the Centre. This was an important component for building a cohesive climate for carrying out professional activities in the Centre.

Madhubhai put the organisational ambition ahead of all personal considerations. Let us take one or two instances to bring home the point. Madhubhai was working on Survey of Research in Education. The main idea was to develop a comprehensive document that can help researchers to consult previous researches in education, since access to such research was restricted because of poor documentation and retrieval systems in India. From the beginning till about the final stage of the project, two young research fellows shouldered the project, whereas at the final stage, he inducted two other senior colleagues and gave them the primary responsibility. The two young researchers felt frustrated. When one of them gathered courage after couple of years to ask Madhubhai, he told that the organisational interest was above all other interests. In this project, what was important was a high-quality document rather than being bothered about who had done what. During the life of a project, it requires different kinds of skills at different phases. The skills that are required to begin with such a massive national project is creativity, rich with new ideas; whereas 'during the last phase, we need people with doggedness and meticulousness'. He involved the two young researchers in the initial phase of the project because of their 'richness in creative ideas', and not necessarily for their meticulousness. Compared to them, the two colleagues, brought in at the last phase could work doggedly on a monotonous activity like language editing and proof reading for hours together with great meticulousness.

Library: Research Support

CASE was financially an impoverished organisation. It had a weak office support—without a stenographer, a computer, a fax or a zerox machine. There was a huge outdated table top calculating machine worth a small calculator today, a cyclostyling machine with none to operate it. Within this impoverished condition, Madhubhai was careful in building one of the richest libraries. It was a strategic decision to support research and nurture research climate. It was a circulating library of approximately 10,000 books continuously updated; it was linked to the main Hansa Mehta Library of the University. CASE library had a large collection of journals from all over the world, much beyond its actual sanctioned budget. It tried all possible means to get extra journals by way of gifts, donations, subscriptions, etc., within the provisions of the UGC fellowships; he encouraged research scholars to subscribe to journals of their interest, and requested them to donate to the library as their gifts.

The library created a small section of research instruments useful for the researchers. It was managed single-handedly and competently by Sarojben, the only professional staff without any assistance. There were many occasions when Madhubhai himself led a group of research scholars, at the end of the day, to clean the library.

Taking People Along

Madhubhai dealt with three categories of people—professionals in various universities and institutions in the country and abroad; research staff and the newly recruited faculty; and his colleagues in the Department and the Faculty. Madhubhai maintained rapport with professionals in different universities and institutions in the country and abroad by his enormously developed social skills and emotional intelligence. To keep them involved in the development of CASE, he consulted them regarding the improvement of quality and relevance of research and other academic programmes in CASE. The guests were treated with great care and honour. His third strategy was to use the knowledgeability of these experts for identifying bright young people to join CASE as research fellows. He also professionally assisted them in their own assignments at their respective institutions. He made himself a major professional support for his contemporary professionals.

His basic strategy of carrying the researchers with him was encouraging them and inspiring them to accept challenge. By exposing them on a weekly and daily basis to serious intellectual discourses, he charged each individual to do his/her best. He took special care about honing their professional skills. There were many instances when at the end of a weekly seminar, he would call a research student in his office and encourage him/her to ask questions. He made no bones about his opinion that asking question is a more competent way of learning in a seminar than making comments and observations. It was quite common for him to say, "I'd like to find you asking two questions in the next weekly seminar". As the research scholars grew in their experiences, they were guided to refine their questions or comments. In the third year, he took one of our colleagues to task. "Is this the quality of question to ask? Is that the way to ask questions? I want to see you improve the skills of questioning and making comments in the next seminar". Along with this kind of intellectual discourses, he insisted on writing. Almost every month, research scholars had to account for not only what they were reading, but also what they were writing.

Once, when I submitted the draft of a paper authored by me under his guidance with his name as the first author he removed his name though he did extensive editing and modification in the text of the paper. I mustered courage and asked him the reason for deleting his name. His response was, "I've done all these corrections because I'm your teacher and I'm your senior. The paper is of good quality. So, it should be published on its own merit. It was not good, I could have lent my name (meaningful smile!) to compensate for the quality of the paper. Since it is already good, putting my name will be stealing your credit which is not fair." Another instance will amply illustrate his professionalism and professional ethics. One of the fellows working on a doctoral study asked his guidance on how to carry out normative and ipsative analyses of certain data. The JRF knew that Madhubhai had taught the same analysis to another fellow a couple of years ago. Madhubhai told him that he might not be able to remember the exact calculation, "but let us meet in the library at 4 p.m.". The research fellow met Madhubhai in the library. Madhubhai took out relevant books, sat down with an exercise book and started working on the analysis. The JRF sat patiently. It was only after sometime that Madhubhai learnt the calculations once again, and taught him how to do that calculation.

There was a considerable amount of effective inputs; he took great personal care about every research fellow. It was quite common for him and Mrs. Buch to personally attend to health and other problems, creating hereby an integrated family-like atmosphere. Another important strategy was creating a network among the researchers themselves as a self-help group. There were several occasions when a postgraduate or a doctoral student was asked to get the first draft of his/her dissertation checked by me, as much as two of the other research fellows were asked to review the draft of my dissertation, before it went for his review, comments and approval. Despite the peer review, he worked hard on each dissertation, as evident from extensive pencil marks, correcting, editing, suggesting changes, improvement, etc.

All the CASE seminars were open to everyone in the Faculty and the Department. All were invited. Although no record was maintained, he did keep an eye on those participating in the research seminars and colloquiums, he also watched the quality of their contributions. Those, who showed enthusiasm, interest and capability, were involved more and more; those who either did not participate or dropped out early, were ignored and Madhubhai did not seem to make any special effort to involve them. In reality, a large majority of faculty members in the Department of Education was not taken along.

Being an old student and teacher in the faculty, he was clear in his assessment of the capabilities and ambitions of the members of the faculty; he possibly did not think that much could be done to upgrade their skills, competence and motivation. Secondly, involving the local faculty would also generate additional resistance because of the need to bring in change in them, whereas, if they were left alone and kept in their own convenient locations, the resistance to innovations and changes would be at its minimum.

Madhubhai also had an enviable position vis-a-vis his counterparts as heads of Departments of Educational Administration and Psychology. At any day, they would have been happy to see him failing. They were visibly peeved at Madhubhai's national and international standing, and in being invited by the University, when others had to come through the normal channel of selection. Naturally, Madhubhai did not make any significant effort to take the members of the Department and Faculty along.

Management of Resistance

The resistance to change and innovation was rather minimized by keeping the faculty members away, since it did not require them to change. They were left to be comfortable with their existing skills and competencies. The major resistance came from his equals, namely the heads of two other departments, one of whom was the dean. Since the dean was a member of several important decision-making bodies of the University, he was a potential tool for resisting the innovative features of the Centre. To counter this power that be, Madhubhai maintained close relationships with the vice-chancellor and pro-vice-chancellors who were instrumental in bringing him to the University. The understanding vice chancellor recognized and appreciated Madhubhai's sincere efforts to build the institution and extended the necessary support.

Success and Failure

The perception of success and failure is a mixed one. He certainly succeeded in creating leadership in educational research as is evident from the large number of his scholars at CASE occupying important positions in different universities and national institutions in the country. Also, he contributed significantly to the high-quality research in selected areas of management of change, teaching and teacher behaviour and programmed learning. Inspired by Madhubhai's strategy, a few other faculty members also accepted areas of their choice like achievement motivation and guided a series of studies, making a comprehensive contribution in that area.

Another important success was documentation of research through the surveys of research in education. During his tenure at CASE, he completed the first and the second surveys of research in education. This was a massive effort managed through a small grant. He continued his efforts on the third and the fourth surveys after his retirement. One of his major efforts was to get it institutionalized in the NCERT which, in fact, published the fourth and the fifth surveys of research in education.

His failures are hidden within his own cherished mission. Strategically, he kept the main department outside the purview of development. He built an alternative structure with the research fellows. As the research fellows completed their doctoral studies, they moved out into different universities in the country. Though this accomplished his mission of creating leadership in the country, it left the department high and dry. As a result, the leadership and the quality of educational research were not sustainable. No wonder, it almost came down like a pack of cards within a few years after he left the institution.

Leadership Style

The contemporary leadership styles and theories have been classified into several categories like situational leadership, transactional leadership, transformational leadership, primal leadership and inspirational leadership. Madhubhai's style was a mixed one, characterized by four distinct elements:

- a hard taskmaster, uncompromising on time and quality for task accomplishment;
- high professional ethics—not exploiting young researchers;
- professional concern focusing on professional development of young research scholars; and
- personal concern focusing on placement, health, economy and personal matters of the scholars like parents.

He was known to be not only a hard taskmaster, but also an uncompromising leader on comprehensiveness, rather completeness of a product, quality and time. Let me take an example. During the project on the first Survey, one of the research fellows submitted his report of the progress. Madhubhai asked, 'how comprehensive and complete is the information'. He said, '99%.' Madhubhai flared up:

'but what about the remaining one per cent?', the young scholar was sensitive. He sent in his resignation to Madhubhai and left the office. Madhubhai kept the paper with him. At the end of the day, he asked one of the research fellows to take him to where the aggrieved research scholar lived. Instead of apologising, Madhubhai scolded him, "haven't you ever worked with your father? Would you leave the home if he had scolded? Here is your paper. You're not going anywhere. You should complete your doctorate before you can resign." The research scholar recognized the relationship better; and he did complete his Ph.D. with Madhubhai. There were several occasions when he worked on a draft for several weeks or even months and would say that 'something was missing'. When the draft came back, it was evident that he was correct; and the draft was substantially richer.

His professional ethics was strong and impeccable. He had a reasonable number of articles to his credit, but not an extraordinary list. However, he never exploited research fellows by asking them to work for him or putting his name on their papers. On the contrary, he removed his name from the papers prepared by research fellows though he had worked hard in editing the paper. This professional ethics created respect for Madhubhai. He preached hard work, he himself being a hardworker. His professed dictum was: 'one who cannot think of education for 24 hours a day has no business to be in education'. Indeed, he breathed education.

There was a strong dictator in him, but a benevolent one. He was concerned about professional development of the young researchers. He used to take journals home and mark articles for different researchers to keep them informed. This resembled what is now known as transactional leadership. That, in each of the selected areas, he encouraged others to lead, was the indication of his transformational style. When the new review committee was appointed by the University Grants Commission, he asked one of the readers, according to their specialization, to defend teaching and teacher behaviour, programmed learning; he called upon a junior research fellow to lead the team on research in management of innovation and change, that should have been led by him. He meticulously monitored writing and professional contributions to journals, quality of participation in professional forums, extensive and intensive reading of professional literature.

He was concerned with the personal affairs of the research

students. There were several occasions when research students were kept at his home to overcome 'change of food' problem; his concern for their economic well-being was no less. There were many occasions when Madhubhai wrote to parents of students in matters of crisis.

With all these 'big qualities', he had a big child always alive in him, that was as mischievous and as innocent as one can imagine. For example, when two young scholars, a lady and a young man, were going out to have coffee, they came across Madhubhai, while entering CASE in the morning. Out of courtesy, they asked, "would you like to join us for coffee?" Without hesitation he accompanied them, and behaved like another research fellow.

He was inspiring, though with an uncompromising attitude so far as professional productivity was concerned. That he was adored much after his retirement by all those who came in contact with him indicates his inspiring qualities. Here is a brief episode. I had accompanied Madhubhai, long after his retirement, to Dr. K Gopalan, the then director of NCERT. I introduced Madhubhai as my teacher. Dr. Gopalan immediately reacted, "He is my teacher, too." I was filled with envy but equally pleased, since I saw sincerity in the statement of Dr. Gopalan.

Lessons Learnt

The development of CASE was a growth march—immediate and short lived. Although Madhubhai could create leaders in educational research in several universities, CASE could not 'stay at the top' as a centre of national eminence, after his departure. An important lesson of creating alternative structure is that it offers immediate solution, but lacks sustainability.

If Madhubhai were to relive the same assignment, he would possibly consider making an effort to develop at least a few members of the regular faculty. His contention, that the newly inducted faculty would provide sustainability was not tenable; for, two of them left almost immediately after Madhubhai. Those who stayed back were comparatively less resourceful. His effort in developing some of the regular members of the faculty might have not only been met with resistance but might have also provided lesser rate of return in short-term. This would have, however, been necessary to maintain the sustainability of the Centre of Advanced Studies with its goal of wresting leadership among the research institutions in education.

14
RIDING THE TIDE
Technical Teachers Training Institute, Bhopal

Technical Teachers Training Institute, Bhopal is one of the four regional institutes set up by the government of India to facilitate quality improvement in polytechnic education. Western region is the jurisdiction of this Institute. The Institute was not functioning well and was classified as a sick institution; government of India, reportedly, was considering its closure. It was at that stage and on an experimental basis, Y Saran was appointed principal of the Institute. Saran enjoyed the reputation of building an institution; e.g. Bhopal Polytechnic. Immediately after taking over the reins of TTTI, Saran swung into action with a series of institution building activities—recruiting new faculty members and initiating a set of innovative activities that are logically linked in a sequence to impact the total polytechnic education system and building the new network with resource institutions within India and abroad. The dying institution was converted into a leading institution among the four TTTIs. Saran's leadership was well-recognized; he was invited to head the Colombo Plan Staff College. This is a case of Saran's inspiring and charismatic leadership style.

Landing Up in the Job

Saran graduated in mechanical engineering from Benaras Hindu University. He was appointed lecturer in mechanical engineering in Bhopal Polytechnic. Within a short period, he became head of the department and finally principal at the early age of 29. This was quite unusual for such a position, particularly, since Bhopal Polytechnic has been one of the best polytechnic colleges in the state. Within a short time, he earned the reputation as a dynamic manager of educational institution. That reputation was reinforced, when the students of all the polytechnics in the state went on strike, but in Bhopal Polytechnic, where Saran was the principal every class was engaged. Because of his reputation, he was asked to take over the polytechnic college in Ujjain, when it was also under a crisis.

Saran had a unique way of networking with people who mattered in the state. His hobbies, particularly bridge and tennis, came handy in developing networks. He combined his hobbies and his 'striving for excellence' together. The tennis court in the Polytechnic was one of the best; it attracted the VIPs including the then chief minister of the state and senior officers in the state administration and bureaucracy.

In the academic circle as well as in the state administration his reputation was because of his tenacious zeal for novelty and innovation. Unusual for a polytechnic, Saran conducted summer school for training of polytechnic teachers; he started curriculum development activities which are normally the domain of either Technical Teachers Training Institute or the Board of Technical Examination of the state. Saran used his initiative and urge for innovation to mobilize people in the polytechnic.

Technical Teachers Training Institute, Bhopal was established as one of the regional institutes, originally known as Western Regional Institute by Government of India in 1962-63 for providing training to polytechnic teachers in the western region. Similar regional institutes were established in Calcutta (Kolkata), Chandigarh, and Madras (Chennai) for the eastern, northern and southern regions, respectively. Although the institutes in the northern and southern regions were doing well, the situation was not so good so far as Bhopal and Calcutta were concerned. In Bhopal TTTI, there were hardly four or five faculty members; a large number of positions were vacant for years together, leading to low and poor quality training output. I was given to understand that Bhopal Institute was also on the list to be closed. In Consideration of Saran's managerial skills and reputation, he was appointed for a short period in 1971, probably to examine whether something could be done about the institute. Saran was 42 when he joined as principal of the Institute.

Vision

There does not seem to be enough evidence to conclude that Saran had a clear documented vision for the Institute. What was evident, however, according to his natural style, was that he wanted to build something outstanding (striving for excellence) out of nothing. Indeed, the only perceivable vision was to rebuild the Institute for which it was originally established, hamper the chances of its closure, and create an impact on the polytechnics in the western region.

He brought in a large number of innovative activities in Bhopal Polytechnic. For many such activities like in-service education of polytechnic teachers or curriculum development, TTTI should have been the natural cradle. His vision was to activate the Institute with a variety of such innovative activities that normally belong to TTTI.

In his enthusiasm of transforming polytechnic education, everyone in the Institute, except a few old hands, got intensely involved. They all made meaningful contributions to the resilient, self renewing process of the Institute.

Strategic Interventions

Instead of allowing the Institute to drift further, Saran led the reverse journey. As a matter of strategy, he decided to fill in all the vacant positions. He invited three of his former talented colleagues in Bhopal Polytechnic—Patil, Balu, and Chandran, to join TTTI as professors. All the three were well-tested innovators and/or early adopters of innovation. Since they were heads of departments in polytechnic, the offer was attractive as a career proposition to them, besides their affiliation to Saran as leader. Patil was an electrical engineer, Balu was a civil engineer and Chandran was a mechanical engineer. Patil was an innovator and early adopter of innovations, Balu had a rich mind with critical and analytical thinking; Chandran was a master translator of ideas into action, a great anchor. Patil had the added advantage of undergoing a professional teachers training programme in Huddersfield in UK. With a receptive mind, Patil made the best professional use of the programme. His capabilities as a specialist in 'education' were quite high.

Saran decided to extend his work of Curriculum Development (CD) in Bhopal Polytechnic and introduced it in TTTI for the entire western region. Besides the strategic importance of CD for innovating and enlivening TTTI, it was an important choice because Patil, Balu and Chandran were involved in CD activities in the Polytechnic. The entire team was familiar and experienced; for them, it was like extending the borders from a smaller to a larger area. The CD project involved job analysis of the technicians. In the project mode, it involved field survey of opinions of the employers as well as the employees. All the faculty members got involved in the fieldwork. They visited a number of industries; interviewed the technicians themselves, their supervisors, their subordinates; got questionnaires filled in. The polytechnic teachers who were then undergoing teachers training programme in TTTI were also involved in the fieldwork as part of their practicum. The entire event witnessed great enthusiasm and a perception of 'something great' being done. The data thus collected were subjected to analysis to identify the job contents and job elements of each category of technicians. Each job element was then used to derive requirement of knowledge, skills, attitudes, etc. In turn, that formed the basis for curriculum development. Decidedly, it was the most scientific and systematic approach to curriculum development.

By the time the CD activities were going on in full swing, first in the field and then in the Institute, the 'think tank' started planning for the next. This resulted into systems thinking that looked for the mechanism of transforming the polytechnic education as a whole. As a natural corollary, the next step was developing learning material based on the newly designed curriculum. Following a typical grammar book approach, the learning materials were developed on the basis of stated objectives at different levels of cognition. Such efforts in generating learning material subsequently led to the development of multimedia material and self-learning modules.

A series of activities was initiated in the student assessment. The major innovation was the new blue print for student evaluation—tests comprising a whole range of objective type test items, very short answers, short answers and short essays, compared to the only essay type tests. The development of new type test items including the objective type, led to several major activities. One such activity was training polytechnic teachers in generating objective and other new types of test items. The training and production workshops created a large pool of test items in different subjects of polytechnic education.

The item pool encouraged the thought of setting up a question bank. A fresh spate of work began in setting up the question bank. One activity rolled on to another, creating larger and larger involvement of the faculty.

While these innovative activities were moving from one stage to another, Saran continued to expand his faculty by recruiting new people into the institution. For example, newly recruited Rao took charge of curriculum development; Verma started working in student assessment and question bank development. Further, as can be seen, as soon as the faculty members developed some expertise in curriculum development, or prepared instructional material, or student assessment, they launched training programmes for polytechnic teachers. With every such action the tempo was building up.

Following the massive activities on curriculum development, preparation of instructional material and student evaluation, the consequential question was improving management of the polytechnics for management of innovation and change. This led to ushering in activities in educational management. In collaboration with Anglian Regional Management Centre, TTTI began training of polytechnic principals and heads of departments in management. Again, Mani, a new faculty member was recruited who took serious interest in management development.

While all the faculty members were involved in numerous activities with tremendous enthusiasm, Saran and his think tank were engrossed in taking a deeper look at activities and its impact on the system as a whole. This particular consideration and concern relate to the identification of research as one of the focused activities in TTTI. Although by this time, quite a few faculty members had been recruited with doctoral degree, all of them had Ph.D. in one of the engineering disciplines, except for one or two in education. Saran decided to recruit a specialist faculty member for supporting educational research activity in the Institute. I joined at this stage to lead research activities in the Institute. Research activities were taken up at two levels. Firstly, teams of faculty members took up major research studies, primarily evaluation studies. Secondly, for contributing to the agenda of change and modernization of polytechnics, it was considered necessary to introduce diagnostic and action research in polytechnics. Training programmes and workshops were organized for training polytechnic teachers in research methods in general, action research in particular. The workshops and training programmes were so designed that they generated research proposals. The polytechnic teachers trained in such workshops were encouraged to submit research proposals, and conduct field-based action researches. A large number of minor studies were thus sponsored and initiated at the polytechnic level. The faculty team undertook major research projects covering the entire western region, and a few national studies in collaboration with other TTTIs.

As these activities were being undertaken with great zeal and enthusiasm one after another, Saran in collaboration with his core team, designed an ambitious comprehensive project, comprising curriculum development, instructional material development, including multimedia and film, research, management, etc. The project was submitted to the UNDP through the nodal ministry of the Government of India. It was an ambitious project. With his skill of negotiation, he got the project approved. However, after the approval of the project, other three TTTIs demanded their share. Although not appreciated, Saran had to concede, since Government of India was involved in taking the decision of sharing the UNDP project funds among all the four TTTIs. There was a very large component of technical assistance in this project, which had brought international experts into the TTTI, including a resident project director from the University of Illinois, USA. In the second component of the technical assistance, there were large number of fellowships for the TTTI faculty to undergo training for six to nine months in any of the Commonwealth countries and specialize in one of the areas in technician education. The majority of the staff from all the four TTTIs chose USA, University of Illinois as the destination. A number of senior faculty members including Balu and others took full postgraduate course in education in the University of Illinois. The UNDP project generated another level of enthusiasm and activity, surpassing all the previous limits of enthusiasm and activities in TTTI.

Saran continued his crusade of innovation. This time, it was Competency-based Teacher Education. Once again, a detailed exercise was undertaken in terms of job analysis and job description of teachers in polytechnics. The TTTI faculty had the experience and expertise on job analysis through its earlier project on CD. The job analysis of teachers led to the identification of 79 different competencies. On each competency, self-instructional, structured learning module was developed. Each and every faculty member was involved in authoring self-instructional modules. The teacher-training programme offered by TTTI underwent a dramatic change. Conventional teacher education programme was replaced by competency-based teacher education. Saran approached the British Council which has been a very important ally in TTTI's development for funding Competency-based Teacher Education. British Council, however, did not agree on two counts, namely Britain did not have relevant expertise, and it did not consider necessary that TTTI should implement CBTE. Saran, persuaded the British Council to fund it and impressed upon TTTI's capability to mobilize expert resources.

These are some of the major innovations carried out between 1971 when Saran joined as principal and 1979 when he left for Colombo Plan Staff College. There are three important components in the strategy described above:

1. there was a large spate of activities, involving all members of the faculty generating an unprecedented enthusiasm in the entire institution;
2. there grew intense interaction between TTTI faculty members and state agencies and institutions enhancing the social acceptability of TTTI as an expert resource institution; and
3. there emerged a clearly defined road map with a systems approach for development of polytechnic education.

Along with systemic innovation, Saran consistently focused on capacity building of the staff. With its old connection with Hudders field in UK, TTTI had developed a close link with several British institutions through British Council. Almost every faculty member had an operation to visit UK and undergo one or two rigorous training programmes. Also, this collaboration led to the visit of British experts to TTTI: for example, the management education activities were developed with the help of experts from the Anglian Regional Management Centre, Sussex. The strategy option in such collaboration was interesting. In the initial phase, management training programmes were designed primarily by the ARMC experts, who also took a lead role in conducting the training programmes. In the following years, they played the role of equals with the TTTI faculty, and subsequently, their role receded to facilitating and critiquing the performance of the TTTI faculty as management trainers.

Drawing lessons from the experience of collaboration with British institutions, with the support of British Council Division, Saran made lavish provision of staff development under the technical assistance component of the UNDP assisted project. This also brought in experts from other countries into TTTI. This continuous interaction of the TTTI faculty with the international experts either in India or abroad contributed significantly to the development of expertise in their respective work areas.

Saran also recognized the problem of dichotomy between enthusiasm and ability to concentrate and specialize. Since all faculty members were involved in all activities of the Institute, specialization was missing; probably, there was also the 'crowd effect' on the quality of the output and the programmes. This concern and realization was further supported by continuous interaction with modern management science, particularly in the training programmes on MBO. This led to reorganizing academic staff into a matrix structure. Although the faculty appointments were in different departments like civil, mechanical, electrical engineering, management, education, educational research, etc., activities like curriculum development, evaluation, development of material and instructional resources including multimedia, educational research that cut interest across disciplines were identified as activity areas. Across the departments, task forces were constituted; faculty members could choose two task areas. Thus, every task force actually came to be an interdisciplinary group of teachers. This also had the effect on the departments looking at all aspects of education, namely curriculum, teaching-learning material preparation, evaluation, management, etc.

Management of Resistance

The level of activism was massive and sweeping for any resistance to be visible. I entered on the scene almost in the last year of the Saran-regime. Things appeared smooth and fine, though differential reactions were perceptible, which could also be due to personal styles, for example, difference between the 'stars' and the 'isolated' in the faculty.

To be more realistic in understanding the dynamics, I cross-checked with other colleagues who worked with Saran for a longer period. We discovered three different sets of resistance.

Firstly, four or five faculty members who were there before Saran entered the scene in 1971, did not seem to be happy with all the 'great innovations' in the Institute. They murmured, but did not necessarily raise their voice of discontent and disapproval. Since they were weak and isolated from one another, there was no 'synergy' among the resisting forces. They did not, hence, make any meaningful impact on the ongoing process. The only difference was their reluctance and slow involvement in the mainstream functions of the institute. They lacked the enthusiasm that was visible everywhere else. Saran literally did nothing to waive off the resistance. Nor did he miss opportunities of involving them in the activities.

The second resistance came from the states. TTTI, Bhopal was established to serve polytechnic education in all the states in the western region. Saran, with his innovative initiatives in Bhopal Polytechnic had already created an 'innovation friendliness' in Madhya Pradesh. In the initial phase of Saran's tenure, Gujarat was reluctant and resistant to accommodate the innovations. Maharashtra was indifferent though not resistant. However, with the change of leadership (director of Technical Education), things changed in Gujarat, particularly after Shri Kalwachwala wala took over as director, Technical Education, followed by another dynamic director, Prof. S B Kumta. Saran's main strategy was to pursue the state authorities, and he effectively used his colleagues like Patil, Balu and others in building the acceptability of the institute.

The third resistance was faced with the introduction of UNDP assisted projects from other TTTIs. Although the project was exclusively conceptualized and designed by Saran and his colleagues for capacity building of TTTI Bhopal, other three TTTIs demanded their share of the pie under the pretext that UNDP supported project can belong only to the government of India, and hence for all four TTTIs. In this struggle for share, TTTI Kolkata was not that important since it had the same condition as Bhopal had, prior to the joining of Saran. However, the principals of northern and southern regional TTTIs raised their voice. Also, they were not very friendly with Saran; Saran's quick rise in fame and prominence in technical education might have also contributed to this jealous reaction. The Ministry of Education of Government of India acceded to this demand; Saran and his colleagues were unhappy but could not stop it. It was, then, decided that Saran would lead the entire project on behalf of the four TTTIs. This, too, was not accepted by the other TTTIs. As a result, the project had to be divided by four. This component of resistance could not be managed by Saran.

Leadership

Leadership is influencing through control, motivation, inspiration of people in the organization for task accomplishment. Let us understand the dynamics and the style of leadership through the following episodes:[1]

- There was a bitter feud between two employees in the institute. It went on for quite sometime and came to a stop. It was at this stage, that Saran intervened and suspended both the employees and instituted an enquiry committee. On the basis of the report of the enquiry committee, both the employees were removed from job. The hushing corridor dialogue, mutual consultations, generated enough anxiety that there might be a staff strike and violent agitation in the Institute. Saran called both of them and was closeted for about half an hour. As they came out, both of them were in smiles. One of the senior faculty members happened to meet them on their way out of Saran's office. One of the two confided with him, "Principal is right. He had no other choice but to remove us from the job."
- After a month of my joining, I found Saran standing at the entrance of the Institute and chatting with Balu. I also joined them. He stood there nearly for half an hour chatting business punched with personal pleasantries. Employees were entering the office; they wished and walked past. I noticed the change in the pattern of employee attendance after this incidence. I raised it with Balu, one of the senior most colleagues. He told me that Saran was standing and chatting with him and me for monitoring employees' attendance. Yet, he never asked any employee about their late coming. Balu said, 'But that's

enough. Employees respect him as a moral standard. They won't be late for some more months'.

- There was a meeting in the Directorate of Technical Education, Gujarat. One of the senior faculty members of good professional standing represented the Institute. During the meeting, he made certain statements, which were not appreciated by the state government officials, and heads of polytechnics. This was reported to some of the senior professors in the Institute. They were of the view that the young professor should not have taken a professional view, and expressed his opinion candidly. The young professor met Saran. He soon realized that Saran had full information about the incidence and views of his colleagues. Without wasting time, the young professor asked whether he should make any amends on the issue and style. Saran responded, "Your professional stand is correct. You are convinced of your views and you have expressed them with all good intentions. Even if some people are not happy, you should not change your principled position for making others happy". The professor asked, "But what if it affected the interest of our Institute?" Saran laughed and said, "I am happy at your concern for the Institute. I'll take care. If I cannot take care of the dignity of my faculty, I have no business to head this Institute. Don't worry, continue your good work."
- One of the states in the region demanded a concept note and a strategy paper on a particular issue of technician education. Saran called three professors—two seniors and one relatively junior. The junior professor was not immediately available. Saran entrusted the assignment to the two senior professors, and asked them to involve the junior professor. It was decided to complete the drafting in three days. Two senior professors went to meet Saran with the draft on the third day. Saran flipped through the draft and asked, "I don't find the young professor's involvement, did you involve him"? The senior most between the two said, "No, Sir, he is too inexperienced in technical education, his inputs will not be of much use to this document". Saran said, "Sorry, I completely disagree with you. I wanted his involvement in

this paper not because of his experience in the system, but because of his freshness of thoughts, analytical skills, and knowledgeability". He returned the paper and asked them to involve him and bring back the document along with the junior professor. On the next day, all the three met Saran. He saw the difference in the draft, and expressed his satisfaction.

- Research department was just opened. I was the first incumbent on the subject in the institute. I developed a research proposal, which in my judgment, was fairly good and sophisticated. When I met Saran and presented my proposal, he glanced through it and returned it saying that this was not a good proposal both in terms of its relevance to the working of the TTTI and the quality of the project. Despite his soft sophisticated style, this hit my self-esteem as a research professor and head. I asked him whether I could have an "argument" on the proposal. Saran was shocked beyond belief—he could not believe that someone in his faculty could confront him and invite him for an academic argument. His view was always unchallenged; this was something new to him. Magnanimous as he was, he asked me to sit down, called for tea, and instructed his office not to telephone or allow any visitor till the time I was inside the office. He asked me to present my views, which he carefully listened, occasionally asking questions; questions were inquisitive without challenging me. After twenty minutes, Saran pulled himself forward on to his decision-making style. Wore a broad smile and said, "I stand convinced. It is an important project. So, this will be an institutional project and not your personal one. You will direct the project, but please involve a few other faculty members so that you may get their help. If they can get involved in such an important sophisticated research project, they can learn, and together we can generate a team of researchers." I came out of his office impressed.
- Balu had submitted a personal leave application for approval to Saran. He wanted to visit Madras (now Chennai) to be with his younger brother and his family. When the application reached Saran, he called Balu. Saran told him that there are

> two important outstanding items with the Directorate of Technical Education in Madras, and asked whether during his visit to Madras, Balu could spare a day and sort these out. Balu was more than happy to do that and readily agreed. While he was about to leave Saran's office, Saran called him back and handed him back his leave application, and asked for his tour proposal. Balu insisted that he would accommodate this work within his personal visit and leave. Saran said, "in any case, we have to send a person to Madras to get this official work done and spend on TA/DA. There is no better person than you for this job. Please send your tour proposal and go on official work. You can take two days' leave along with the work to visit your brother".

The above episodes and many others shed tremendous light on the style of conflict resolution to influencing colleagues, which indeed is leadership. He was charismatic in style. Despite all the warmth, generosity and comfort, he was equi-distant from everyone in the Institute including Patil, Balu, Chandran, and others. He never raised his voice; yet, if he ever used statements like, "I thought this was to be done yesterday", people hung their head with shame, as if they had committed a blunder.

His task orientation and emphasis was little. His emphasis was on task accomplishment on time with quality. He hardly ever compromised with any of the three criteria. Patil brought a large number of new ideas in curriculum development, production of instructional material, etc. Similarly after my introduction, I brought new thrust and new ways of approaching research. Others introduced educational films and videos, etc. He enthusiastically received all such innovations and innovative ways; provided all possible support removing the roadblocks on the way. His leadership style also included protection and paternalistic behaviour; he protected people from external criticisms, taking the brunt on himself. Through this, he owned the trust of the staff.

He had rich skills of communication and presence. His sophistication and style provided him an air—he carried himself with dignity earning respect and adoration.

His inter-personal relationships and skills were extensively used for developing networks. This was evident from his ability to network

TTTI with British Universities, British Councils and finally securing a massive project from UNDP. Many senior faculty members held that Saran had an overarching style, and he could get almost anything done. Yet, there is not a single evidence where he used his influencing style and position for himself, or for his near and dear ones. His leadership style was full of ethics.

Success and Failures

From almost every angle, this is an eminently successful case of institution building. Saran's journey began in 1971, with the prospect of closing down the Institute looming large on the horizon. He successfully turned it around for TTTI to occupy a place of prominence. Not only had the Institute a turnaround, but it also became the leader among the four TTTIs. The story of his success as an institution builder spread beyond the boundaries of India. He was invited to lead as director of Colombo Plan Staff College for technical education.

His major success was building a competent and committed academic staff. The competent staff recruited from time to time was inducted to build the culture of innovation and sustainability. His greatest success was his ability to inspire and get everyone involved in building the institute. That the Institute has been able to maintain its innovative culture even after two decades of Saran's departure provides enough basis to draw conclusions about his success.

However, despite massive work and innovation over the years, the Institute did not to get the national or international recognition as a leader in the field, the way CASE or NIEPA carved out their respective spaces in the international arena. This was largely due to lack of professionalisation of the academic staff. They were hard working, loyal to the Institute and their leader. They missed out on the intellectual culture backed by research, documentation and authoring. Developmental activities without research and evaluation and a critical documentation get lost as lamented by Ronald Havelock in his classical work, Planning for Innovations. Though rarely, Saran was also the victim of human weaknesses. Under recommendation, his selection of the staff in certain core areas affected the institute's journey towards excellence.

More importantly, Saran did not build the second line of

leadership, what transformational leaders do for sustainability of innovations. Patil, Balu, Chandran and others closer to him were of the same age group. They could not imagine assuming leadership position although some of them had the necessary skills and qualities. The intriguing phenomenon during Saran's regime was riding the tide, what some faculty members termed "survival of the latest". There was hardly any effort for consolidation. For example, properly researched, evaluated and consolidated, TTTI's Competency-based Teacher Education would have provided the Institute a world-class stature and recognition, whereas such an important innovation is not even known in the mainframe teacher education system in India itself.

Revisiting TTTI

Saran did come back to TTTI after his tenure in Colombo Plan Staff College only for a short while, before he left for another assignment with the World Bank. His experience at the Colombo Plan Staff College did not seem to have any serious impact on his second tenure in the TTTI. Deriving lessons from international experiences, almost every Institute that reached great heights, reached primarily because of its research, documentation and high-quality training that generated reputation. If TTTI could be revisited, the high-quality committed academic staff need to be given professional orientation culture of research, intellectual debates and discussions, research and critical writing, may be even moving towards theorizing. It had a significant opportunity of professionalisation through its contact with international institutions of repute. It failed to encash primarily due to the culture of bandwagoning, instead of standing up as individual intellectuals within a team.

His strategy of recruiting his old colleagues from the polytechnic provided him with unenviable 'catch 22' situation. They were committed; their experience in polytechnic education was an asset. Polytechnic teachers in the region, however, had reservation. According to them, TTTI professors have the same qualifications and experience as they had, but being in TTTI they enjoyed better job privileges, though hardly anyone of such complainants could actually match the skills and competence of the people Saran brought from the polytechnic system. This jealous reaction affected the acceptability of TTTI and its reputation. Saran rectified it later by recruiting some highly qualified engineers and educationists and asking the first generation recruits to go through M.Ed. programme during their UNDP fellowship. If TTTI could be revisited, the graduate engineer teachers with experience in polytechnic education, with enriched education leading to postgraduation and doctoral degrees in education/technical education would still be the best choice.

Saran's is a case of fast sweep that roped everyone in an inspired spell; a case of endless energy and creativity that provided his colleagues with a new meaning to work.

NOTE

1. Literary criticism tells us that short stories are windows to the life of individuals. These episodes are like those short stories that shed light on the life of the leader.

15

SELF-REGULATION, THE KEY TO INSTITUTION BUILDING

INDIAN INSTITUTE OF MANAGEMENT, AHMEDABAD[1]

The Indian Institute of Management, Ahmedabad, was founded in 1962. Vikram Sarabhai acted as the part-time honorary director while the Board of Governors searched for a full-time Director. Ravi J Matthai, the first full-time director, took over in 1965. The Indian Institute of Management, Ahmedabad, has come to symbolise various innovative practices in the management of institutes of higher learning. Stress was placed on maintaining the autonomy of the Institute, developing the culture of professional and non-hierarchical relationships, with an emphasis on a matrix-type of organization, in which people performed various roles and their significance depended on the roles they performed in the institute, rather than on hierarchical status. A deliberate attempt was made to build a culture of self-reliance and competent creativity in diverse roles. Several innovative practices were introduced in the institute which would be difficult to conceive in the general Indian structure of higher education. These innovations have helped the institute to acquire an internal strength. The principal architect of this system was Matthai who, during the eight years (1965-72) of his directorship, created and nurtured the peer-group and a professional culture and sustained the self-renewing process in the institute. The following interview between Udai Pareek (UP) and Ravi J Matthai (RJM) gives some idea about the thoughts of a person who has been a great institution builder.

UP: The purpose of this interview is to see what we can learn from some insightful experience of one who has contributed to the institution building process. A question I may like to ask you, in the beginning, is: What is the most important thing in institution building? What contributes to institution building?

RJM: As far as the Indian Institute of Management, Ahmedabad, is concerned, I think the single most important aspect was building a self-regulating culture, within the institute, built upon building people. This meant trying to build attitudes within the institute community that would foster and sustain self-discipline. It also meant building attitudes of people outside the institute such that they expect a high degree of self-discipline from those within. Influencing the external expectation was important because it reinforced integrity within the institute, and it reduced pressures for procedures and rules that would have resulted in imposed regulation. By self-regulation based on self-discipline I mean our capability of being able to evolve norms of behaviour regarding the institute's goals, tasks, cooperation in work, interpersonal relations, innovation, the use of authority, acceptance of responsibility, etc. For example, we have a two-year Post-Graduate Programme (PGP) as one of the important programmes of the institute. But when, for example, consulting executive programmes or research came into conflict with the faculty schedule of the Post-Graduate Programme, it was the faculty that laid down the norm of not tinkering with the PGP schedule. The important point was that the chief executive of IIMA should not impose rules on the faculty but that the faculty should develop norms such that the chief executive would not, hopefully, have to haul up faculty members for missing classes. The weight of faculty opinion influenced a faculty member's priorities and as to how he should behave. Again, as far as consulting is concerned, it was not that the rules mattered so much as the fact that the members of the faculty did exercise their own sense of responsibility in regulating the time to be spent on consulting. Self-regulation was also developed through the way in which committees functioned, the way in which individuals took responsibility without authority. This made the committee's job and the job of the chairman doubly difficult. Unless there was a very strong sense of self-discipline, the faculty member could easily have regarded the job as much too difficult for him, and also a waste of time.

In fact, a few faculty members did protest against responsibility without authority. Colleagues and groups exercised pressures. People in the various roles acted because of such norms, rather than the imposed regulation of the chief executive. The Board, Government of India and the state government—all had a tendency to ask for clarity in relation to statutes, rules, regulations, procedures and expected large documents to be compiled which would state how every faculty member would behave under every circumstance.

This was resisted. Again, through meetings with the government and with the Board, the idea was put across and accepted that we, within the institute, would try to evolve this self-regulating culture and, therefore, the expectation of the government and the Board in relation to the institute also became one of the self-regulation measures, within the institute. So, thereafter, neither of them pressed for these rules and they accepted the idea of the institute developing norms for such self-regulation.

UP: You have stressed the value of self-regulating mechanisms, and you have also indicated what mechanisms you used to work towards this goal. What were your main concerns in the beginning while you were working towards self-regulating norms and mechanisms?

RJM: To my mind, self-regulation depended on the sense of responsibility which each faculty member felt for the institutional, organizational and individual tasks that he undertook—academic, administrative or whatever they might be. This sense of responsibility, it was hoped, would evolve only with a very high sense of autonomy in relation to both individuals and groups of individuals. In a sense, it meant, trying to develop the individual faculty member's initiative, ability and confidence to satisfy his own creative expression without losing sight of the difference between the freedom implied in autonomy and licence.

One of the regulating factors built into the system, was that individual faculty members in-charge of tasks always had to work with a group. Every individual who had a task had to work with a committee. The objective of having such a large number of committees was that, in the course of trying to build this institute, every faculty member, one way or other, should be involved in the administration of the institute and so develop an organizational and an institutional points of view. This involvement was not in any hierarchical sense but in the sense of equal participation, despite differences in academic status in terms of being a professor, or an assistant professor. Both the individual and the committee, it was felt, should develop a sense of autonomy. It was hoped that developing an organizational and an institutional point of view through creative and innovative academic administration in a committee system would result in the individual's self-restraint. This did not, however, mean that there would be no "organizational space" for individual innovation; quite the reverse, such "organizational space" must be available.

Another assumption made was that unless the individual gains some understanding of how to use his freedom and some degree of self-confidence in his own individual functioning, his functioning in a group becomes less effective. Some of us who were not used to a high degree of free self-expression, I think, sometimes found our own sense of discrimination lacking. Perhaps, we were not able to distinguish always between freedom and licence, or between frankness and rudeness, or between freely expressed opinions and "as-a-matter-of principle", self-righteousness. I think that the exercise of autonomy and the implicit freedom require a great deal of interpersonal sensitivity, understanding and consideration. Insensitivity and intolerance vitiate the culture. It was hoped that the organizational and the institutional points of view and regard for others would be brought about to some degree by the shared experience of group work through committees and other task teams.

UP: As I understand, the two major concerns were to develop true autonomy of individuals as persons, as well as to develop respect for one another, contributing to a culture in which groups could work out self-regulating mechanisms. Is that so?

RJM: Sometimes, a lack of mutual respect was evident. The crucial aspect was whether there could be a strong enough sense of expectation amongst the rest of the faculty that would succeed in dampening the negative effect of the lack of mutual regard in the performance of organizational tasks. For example, some faculty members had interpersonal problems and, at the slightest provocation, would quarrel with one another and introduce personal issues into general discussions. These instances in the early years were not uncommon at faculty meetings. There were occasions where we had deliberately stopped the substantive discussion during faculty meetings in order to discuss, not the substantive issue, but the manner in which we were discussing it and whether people were using the discussions for personal issues and hidden agendas.

UP: Was this in tune with the process?

RJM: Yes, in the sense that we were trying to get individual and group identities and autonomy established. The endeavour was, despite interpersonal problems, to get groups to organize their own work such that the faculty reaction to a display of autonomy on the part of the group was met with approbation—"Good for them! They have decided what their own job would be and are doing it!, as distinct from the director deciding what they should do," which they are then expected to do because the director said so. The phrase frequently used was "academic entrepreneurship".

UP: Which also means making the group both responsible and accountable as an entity, in addition to the individuals.

RJM: This related to the individuals', the groups', the committees' and the whole faculty's sense of getting a job done. As far as the task was concerned, there was initially a demand for power and authority in relation to the role of those in-charge of the task. This authority was not given. The persons in-charge used to complain: "How can I do this job and get the task done, when you give me no authority to tell the faculty members what to do?" The answer was: "Persuade them. If you can't persuade them, however, you have problems."

UP: This is a very intriguing phenomenon. How do you develop a power which creates more influence but does not restrict others? Instead of giving power, in the sense of sanctioned authority which people use to apply further sanctions downwards, how do you create power which is more liberating and also helps to release an individual's energy for productive purposes? How did the culture of this kind of power develop? How did you operate in relation to the chairmen of various activities and other people to help produce this power?

RJM: The first step was in trying to build the individual's sense of autonomy and self-confidence which would allow this power, in the sense you have described it, to evolve without threatening individuals or other groups within the community. So, endeavouring to build self-confidence was a major aspect. There were both internal and external factors which one used in order to develop this. Every opportunity was used. At the Executive Development Programmes, for example, the effort was to try to develop a very strong self-respect amongst faculty members in front of outsiders. Other instances were the inclusion of faculty members in all sorts of meetings in which they would not have normally been included, constantly giving them responsibilities which they would otherwise expect the director to handle by himself.

The second aspect was that whenever the responsibility for a task was given to a committee and a chairman, there was a very definite endeavour not to allow the buck to be passed back to the director. So, if ever a committee within its framework tried this, the effort of the director was to throw it straight back to the committee and tell them to get on with the job. This policy was followed to the extent that some faculty members even accused the director of not fulfilling his function because he refused to take many decisions which the faculty and groups were finding difficult to take. But the assumption was that unless the faculty persevered, they would never be able to earn autonomy. Initially, as had always been happening, a great deal would come back to the director's table. Decisions about the PCP, Executive Development Programmes, Research, etc., would find their way back to the director's table. Within about 3 or 4 years, very little of this used to come to the director's table. The simple fact was that the faculty members were very capable people.

A third aspect was delegation "upwards". The PGP was an example. The programme was conducted by a committee consisting of all the faculty members who taught in the programme. This meant that nearly the entire faculty was involved. This large committee used to meet frequently to make all programme decisions, even minor decisions. Obviously, decisions were very difficult to make in this large group and often, in desperation, or disgust, they wanted to leave the decision to the director: The "buck" was thrown back. Undoubtedly, a large number of faculty members wasted a great deal of their time and the entire process created a high degree of frustration. A simple solution would have been for the director to re-organize this arrangement in obvious ways. This was not done. After a while, the large committee delegated a considerable part of its decision-making to a smaller executive committee, which later, in turn, delegated more power to the PGP chairman, thinking that this process rendered the chairman and his committee far more effective than they would have been, had the director delegated authority to them in order to get decisions made and save on faculty time.

UP: Those who have worked with you continuously refer to your behaviour of letting the people take the decision, giving them a sense of autonomy and respect in taking those decisions. May I ask you a personal question? To what do you attribute this quality which, I think, is one of the rarest qualities? How did you develop this quality of helping people to take on independent respectable roles when they are working with you and not leaning on your shoulders? The reason why I refer to it as a quality is that a person would not be able to behave that way, unless he socialises in a culture, in which he experiences such a behaviour. Do you, for example, attribute this quality to your experience in relation to your father, or the way you grew up in the culture, or your experiences in the institutions and knowledge of the theory people find it difficult to behave this way, and, without being aware, may rush into controlling things in the hope that they are doing it in the interest of the organization. That is why I refer to it as an intrinsic quality.

RJM: Well, this sort of question, I find it very difficult to answer. I do not know whether it is a quality or whether it is merely a way in which I saw the task I had undertaken, when I agreed to the Board's invitation to come here. I had lots of misgivings about coming over here. But I decided to take it on, because I was intrigued by the thought of building an institution, practically from scratch. So, what always dominated was the objective to build an institution. So, I did make deliberate choices in terms of what I set about. I imposed on myself, for example, the limitations that I would not accept any external work, i.e., work concerned with any external agency outside the institute, unless that work had a very direct bearing on the functioning of the institute. These links, not just tasks, the other faculty should take over. I respected all other types of involvement. All the links that were built in relation to the institute always and, without exception, had a primary bearing on the functioning of the institute and these links were soon managed by others than the director. I do not attach any normativity to what was done at this institute, in the sense of its being right or wrong.

UP: But it is in relation to effectiveness.

RJM: In relation to how all of us saw the task. Let me illustrate this. One aspect was that the more the power, implicitly or explicitly, I kept to myself, the more the faculty members would be dependent on me, the more aspects of the institute I would get involved with, in greater detail. I would, therefore, have that much less time to spend on major aspects of development on which I thought a director should spend his time; for example, in terms of new activities or building external links, support and resources, searching for the faculty and spending time with it in trying to develop this sort of culture in an institution, without getting bogged down in operational details, in terms of my own "Dhobi Book" planning. Planning inside the institution, as we all knew, was perceived as fairly weak. This war is deliberate.

UP: What is this "Dhobi Book" planning?

RJM: "Dhobi Book" planning is the sort of planning I did in a little black book, covering periods of 5 to 20 years in terms of how I saw the institution developing. I did not discuss the plans either inside the institute with the faculty or with the Board members or with the government. I just kept these plans to myself, the way I kept my "Dhobi Book". This I did deliberately, because I did not want people to be made, self-conscious by planned targets. Nor did I wish to be constrained by other people's expectations of targets I set for myself. My view was that, at an early stage of institutional development, laying down planned targets forces people to achieve an artificial number of targets, without giving them time to develop their capacity to undertake responsibility, as a way of expressing themselves, creatively. Building this sense of responsibility, I saw as being more important for the institute than the obviously necessary accomplishments of tasks. Most of the explicit planning was short-term and operational, which each faculty task group did for itself rather than having it imposed.

There are, then, our five-year plans and annual budgets which make the bases for negotiating government funds. Other short-term plans were in relation to specific activities. As all of us evolved our own ways of handling functions, which influenced various longer-term aspects of development, I altered my plan in my "Dhobi Book", if I found that the ideas, directions and pace, as they had evolved, were more effective than my own. In a sense, I am emphasising the fact that there was no particular person who "directed development". All of us were growing up together.

UP: Now coming back to the origin of the quality of giving autonomy to people, it seems to me that either you are evading the question, or I have seen you in other roles and I have found a similar concern and approach which helps people to take on responsibility with dignity. That is why I have been raising this question. Only a deep sense of internal security can contribute to such an attitude, and internal security may be a part of some processes in early life.

RJM: It is not so much a question of security. If you ask somebody for something and you are uncertain as to whether the answer will be "yes" or "no", you may be uncertain as to whether you should ask him the question in the first place. My reaction to that has always been that the worst he can do is to say "No". The worst that could happen was that I would fall flat on my face. So might we all. But, we pick ourselves up and go on again. I think my father did try to make us self-reliant and while I doubt my own degree of self-reliance, I seem to regard it as a virtue! My naive rationalisation was that self-reliance and self-regulation would make the task of building the institution possible.

UP: All right, may I take another angle and ask you one more personal question? I am sure it would be difficult to get an answer, but let me try. What were your main strengths as an institution builder?

RJM: My main strength was my ignorance.

UP: Was it?

RJM: I am not being entirely facetious. Even though I worked in industry for quite a few years, I had no formal education in management whatsoever, not even a one-day seminar. Beyond the fact that I thought it referred to running a company, which I had been doing, I did not know what occurred between the first and the last pages of any management textbook. Secondly, apart from my two years' experience at IIMC and MIT before coming to Ahmedabad, I had never worked in an educational institution. I knew nothing about building an educational institution, let alone managing an educational institution. So, may be the strength is my ignorance, in that I had no structural preconceptions. On the other hand, 1 did have attitudinal biases towards education arising from my experiences as a student, as an employer when I was in industry, and as a faculty member for a very short while. These biases were the very common "motherhood" types of norms. I thought that creativity and innovation were "good"; this required "freedom of views and expression"; this required self-discipline which required self-confidence, which, again, required self-esteem and mutual self-respect between colleagues and so on. But I had no preconceptions as and how all this could be achieved. All I had were biases in favour of self-reliance of individuals, groups and the institute. So, when I accepted the invitation to come over here, we had to generate our own and the institute community's ideas of what an institution should be, of what an educational institution should be and what the management of educational institution should be. We also had to generate thinking not merely about "what", but also about "how" to develop and sustain the "strengths", without an over-dependence on—leadership, or external patronage of regulation. It really all started from a point of ignorance, a lack of experience. Perhaps, experience might have constrained me. Today, I have more experience. I do not know whether this would make me more or less constrained. Perhaps, the more one's attitude towards the value of experience changes, the greater the variety.

UP: If ignorance, as you put it, which I would like to translate as openness, creativity and not going by the stereotyped understanding, as your strength, what was your weakness?

RJM: One weakness which I think harmed the institution was my lack of socialising within the institute. I had a very strong need for privacy. If the whole day from early morning to about seven in the evening was spent primarily on discussions with the institute's community, groups, individuals, outsiders and so on, the whole day had been spent in talking about important problems that were of concern to all of us who raised them. On the other hand, I had to be alone to think about longer-term aspects of the institute, and about what I regarded were the basic problems of developing the culture of the institute. So, ever)' evening, I barred and bolted myself in the house, with no meetings, and no one was allowed to see me. I would not be sociable. I think problems were created by this lack of socialisation.

The second aspect is that I cannot do a task effectively unless I am emotionally involved with it. I suppose this might mean that I have instinctive attitudinal traits. With the best of intentions, for me, reasoning is necessary but not sufficient. More often than not, I need to get emotionally involved. When I get emotionally involved in the task, it is very difficult to remain "objective", or "unbiased" and to satisfy all the other requirements of rationality. Apart from being in my thinking time, perhaps my need for privacy was also dominant because of my coping mechanism. Sometimes, I found this emotional involvement somewhat an inhibiting factor. On occasions, I found it necessary to deliberately delay making a decision, until I felt that I was emotionally calm enough to make a reasonably unbiased decision. The expression of the emotional involvement was something. I had to keep under control. This could be regarded as a weakness in my functioning, but it was also necessary for me.

A third aspect was not so much a weakness as a debatable tactic. I was not as open as I might have been with the faculty or not as open as they might have thought me to be. I mentioned my long-term planning. 1 was also close-mouthed about finances. Sometimes I did not take the faculty into confidence when starting new activities. There were other instances also. I was generally reluctant to confide in people, in case it bothered or embarrassed them to become involved in my problems. Nor did I like the idea of confiding in some and not in others. Perhaps, 1 appeared withdrawn. After I resigned, a faculty member remarked in my presence: "As director, Professor Matthai was a friend of everyone. But no one knew him!"

UP: Coming back to the IIM, what phases have you seen in the development of this institute?

RJM: The first phase consisted of determining the need for management education. This process started in the late forties. It stretched over the fifties and early sixties into the discussion about and decision of starting management education in institutes outside the university structure. Then, came the decision to locate this institute at Ahmedabad and its establishment in 1962. This was followed by the logistics of obtaining sanctions from the governments of India and Gujarat, obtaining land, arranging Harvard's collaboration, and Louis Kahn as the architect. Then, followed the recruitment of the early faculty and their development through Harvard's nine-month International Teachers' Programme. In terms of activities, the Post-Graduate Programme was started in 1964. The collection of case material for teaching had started. A three-tier executive programme was started. A small group of faculty and research staff was being developed to work OQ agro-based industries, and more particularly, on the dairy cooperatives.

The second phase started in widening the base of the institution in terms of a greater diversity in attitudes, directions, skills and activities. There was a desire not to be dominated by a single foreign culture. Many faculty members were concerned as to whether the case method was being thrown out and whether all that Harvard had done for the institute was being undone. This was not so. The question was how much diversity could the institution contain and use that diversity as a strength rather than as a dissipating or divisive aspect of our functioning. At the institute, we were quite sure that we could establish our own identity, set our own goals, develop our own culture and form of management education. In the very long-term of 20 or 30 years from then, we wondered whether we could view the country as a whole as an integrated operating management system. To do this, we had to know the operations of the parts without compartmentalising this knowledge. The second phase was, therefore, characterised by beginning to work in many sectors such as industry, agriculture, banking, government system, education research systems, transport, energy, population, etc. A wide range of general, functional and sectoral programmes was started for practitioners. Research and consultancy work were also started. This resulted into changing the pattern of faculty recruitment and development in relation to a much greater diversity of backgrounds and experiences. Since this phase emphasised a greater diversity, it also laid emphasis on what I call "academic entrepreneurship" on the part of all of us. Out of this evolved a set of new directions for the institute. The process helped us to evolve the then very controversial, sectoral approach to management rather than the traditional business school in relation to industry. I think seven years, the time for which I was the director, is too short a period to break the institute's development into more detailed phases. This phase is growing from strength to strength.

UP: Finally, in terms of the institution building process, what would you like to say to those who are involved and engaged in such a process, based on your experience not only with this institute, but with other institutes?

RJM: I would first stress the building of people, their relationships, attitudes and behavioural norms. I would stress the development of conditions in the institution conducive to the development of individual, and group self-esteem, autonomy and creativity. This should be characteristic of the institution itself. I think it is important for the builder to spend time thinking about his own perception of the task he has accepted. I do not mean this in terms of five-year plans, budgeting, faculty numbers, number of research projects, number of courses, etc., but to really spend time on thinking about the philosophy of developing the institution, viewing this as an essential part of his task. He must be able to judge for himself, whether or not he can adjust his need to the task, and therefore, be honest with himself. When there is a high degree of ambiguity, there is a tremendous temptation to rationalise what has been done with a certain degree of intellectual dishonesty. It is, in this sense, possible to "use" institutions rather than build them. This is commonly done. I think that with jobs of this sort, a major qualification is that the man must not basically need the job. While I do not suggest a threatening attitude, or a sense of artificial humility, I feel the individual should be able to carry, metaphorically, his resignation in his pocket. While he would have no basic intention of using it, he should be absolutely certain in his mind that if he had to do so, he would have no hesitation at all in doing so. The person should not be vulnerable by being dependent on the job. Another important aspect, to my mind, is thinking about the institution far beyond the period for which an individual might be the head of it, and therefore, beyond his own commitment. One must see oneself neither as a phase of institutional development nor as a period of institution building with a definite boundary around it, but as a part of a continuum, whether it eventually works out the way the individual planned or not. The fact would remain that the individual had thought of himself as only a part of a very very long process. This way, one is less inhibited and less threatened, perhaps, about whether something should go wrong. If, however, the individual's need is that, by the end of his tenure, he must be regarded as a builder of institutions, it would become self-defeating, because his priority-would be to achieve his personal success. It is unlikely that such a person would be able to face the risk of failure.

UP: Thank you very much. This talk with you has been extremely useful.

NOTE

1. Reprinted with the permission of the author, Dr. Udai Pareek.

16
LEADERSHIP SEAMLESS
National Institute of Educational Planning and Administration

Beginning in 1961-62, as UNESCO's Regional Centre for Educational Planning and Administration, NIEPA became a newly registered society in 1978. The Memorandum of Association positioned the Institute as a research Institute to provide professional support to the government in educational policies, planning and management and also reach out to other developing countries. Professor Moonis Raza, credited to be the architect of NIEPA, built up the institution through inducting high-quality faculty, establishing a research culture and culture of quality with pace-setting, walking-the-talk leadership. In the process of institution building, his emphasis was on developing academic support infrastructure, decentralization of authority and responsibility, and inspiring staff through celebration of success and ignoring or redirecting failings. The mission was successful—it reached out to the Central and the state governments, the Central and the state institutions and attracted a large number of developing countries to take advantage of the strengths of NIEPA for upgrading the capability of their educational planners and managers.

The Assignment

The National Institute of Educational Planning and Administration (NIEPA) had its origin as UNESCO's Regional Centre for Educational Planners and Administrators, established in collaboration with government of India in 1961-62. In 1965, the Institute was renamed Asian Institute of Educational Planning and Administration. At the completion of its 10-year contract with UNESCO, the government of India decided to take over the Institute and continue. It was renamed National Staff College for Educational Planners and Administrators. At a later stage, in 1978, the organization was registered as a society under Society's Registration Act of 1861 and was renamed as National Institute of Educational Planning and Administration. Professor Moonis Raza (Moonis), the main architect of the new Institute, NIEPA, directed the Institute for three years during 1980-81 to 1983-84.

Immediately preceding this assignment, Moonis was the principal of the Regional Engineering College in Srinagar. His substantive position was in Jawaharlal Nehru University (JNU), one of the most prestigious universities of India. He was nicknamed as the 'blue-eyed' boy of the first vice-chancellor, Sri Parthasarathy, who is credited as the architect of JNU. Moonis was known and admired for his scholarship, imaginativeness, positive orientation and professionalism. He was a geographer, specializing in regional planning.

Moonis was the choice of Professor Nurul Hasan, an eminent scholar and Professor of History, the then minister of Education in government of India. Prof. Hasan and Moonis were together in Aligarh Muslim University. Moonis was invited for his specialization in regional planning, long and meaningful experience in university education, including technical education, imaginativeness and magnetic personal attributes to create a new organization out of NIEPA. Moonis accepted the assignment for the very same set of reasons. He saw an opportunity in NIEPA to be developed as a major research institution—not only the best in the country, but also favourably comparable to international standards.

Missions

Before Moonis, the Institute, as National Staff College for Educational Planners and Administrators, was headed by professor M V Mathur, another eminent economist, administrator and educationist. Professor Mathur had already laid the foundation of the new organisation. He was instrumental in defining the organizational goals of NIEPA as a newly conceptualized institution, as evident from the Memorandum of Association; he was signatory to this MoU. Prof. Mathur began the building of an unenviable library, the heart of any good academic institution. His emphasis on quality of training was another landmark. In the same breath, I must mention that National Staff College was largely a training institution that managed training activities primarily with the help of a few retired professionals and a few regular staff members. Research, publications and dissemination were added later. The newly conceptualized institution warranted research, documentation, dissemination, publications and other scholarly activities along with capability building of educational planners and administrators.

Moonis internalized the new set of goals and objectives of the Institute and translated them effectively into action. His primary mission was to transform the Institute from a training organization to a research institution. He also looked at NIEPA emerging as a major international institution, specializing in educational planning and administration, which had already a background as Asian Institute. But his organizational ambition and imagination went much beyond. This is indicated by the fact that social science teachers from the USA used to come to NIEPA for training.

His second important mission was linking research with training and capability building activities, ensuring research as an input for modernization of training and improving its relevance. To match the international standards, research was seen as a means of quality assurance. His mission of high quality was equally visible in documentation and publications.

Mission Formulation

Moonis derived NIEPA's mission out of its Memorandum of Association that clearly spelt out the objectives of the Institute. Moonis internalized the missions and made the organization breathe those missions. He did not miss a single opportunity to mention the organizational goals and missions for people to inhale and internalize. In the process, he hardly ever followed the conventional route that is described in the corporate sector management textbooks like organizational diagnosis, collective visioning, etc. His inspiring style made people fall in line; also, because his personal agenda was never there and visible in managing the organisation.

Also, his mission was not static; it did not stand at one point during his entire period of three years. It moved on adding new dimensions and higher ambitions. Like any creative doer, he enjoyed what he was doing. He was deeply involved in the process of creation. Consequently, his missions of the Institute moved from one level to another in terms of quality and performance, inducing the organizational ambition to be the best in the field and to stay there.

Strategies

His strategies for institution building, converting his missions into action can be largely classified into a few categories. These are:

- Pace-setting and being source-credible
- Ensure high-quality manpower
- Inspire and enthuse leadership
- Develop academic support infrastructure
- Decentralize authority and responsibility
- Celebrate success, ignore and protect failings.

Pace-setter

Moonis was known for his scholarship, oratory and imaginativeness. He was an established author and a first-rate classroom teacher. He was one of the best that a teacher in a university or a research institution could always aspire to be. Thereby, he acted as a pace-setter for the young faculty that was inducted into the Institute. There were several instances when this was visible to the rest of the faculty. Faculty members were expected to conduct research, write and publish. Along with his responsibility as Director of the Institute, Moonis consistently worked on one or the other research problem in educational planning and administration. He documented his researches and published them. Those days, there was an old huge computer, with the power of hardly a calculator today. Moonis was a regular user of the computer to the extent that he could be blamed for monopolizing the computing facilities.

In his various research and writing projects, he involved the younger faculty and recognized them as co-authors, rather than 'acknowledging them in the preface'. For the young faculty member it was a dream come true to be a co-author with Moonis Raza.

Similarly, along with his duties as Director, he used to take classes on the training programmes in the Institute. Each programme was evaluated and Moonis was evaluated as one of the best faculty in NIEPA. When he addressed such programmes and public gatherings on education, either as a keynote speaker, or as a chairperson, it was a feast for the participants; it was extremely educative and inspiring to the bright new younger faculty of the Institute.

Though a pace-setter, he rarely, if ever, insisted on people following his style or his way of working. In the emerging new literature on the primal leadership, 'pace-setting' has been considered a dissonant leadership. Moonis carefully avoided dissonance, by allowing people to observe him and choose their own styles as they pleased.

Ensuring High-Quality Manpower

Before Moonis, NIEPA had a skeleton regular staff, primarily supported by the retired educational personnel. Moonis brought in a major shift by inducting bright young faculty at various levels in the organisation, steadily replacing the old retired people. Although it was obligatory for the Institute to recruit through advertisement and interview, Moonis had his own ways to ensure that everyone entering the Institute did not come through a fluke of a 15/20-minute interview. Either he brought in young fresh students from the universities through his personal knowledge or searching through friends who could be trusted for their academic excellence. He took extreme care, when it was a question of inducting a person at the level of professor. Let me illustrate the point. I was then professor in TTTI, Bhopal. When I visited Delhi, I met him at the instance of a common friend, Dr. D V Chandrasekhara, who simply mentioned that Moonis was an interesting person. Within five minutes of our first meeting in his office in NIEPA, Moonis invited me to present a seminar to the faculty, and offered me to and fro travel costs from Bhopal. When I came back and presented the seminar, Moonis was personally not present. Within a fortnight, I received another invitation from Moonis to help in designing a module for a group of trainees from Sri Lanka. I helped him in designing the programme when Professor Udai Pareek, an eminent management scientist was also present. After about a month, I was invited to implement the module. Professor T V Rao, another eminent management scientist of Indian Institute of Management, Ahmedabad, was present during the module implementation. On both the occasions, Moonis invited me for lunch. We were one-to-one. He was a slow eater. So we took more than an hour each time. Hardly ever did I realize what was happening, till I received a letter from Moonis saying, NIEPA was looking for a professor of management, if I would be 'kind enough to send my bio-data'. Subsequently, I was called for "a discussion" with a group of experts including Nitish Ranjan De and Abad Ahmed, two of the outstanding scholars in management science. I was offered the appointment.

After joining the Institute, I asked Moonis about this elaborate process of selecting a person. His response was exemplary. According to him, bringing a full professor is like transplanting a full-grown tree. "If we don't choose the right tree for the right soil, either the tree will die or it will damage the soil. A lecturer is like a small sapling that knows how to adapt to the soil, also the soil knows how to nurture it". Almost every professor in the Institute came through this kind of a rigorous channel of selection and testing, with full dignity and honour. The bright young people inducted at comparatively junior levels were carefully nurtured, many of whom are now internationally reputed professors. His major contention was that second-rate people could never make a first-rate academic institution to be internationally competitive and comparable.

The second important strategy of managing quality was his choice of external experts for the training programmes. While, conventionally, the training programmes in NIEPA were being inaugurated and valedicted by the director, Moonis held a different view. There are more than fifty programmes a year; there are, hence, 100 inauguration-valediction events. How can one person manage 100 meaningful speeches each year? He insisted on inviting specialist-scholars from outside to inaugurate, where 'Director is there to chair' and make his own input. These were the rare occasions, when the participants and the NIEPA faculty were exposed to outstanding scholars of the country. He took special care in designing and developing each programme.

Similar strategies were adopted when it came to the review of research proposals. He invariably involved outstanding scholars in reviewing research proposals and publication programmes. His basic strategy was to put the best of the human beings in the organisation, such that the organization would learn to grow.

The complementary strategy to the induction of high-quality manpower was enthusiasm and inspirational activities. Moonis not only continued to work in his own areas of professional specialization, but also encouraged the young faculty at all levels to undertake activities and to bring in their proposals. He ensured that the proposals were processed fast and in a transparent manner. There were many occasions, when Moonis called upon a young faculty member encouraged him/her to submit a research proposal; as soon as the proposal was submitted, he took it to the Executive Committee, got it approved and informed that they should start working. Some of his important styles of inspiring and encouraging and simultaneously protecting the young persons were exemplary. Let me take a leaf out of my own diary. A senior professor came to Moonis complaining about his research assistant. His main contention and complaint was that the research assistant was a shirker, and was incompetent. The project was not progressing, primarily because of this kind of research assistant. Moonis asked the professor to replace the research assistant for a better one. The professor had come prepared. He immediately put out his note before Moonis. Moonis took no time to stamp his approval with his signature. I was witness to the entire episode. As soon as the professor left, Moonis looked at me and said, "for your research project, you need a project assistant. I have a recommendation or a request; please take this young researcher." I felt uneasy. What do I do with a shirker and an incompetent worker!' So I asked, 'how is it that you agreed with the professor to remove him, because he is a shirker and an incompetent person, but you are recommending the same person to me?" Moonis immediately went back to his favourite agricultural example: "Certain plants can grow only in certain soils; only certain soils know how to nurture a plant. That was not the right soil for the young boy. I assure you, he is a good worker and will do a good job and develop faster with you." I had this boy with me, and I must admit that Moonis was completely correct.

Develop Academic Support Infrastructure

In order to convert his mission of generating a first-rate research institution out of NIEPA, Moonis carefully developed the academic support infrastructure. While the foundation for a modern library had already been laid by his predecessor professor Mathur, it is to the credit of Moonis to have set up the Documentation Centre that contains all possible state, national and international documents for consultation by the researchers, which is necessary for educational policy and for planning related research.

Whereas a Library, and a good library at that, is a common place, the Documentation Centre is a unique entity in itself.

He had a number of small group rooms built for interactive training and learning sessions, which were necessary in order to build skills; and which could not be done through lectures in large classrooms. One of his finest gestures was creating a Committee Room out of his own office. When he joined the Institute, the director had a big room. His first question was: "why should the director need such a big room, when the institute is small and there are very few group rooms?" He put a partition right in the middle of his office, creating a committee room. This was called Director's Committee Room, indicating priority of the director, in case there were more than one claimants for the room at the same time.

His concept of support structure did not stop at the academic activities alone. His fascination for agricultural examples came from his rural background with significant taste and expertise in gardening. He took special personal care in creating flower gardens, lawns and greenery around the staff quarters and the Institute. He regularly visited the garden and lawns; spent time with the gardeners and asked inquisitive questions, and uttered words of appreciation that enthused them. Whenever a programme was to begin, he took special care to supervise the arrangement in the classroom that included the colour of the choir mattresses, the colour of the flowerpots and the flowers. He showed interest and supervised the academic support structure that enthused the faculty, and provided them the necessary academic support.

Decentralized Authority and Responsibility

Another important strategy of development was decentralization of not only the responsibility, but also the authority, which created a new responsibility-framework. There were two different categories of decentralization. The administrative decentralization was carried out with the executive director and registrar who was the head of administration. This was evident by the process of file movement. The majority of the files were disposed of at the registrar's level, and a large number of remaining files that moved beyond the registrar were disposed of at the level of the joint director. Only a tiny percentage of the files reached the director for his decisions. Effectively, the registrar and the joint director were asked to take decisions. The whole concept was built around, 'higher the implications of the decision, higher the strata for the principle to reach out'. As director, he could reach out to any level; respecting the administrative protocol and the spirit of decentralization, he never reached out to administrative officers or section officers for administrative reasons.

The second category of decentralization was academic decentralization. With the same spirit, the authority for academic programme designing, implementation and evaluation was left to the heads of the units and individual members of the faculty concerned. Most important repercussion of the academic decentralization was the participation of NIEPA in important meetings of the Ministry of Human Resource Development, Planning Commission, University Grants Commission and such other organisations. Moonis hardly participated in such meetings. Depending upon the subject of the discussion, it was one of the senior specialist faculty members who participated in the meeting. During one of our personal discussions, I asked this question about his participation in the Ministry. His answer is an important landmark in management. He said, "if the meeting is on educational finance, we have Dr. Brahm Prakash or Dr. Tilak; if it is on management or technical education, we have you; if it is on higher education, we have Dr. G D Sharma. They should participate and provide an expert view on the subject. However, if education secretary conducts a meeting on broader issues of educational policy, I would definitely participate." It had two advantages; firstly, colleagues with expertise being involved in the national policy-making and planning, felt encouraged. Secondly, "as an institute, we put our best foot forward. I may have reasonable smattering on educational financing or technical education or higher education, but each one of you is a better specialist in your own area than me. It is the responsibility of the national institute to provide the best that it has in educational planning and policy making to the country."

The delegation of responsibility and rights were based on trust. This is indicated by the rare occasion, if ever, of monitoring faculty activities. Dr. Singhal narrated to me an interesting episode that sheds significant light op Moonis' management style. Dr. R P

Singhal, then executive director, completed a research report. He showed a copy to Moonis. Moonis turned over the pages and expressed his desire that 'this should come out as a book', "a good publication". Dr. Singhal mentioned that to make it a publishable volume, he had to work on the manuscript. And, it would take almost a year with his other assignments as executive director of the Institute. Moonis immediately agreed. During the next few months, Moonis and Dr. Singhal met several times every day on a variety of organizational matters. Moonis never asked about the project. Although Dr. Singhal anticipated that it would take one full year, he finished it in nine months. At the end of nine months, he went and showed the copy to Moonis. He once again, turned over the pages, did not make any suggestion, called up a publisher and handed over the manuscript.

The delegation of the authority automatically created a sense of responsibility and involvement in administration as well as the faculty. Every faculty undertook research projects, training programmes and publication activities. Hardly anyone of them was ever monitored by the director. On the contrary, he was available to assist, thus making project management easier by removing the road blocks.

Celebrating Success, Ignoring Failures

Celebrating success is a common feature in all organisations. It was there with Moonis as well; and it was not something special. What was special with him was either ignoring mistakes and failures or even protecting them to defend the self-image and self-esteem of the person. Hardly ever, one came across a situation where Moonis was found either angry or criticizing a person. On the contrary, there were many occasions when members of the faculty and administration expressed their regret for their failure; it was the large-heartedness of Moonis that extended a cover, "Doesn't matter. One who doesn't experiment, doesn't fail. One who doesn't fail, doesn't learn. We are here to learn, and we will experiment".

Managing Resistance

Looking back, the kind of resistance that one experiences in many other organisations was almost absent in NIEPA during Moonis' tenure. Resistance originates when a person is burdened with a new set of ideas and practices without his/her conviction. In this case, since everybody was empowered to decide the kind of activities that he/she wanted to carry out, there was hardly any perception of being imposed. At the same time, if there was a difference of opinion, he magnificently accommodated the opinion of others. NIEPA maintained a tradition of using the word 'programme director' for those who conceptualized, designed and conducted the programmes. The registrar proposed that the Institute should have only one director, the others should be 'programme coordinators' or conveners.' The registrar, with the permission of Moonis, submitted the proposal in a meeting of heads of Units with Moonis in the chair. There was a serious argument where all the heads of departments unanimously rejected the concept of converting the designation from programme director to programme coordinator. Although the registrar was unhappy with the discussion, Moonis never missed his smile and concluded that NIEPA will have 'one director' but many 'programme directors'. Almost no resistance was visible in the administrative level, primarily because of his style, which, on the one hand, was overwhelming and on the other, extremely caring and protective.

Leadership Style

Moonis' leadership style is characterised by several attributes. The first and foremost of the characteristics is his pace-setting style, where he excelled in every department that the academic faculty would look forward to. At the same time, he carefully protected himself from any kind of preaching to the faculty or citing himself as an example or a role model. To that extent, he was more normative than prescriptive; he set norms by his actions, but did not impose on others. His second important attribute was directing the Institute, without directing the faculty. Compared to the average heads of institutions who instruct the faculty what to do, how to do, and when to do, his style was much more encouraging; the faculty would do something that they wished to do to promote institutional goals and objectives. Let me illustrate this point. Immediately after my joining, in one of our personal meetings, he encouraged me to undertake research projects that I would like to undertake. At the same time, he did not miss this opportunity to point out that I came from technical education; he was also Principal of a Regional Engineering College, and he would like to bring in research and training activities in technical education, if I wished. He never elaborated what kind of research was expected. I submitted a prospectus of two research projects which were approved by the Executive Committee, chaired by him. He was enthusiastic and encouraging. He took special care of every activity conducted in the Institute asking, 'Can I help you'?

This inspiring and encouraging leadership style was closely supported by emotional attachment. He visited almost every home of the faculty; where he hardly talked about academics on research. He would chit-chat and be naughty with the children of the faculty members. There were many occasions when he would walk over to the office of a junior faculty or a supporting staff and share the food. This emotional equality along with colossal academic superiority was not only another unusual combination, but also made people feel attached to him.

Learning

There were two or three important components in the institution building process of NIEPA: the Moonis style. One component is his personal style, characterized by excellence in academics, communication, interpersonal relationships and fatherly concern for all in the Institute. Such quality can be admired but is difficult to imbibe. So, none is sure whether this can be learnt at all.

It is possible to derive some learning from his strategic planning and action. Firstly, excellence in a research institution requires excellent human characters, who are excellent in academics, personal ethics and values. Moonis was careful in choosing each of his colleagues over a long period of time, allowing him to judge a person not only on the basis of academic excellence, but also on values and ethics. This has survived in the Institute over a long period of time. Let me illustrate this point with a post-Moonis-era event. There was a major national project on Survey of Educational Administration in India, initiated by one of the senior colleagues, Professor M M Kapoor. When the first report was submitted and sent to the press for publication, Professor Kapoor expired unfortunately. Then, the executive director was asked to look after the project. The projects were implemented by a team of researchers in collaboration with a state official. In fourteen such state reports prepared by the project staff, the then joint director appeared as the first author. This tradition was followed by his successor joint director. At a later stage, when Professor Kuldeep Mathur, the then director was leaving the Institute, he called upon six senior faculty members, and requested each one of them to take charge of one of the six remaining states. All of them agreed to help out the project. When the draft reports were ready and the research staff submitted the reports to the concerned senior faculty, each one of them took great care to edit, modified wherever necessary and finalized the document. In all the state reports, the young research staff had put the name of the senior faculty member as the first author, in keeping with the tradition of the previous two joint directors. Without variation, every senior faculty member removed his/her name from the document, though some of them wrote the preface to the volume. The director who succeeded Prof. Mathur tried to persuade many of them to continue the practice of lending their names to the reports. Without any mutual consultation, all of them had one single response, 'the credit should go to those who have actually worked; we accepted the responsibility and finalized the manuscript, because we are senior faculty members in this organisation. It was our responsibility and duty.' This indicates a sound footing of the institution that Moonis left so far as values and professional ethics were concerned. Organizational growth and health is indicated by organizational ethics—interactive product of individual ethics. Moonis led it from the front with transparency, personal ethics, and values.

The second important learning for institution building was to facilitate individual growth within the perspective of organizational goals through encouragement and recognition. In the process, it was important to remove the roadblocks which often discourage the academic faculty to move ahead.

A third significant learning is developing compatibility of management style with Indian ethos and culture. Unlike the western world, Indian mind provides larger emotional qualities than only intellectual qualities. This is equally true in Indian organisations. The personal care and concern of Moonis for every individual as well as his concern for every detail without overbearing, is an important strategy and style to make an Indian organization resurgent in so short a period of time.

17
A NEW MODEL OF PRIVATE UNIVERSITY
KATHMANDU UNIVERSITY

During my visit to the Kathmandu University, I was deeply impressed the infrastructure and facilities in the sprawling campus high on the hills, away from the humdrum of the city. This is a private university with a difference. Considering the enthusiasm evinced by the Vice Chancellor and a few others, the Minister of Education called upon the team to set up a private university. Unlike the Indian experience, there is no industrial house behind this establishment. The government has allotted the land and a core grant for the initial infrastructure. The Nepalese diaspora mobilised a massive amount of funds from themselves and the donors. Students pay for their education that is priced at a breakeven point. Emphasis is on quality—quality faculty, quality facilities, quality programmes, etc. The university was built from scratch by Professor Sharma and his team in a rather short span.

Early Years

Vice Chancellor, Prof. Sharma was born in a conventional family in Nepal. However, even in this conventional situation arose the major difference. The parents and grandparents had high respect for scholars. Professor Sharma, as a child, grew up in the ambience of great expectations from parents and grandparents to emerge as a scholar despite the environment, which was not really conducive to such extraordinary achievements. However, Professor Sharma admits the influence of such expectations in moulding his destiny. In his own words, "the only thing I could do was to keep on struggling". In fact, the truth of this statement is visible in the way he built up the university almost out of nothing.

He went through a simple traditional type of education where 'good education meant good rote learning'. There was hardly any scope for creative activities, social activities and innovations and experimentations. Emphasis was laid on academic learning and performing well in the conventional examinations. The other important associated features which influenced his lifestyle later were emphasis on patriotism and nationalistic feelings, developing a moral character, building a larger framework of academics through study of literature and mathematics. Since school drop-out was rampant in those days, the ability to survive in an academic system was another dominant concern in the development of Prof. Sharma. Later, Professor Sharma had the opportunity of studying further in the western universities.

Assignment

Nepal was one of the few countries ruled by a monarch. It was finding it difficult to seek out methods to improve the condition of the people. It was struggling hard to make economic progress, which is the key to economic development and improvement of quality of life of the people. Its physical infrastructure was underdeveloped—few roads, few irrigation canals, poor power base, poor health system, traditional agriculture system, poor technical manpower base, etc. The government was struggling to make improvements in these areas. It was proved that only visionary leadership, efficient management system and improved and skilled workforce were essential to bring about the desired changes.

Some of the Nepalese scholar diasporas were keenly watching the struggles, the frustrations and the changing scenario in Nepal. Because of their sense of pride and patriotism, a small group of foreign-returned Nepalese graduates felt rather restless for not finding meaningful roles for the trained youths who were full of enthusiasm and were keen on developing the country. It was also evident that the education system was expanding fast, though the quality and relevance of the educational programmes including the quality of delivery were far from desirable.

'On the other hand, bright young school graduates were seen

desperately looking for quality institutions in the country for further studies in the technical fields of their choice. Their aspirations could not be met within the country; consequently, these youngsters opted for colleges outside, like India, Bangladesh, Russia and the Philippines, because admissions were easy and one could afford to pay. Similarly, the demand for new skills in IT-industries, engineering based industries, agriculture based industries, health services sector was rapidly increasing'. The training system was, however, not at all geared up to generate adequate skilled workers and professionals in those areas. There was a gross mismatch between demand and supply of trained manpower. Education system was ill-equipped to respond to the developmental needs of the country.

Many of the graduates educated abroad did not return to the country, but settled down there. Those who returned did not find adequate opportunity and placement, equivalent to their knowledge and satisfaction, as well as for the development of the country. Nepal's human resource development and human resource management were not tuned to each other.

The government was able to set up a few technical and professional institutions for education and training in selected areas like medicine, engineering, agriculture, forestry and some natural science subjects. 'Some research centers were also created for medicinal plants, food research and mineral exploration under the government departments. Ministry of Science and Technology, Ministry of Environment, Royal Nepal Academy of Science and Technology were also created. Although such institutions and centres were set up, because of lack of direction and funds, many of them remained dormant for long.

There was an excessive dependence on foreign assistance for HRD. Whether for training Nepalese nationals abroad or for setting up and running the institutions, the government looked for external assistance. The country was not only slow in making education adaptable to meet the emerging needs, but it also could not keep the academic calendar intact and political interests out of academic institutions.

Nepalese scholars like Professor Sharma were also watching the growing competition in the region, and were concerned about the dismal capacity for facing such competitions. 'We were also noticing

Pt. Nehru's vision yielding results in India. India's strength in IT, biotechnology, engineering, alternative energy, agricultural growth etc. are the results of Pt. Nehru's vision to create a chain of world class technical institutes to produce technical manpower; national research laboratories and research centers to promote indigenous scientific capacity and making application of S&T developments for the economic development as well.'

These developments in the neighbourhood were inspiring to the nationalist scholars. There was a dilemma, however, whether they should wait for some visionary leadership to be born in Nepal, or move forward to take up on their own, the responsibility of reconstructing Nepal, by undertaking, meaningful, human development projects, large enough to impact and small enough to be feasible. As pronounced by President A P J Abdul Kalam, they decided to lead themselves.

The vision was getting clearer that Nepal needed institutions of high-quality, relevance and strength in research and development. If the government was unable to respond to these challenges and demands of the society, the civil society must create itself alternative mechanisms to respond to the challenge. This perception or conviction to produce and provide an alternative framework to the existing system to create expert manpower that Nepal needed urgently, drove Professor Sharma and his team to come forward to create Kathmandu University. 'We strongly felt that nature has given us enough resources and also the talents to harness them.' Only the Nepalese own efforts were called for. There was a perceived helplessness; they had to overcome this immobilizing perception.

Vision and Missions

The vision was to create a world class institution, a new generation of professional manpower that could match the quality of comparable manpower in the rapidly advancing developing countries and optimize the capabilities of Nepalese brains to do their best.

While defining the missions, we first wanted to demonstrate that we have the capability to prepare good quality human resource here, to harness the natural resources for alternative energy development, to make the best use of renewable resources with due care to the environment, for the overall upliftment of the quality of life of the people and also be able to bring the benefits of globalization of economy to the Nepalese people.

The founders of Kathmandu University were confident that their ability to offer high-quality programmes would attract qualified faculty members and donors; such programmes would also attract and win the hearts of students. In turn, their efforts would help development of suitable physical and human resource base. Indeed, the mission of the institution was directly linked to the larger social concern and national ambition. The team led by Professor Sharma believed that with clear vision, determined efforts, hard work, tidy management, result oriented approach, etc., the university could fulfill its commitment.

Another important mission of the university was to create an educated and trained manpower for global competitiveness by transforming the youth force into an economic force through interdisciplinary approach. The mission was to bring science closer to people, hence, be of service to mankind through the efficient use of available natural resources. Finally, the mission was to attract the support of the government, the community, and the donors to create a synergy and ownership of the university.

Innovations and Action Strategies

One of the major innovations was to offer courses in applied sciences with the combined efforts of the faculty specializing in pure and applied sciences. This was necessitated by an interesting situation of paradox. People specialising in pure science were encountering difficulty in finding placement in teaching, research, and application oriented assignments. On the contrary, those who specialised in applied sciences had more market value; but, they were not interested in taking up teaching positions in the universities. The university brought together people specialising in pure and applied sciences, to upgrade the quality of programmes and ensure the transfer of science to society for improving the quality of life.

For example, the first courses drawn up were honours type bachelor level courses in areas like physics and electronics/energy studies, chemistry and applied chemistry, mathematics and computer science, biology and environmental biology.

The associated innovation was to introduce subjects with high employability, namely pharmacy (chemistry, biology), electronics engineering (physics, mathematics), computer engineering (physics, mathematics), and environmental science (biology, chemistry, mechanical engineering).

The third curricular innovation was intended to offer high level courses to meet the needs of business sector, namely backing up of the manufacturing and service industries; business management courses for the management of technology and for entrepreneurship development, courses for banking sector and community development.

Nepalese education and development framework was conventional, often stuck to a specific branch of knowledge or subjects, where interdisciplinarity was rare to find. Adopting interdisciplinary character right from the beginning was considered necessary. How to accomplish the interdisciplinarity within a conventional framework was a major challenge. It needed serious rethinking. Accordingly, the strategy was to provide equal weightage to pure and applied sciences; emphasis was laid on practical application at the undergraduate level and research focus at the postgraduate level courses. In order to build skills of application and problem-solving, the university decided to adopt project-based approach, where such projects were to be carried out in collaboration with the industry and other employing organizations.

Taking People Along

As mentioned earlier, the university was built from scratch, and Professor Sharma was involved throughout. The people who were involved from the phase of developing the vision, i.e., the stage of setting up of the Kathmandu Valley Campus, consisted of like minded, dedicated, hard working people with clean personal image. Most of them were ready to plunge into the long arduous journey together.

The people on the mission included committed academicians, some management experts, some social workers, donors both internal and external, experts, etc. Professor Sharma worked at the National Education Committee and Council for Technical Education and Vocational Training. These provided him some contacts with such people; and also the experience to judge the visibility and possible resistance.

In the initial phase, the journey was undertaken together. It was comparatively easier, since the group comprised people of genius. As the university expanded, it brought in new faces in the faculty and administrative staff. Great care was taken in selecting such staff, so that the university's mission did not get adversely affected. Also, as a matter of fact, the staff, in the initial phase of development of the university, found a new meaning in their job, since they also contributed to the development of the university. They felt a more engaging relationship than that of an employer and an employee.

Managing Resistance

A big resistance was seen at the stage of obtaining the charter of the university, particularly from the parliamentarians. Government agencies were unwilling to allow alternative authority in the field of education. It was a powerful resistance. Many were apprehensive, that establishing university type institutions with the authority of setting up technical and management institutions without confirmed financial resources would be impractical and risky. Resistance also came from the existing university, as it saw a competitor in the new university, which was only natural.

The most intriguing situation was the fact that for preparing plans for the new university, and also for executing them, it needed the manpower from the existing university. The new university trod a difficult path of managing the egos and the ethos of such people, keeping the patience and hope alive. The university learned to tolerate and accommodate as much as possible. At the initiative of the team led by Professor Sharma, the university established a good working relationship with Dhulikhel Municipality, which helped the university to create and make available certain physical infrastructure like land, road, water supply, etc. Besides the physical facilities, these provided moral support, too.

On the academic front, special efforts were made to mobilise the support of some of the prestigious institutions abroad like Birla Institute of Science and Technology, Pilani, Manipal Academy of Higher Education, Indian Institute of Management, Calcutta, Norwegian University of Science and Technology, United Mission to Nepal, etc., right from the early stages of its development. The support was particularly obtained for designing and offering the new courses, and training of the newly recruited young teachers in their institutions. Several outstanding teachers of the prestigious institutions abroad spent a considerable amount of time in the university campus, teaching courses on a full-time basis. Not only the students benefited from their interaction, but also the new teachers recruited locally.

Leadership Style

Although leadership theories have offered leadership typologies, it is often difficult to classify an institutional builder into one single typology. Same is the case with Professor Sharma's style. On the one hand, he is a leader with production emphasis where he means business; on the other hand, he wields a magnetic personality to attract and retain people over a longer period of time. In the process, he is able to build teams and work with them. He trusts people—their capabilities as well as their intentions; he invests in building the capability of the people. At the same time, he is concerned with quality in every aspect of the university life. His emphasis on production coupled with trust in people and his ability to build teams, provided a sound basis to be a resonant leader and build the institution within a short span.

Another interesting style of Professor Sharma is his down-to-earth approach to the environment, providing strategic leadership. He is aware of the powers of the government, and also the capability of sister institutions and the community to derail the mission and the very existence of the new university. Without sacrificing the dignity of the university, he carefully avoids confrontation. Similarly, he nurtures and respects the feelings of the partners, and those who are potential partners. In other words, as a strategic leader, he indicates his sensitivity to and understanding of the powerful elements in the environment. He tries to take them along. Internally, he is a resonant leader; with the environment, he is a strategic leader.

Successes and Failures

Success and failure are the partners in such enterpreneurship in education. Here too, there are success and failure.

Professor Sharma could watch the emerging trends in time; therefore, many new plans and programs could be developed and initiated even before the government could think of them it. He was also successful in making the faculty aware of the upcoming challenges by repeating them time and again to make them feel the urgency and credibility of the university management and leadership at the highest level. The success was in his ability to create seriousness among the faculty about the upcoming challenges. Another important success was putting the education, science and technical studies on a sound footing and establishing the university's priority and conviction to provide science and technology as the foundation for national development. A further significant success was integrating social science studies and the courses focused on technology.

It is not easy to accomplish the tasks in time with assured quality. The university succeeded in taking up the activities which were on demand, and created facilities to make them feasible and popular. It was able to keep most of the programs in right gears. It also succeeded in making it a research-cum-teaching university. This vision had to be understood and accepted by those in the leadership positions, particularly the deans, directors, chief administrators, professors, and appropriate strategies had to be adopted so that it did not become a conventional, technical education course driven teaching university.

The university also succeeded in generating adequate resources for its programs. In the process, it also learned to involve all sections of the society in its physical development. The most significant success, according to Professor Sharma and his colleagues, was the university's ability to keep politics away from the campus, yet winning the confidence of leaders of all major political parties.

The university experienced failures too, in certain areas. It could not convince the people that the new university was a public institution and not for profit, yet a self-financing one. Professor Sharma considers it to be a failure because of the mindset of the people conditioned for decades and centuries.

At the budding stage, the vice chancellor thinks that working hard for long hours is necessary for its development, particularly for quality. He is concerned that the workforce has not absorbed this work culture and spirit. Similarly, it took a long time for the faculty to accept the university as a research university and not just a teaching university; accordingly, the faculty of the university had to accept the responsibility of research and academic administration for faster growth of the university.

In Professor Sharma's assessment, the university could not make use of the capabilities of people with research background. Such people felt unutilized, undervalued and frustrated.

Despite significant achievements in developing collaborations and network with various academic institutions in various countries, the vice chancellor felt that the university was still weak in planning, international relations, student services, recreational facilities, etc.

Lessons Learnt

Professor Sharma provides an interesting list of lessons learnt from his experience of building this university. These are:

- don't take all the responsibilities on your shoulders, delegate responsibilities to others at the right time;
- strengthen planning and implementation aspects even at the department levels;
- work harder to make good use of people returning from advanced training abroad or make a better use of the available well-trained people;
- people coming with research based training were not being put in right places; they need special attention and care, since they are the potential assets of the university; and
- there is still a shortage of the right type of fresh people in the job market. People with experience seem to have lost the vigour. There is a vacuum which the university is still trying to fill in, without much success.

Succession Planning

The Vice Chancellor has spent quite a few years now. A very common feature of the universities and academic institutions is the standard, once the person or the leadership position changes. The university either deteriorates or continues at the same pace, or grows to new heights. But this is a practical agony that bothers the institution builders, who are engaged themselves emotionally in the process of institution building. I asked Professor Sharma his views about succession planning; what kind of a person should succeed him was my question. His responses were categorical. The new incumbent:

- must be very alert and vigilant about the emerging challenges and opportunities;
- must have the strength to make the best use of the available resources including trained manpower;
- must keep the whole institution prepared for bigger challenges including international competition;
- must be able to mobilise financial resources through competitive research projects on merit, rather than depending upon financial support from the government;
- should have the strength of an academic leader with competence of mobilising and managing financial resources, maintaining strong network with local as well as national and international organisations; and
- must be able to strengthen the community services.

Prof. Shrama has preference for a successor to be young, dynamic and able to provide ethical leadership, projecting clean and forward-looking colleagues to important positions.

Conclusion

The evolution of Kathmandu University is an interesting story of nationalistic concern of a few scholars to provide high-quality professional manpower for the development of the country. They created a new model of private university, where the government, the local community, Nepalese diaspora and donors joined hands. There is no business house involved, thus, making it self-financing but not profiteering. Its concern for quality provided a new dimension to institution building, when it sought collaboration of major international institutions in curriculum design and implementation, and training of the younger faculty. Erecting an innovative university in a conventional society with a strong and jealous competitiveness is not an easy task. The university has been able to accomplish this with the Vice Chancellor's formula—combination of resonance and strategic leadership.

Lessons Learnt

18
ETHICS OF LEADERSHIP

Ethics and values are two guiding stars of leadership in all kinds of social organizations. 'Leadership and ethics are inseparable, unethical leadership is an oxymoron' (James MacGregor Burns, 1978). Ciulla (2004) caught this spirit of inseparability of ethics from leadership or leadership from ethics in her book, 'Ethics: The Heart of Leadership'. Gandhi's talisman of 'walking the talk' points to the same spirit. Warren Hoffman, however, struck a different note, 'There are no universally agreed upon rules of ethics in leadership, no absolute standards or controls, and no fixed and firm reference points. This is fascinating given how hugely important ethics have now become in modern life and society'. The demand on ethical leadership is probably loudest in education since, here, the business is shaping human minds and consciousness. Hence a discourse on leadership would remain incomplete without inclusion of ethics and values.

Ethics is not what we think, feel or speak. Ethics is how we behave. 'Thoughts and feelings are neither right nor wrong, they just are. Actions driven by those thoughts and feelings are what will be judged in the context of social acceptability, resulting in labels of "ethical" or "unethical" behavior. Leadership, too, has no real meaning without action; it is effective behavior manifest in desired results' (Cornett and Thomas, 1995). I concur with Kidder (1994) when he says, 'in some way, every one teaches moral values to others'. The way we live 'broadcast potent, clear signals to all within our radius'. The way people live today sets examples for newer generations to emulate for future (The Bhagavat Gita, Ch. 3/Sloka 22-24[1]). Leaders' life styles thus create the organizational values and ethics.

Hence, ethics of leadership is a way of living; knowing what is right and what is not. Robert Terry's curt and right approach, 'If you do not do your job right, you have no right to do your job. This is critical for those in leadership positions and, especially, for government leaders and corporate officers. You lose all credibility when your ethics are questioned, when you are even suspected of breaking the law, and, finally, when you are actually found guilty of missteps of judgment. You lose any ability to enforce your authority...and you should'. Thus, ethics must find a place in the construct of leadership.

Construct of Ethics and Values

Ethics is choice between right and wrong. In social situations, these choices may not be in black and white. There can be many shades of gray painted by broad social culture and even peers. Drawing from Stephen Covey's (1995) concept of integrity as 'mother of humility and father of courage', it is safe to infer that choosing to act with integrity requires lot of courage to stay beyond the win-lose games common in organizations and also the dictates of the ego.

According to the Western philosophy, ethics are virtues like justice, charity, generosity; ethics comprise morality based on mutual respect; conduct rules that benefit greatest number of people. According to Indian philosophy, some important ethical behaviour are Austerities, Straight-forwardness, Harmlessness, Veracity, Angerlessness, Renunciation, Tranquility, Broadmindedness, Kindness, Absence of avarice, Mildness, Shame on evil action, Forgiveness, Non-hatred, Non-overdignifying, Balance of knowledge and action (largely based on divine qualities presented in The Bhagavat Gita (Chapter 16).

Connecting leadership with ethics, Terry (1993) offers Action Wheel model suggesting six areas of reflective ethical action, namely ethical sensibility (existence), ethical tools (resources), ethical methods (structure), ethical motivation (power), ethical principles (mission) and meta-ethics (meaning).

- Ethical sensibility (existence): Without the socialization that produces values, we could not recognize any situation as an ethical dilemma requiring reflective action.
- Ethical tools (resources): Just as the science of economics uses such concepts as supply and demand, marginal utility,

and cost-benefit to analyze economic issues, ethical reflection has its tools of analysis. These tools are such concepts as love, justice and freedom which must be built into any comprehensive ethical framework.

- Ethical methods (structure): Methods link tools to issues, reflection to action. Appeals to scripture, third-party scrutiny, or recognized social standards fit this category.
- Ethical motivation (power): Motivation, or commitment, is the energizer. It engages the methods and links methods to principles. Without commitment, there is no spur to engagement.
- Ethical principles (mission): Principles point the way to ethical action. Without ethical principles, particular actions get lost in details or stray away off-course.

Meta-ethics (meaning): Doubt accompanies ethical reflection and action. Why be ethical? What supports ethical action and encourages it to endure? Not everyone asks meta-ethical questions. Yet in times of great distress, these questions demand action.

Learning from the Case Studies

From the case studies presented in this book, we found that leaders who build institutions maintain high moral standards. There are intrinsic and extrinsic reasons. From the angle of genesis of personality, values and ethics are part of the DNA of the human psyche. Just as an incorruptible person cannot be corrupted, a corrupt person cannot be de-corrupted. It can be called behavioural determinism.

Institution building is a function of the synergy amongst the creative and positive energies of its constituents, people and the processes. It is built by contributions by individuals; in sharp contrast to exploitation of institutional resources and positions by those in the leadership positions. For example, 'entitlement' is a common item in organizations. The difference between institution builders from the rest is the difference between 'entitlement of the organization,' versus 'entitlements of the person' in leadership position. Institution building is sharing the achievement and happiness by giving, as compared to personal gratification through exploiting the institution.

Lord Sri Krsna told Arjuna, in Karma Yoga (chapter 3, The

Bhagavat Gita), that youngsters follow the elders. Lord had nothing to gain, still he worked; if He did not, others would stop working, resulting in great chaos. This is ethics and values of a leader (Lord Krsna). There is great relevance of this statement in institution building. The people in leadership positions set the tone of an organization. People follow the seniors in the organization; seniors create role models and the unwritten code of conduct. Research literature on management of change indicates that other things remaining the same, institutions change for better or for worse with the change of guard at the top. It is the head of an institution that creates or destroys an institution. Institution builders create values in the organization. The people in leadership positions with poor values steadily debilitate the organization.

Ethics is an abstract concept. In order to build up the case of importance of ethics in an organization, I shall take help of contrasting examples of ethical and non-ethical behaviours in organizations within the range of our experience. I shall refer to actual cases and episodes of ethics and values as benchmarks to indicate how institution builders differ from others in the comparable positions.

We must also appreciate that there are many instances that obstruct our vision. Just as a courteous and sophisticated behaviour can put a veil on an unethical head of an institution, there are also instances where apparent incompetence and gross/rustic behaviour obstruct the view of a gem of a human being in the head of an institution. We need to piece both to understand the value of ethics in leadership.

An Episode

I joined my village school as an assistant teacher. My village school headmaster was my teacher; he taught us Bengali literature during my school days. He was a lethargic teacher who would come to the class, ask us to read, and sleep with his head on the table. Obviously, we did not have a great opinion about this teacher. After I joined the school as a teacher, I met another person in him. I was the class teacher of standard eight and was responsible for compiling and preparing the results for the annual class promotions. As a matter of tradition, after preparing the results, we used to hand over the papers to the headmaster; he would go to every class and declare the results. After the results were declared, the school witnessed both joy and sorrow. When I came out of the staff room, I found Ashok weeping, hiding himself behind one of the pillars. As class teacher, I knew that he had stood first. I asked him why was he crying. He told me that his results had not been declared because he was not able to pay his dues which was, if I remember correctly, Rs.3.50. There was a provision, then, that the headmaster could waive the outstanding fees of deserving students. Hence, I approached the headmaster to waive off the fees of Ashok. The headmaster politely declined saying that he had reached the limit of waiving the outstanding fees. Without understanding what he meant, I expressed my anger giving the impression that he was partial and biased towards certain student. At this point, he called his office clerk and asked him to 'write down the outstanding fees of Ashok in his name and declare the result'. The office clerk told him that two-months equivalent of his salary had already been written off. I asked the office clerk, 'what does that mean?' The clerk explained to me that, according to government regulation, there was a ceiling to which the headmaster could waive off the fees. That limit was over. When I asked him, 'what is this writing of fees in his name?', the office clerk explained that because a large number of students come from very poor families and they are not able to pay even the small amount of fees, this money is adjusted against the salary of the headmaster, and then the result is declared. I was really moved at this gesture. The headmaster pointed out that it was done not only by him, but also by several other teachers who paid for defaulting students and the fees was adjusted against their salary, when the salary was released by the government after three months. Ashamed of myself, I asked the headmaster to write down Ashok's fees against my salary. The headmaster pointed out that my father was retired and my salary was the only source of income for the whole family, and that, too, the school was unable to pay regularly. So, he was unable to adjust Ashok's fees against my salary. I politely confronted; "how about you?" He pointed out that he had a small plot of land that grew paddy and some vegetables, so his 'family would never starve, they would get the minimum quantity of rice and vegetables.' Our family being landless and exclusively dependent upon teaching as a source of income would really starve without the salary. When I was unable to convince the headmaster despite my deep-seated feelings, it was the clerk who declared the verdict saying: 'if he has to work here, it is better he learns the way of working of this school'. The Clerk continued, 'In any case, he will get his salary after three months, it won't matter if that small amount is adjusted against his salary.' The headmaster agreed. I was relieved. But before I left his room, he told me that this tradition was set up by my father, the founding headmaster of the school. 'We're all following his footsteps', he said.

This is one instance, where his incompetence as a classroom teacher obstructed our view of the soft, warm hearted headmaster that bleeds for the poor students of the school. There are counter incidences, where competence and sophisticated behaviour are used to exploit others and practise unethical behaviour. In this Chapter, I will flag a few aspects of ethics in leadership behaviour contrasting with unethical actions.

Gratitude and Obligations

Gratitude is 'sincere appreciation of help received' and in spiritual context, 'appreciation for the blessings of the God'. Best expression of gratitude is a sincere thanks, and reciprocating help to the benefactor when in need and reaching out to others in need as gratitude for the blessings of the God. It is an important value and human quality. In a way, this differentiates between humans and animals; qualitative difference in expression of gratitude indicates the level of human quality. This is an important issue in institution building. The problem is that gratitude is not uni-polar; it is a multiplex—gratitude to individuals, organization, immediate neighbourhood and community, (national)/society (patriotism), human society at large (international understanding), and God, the creator. It is more like a hierarchy:

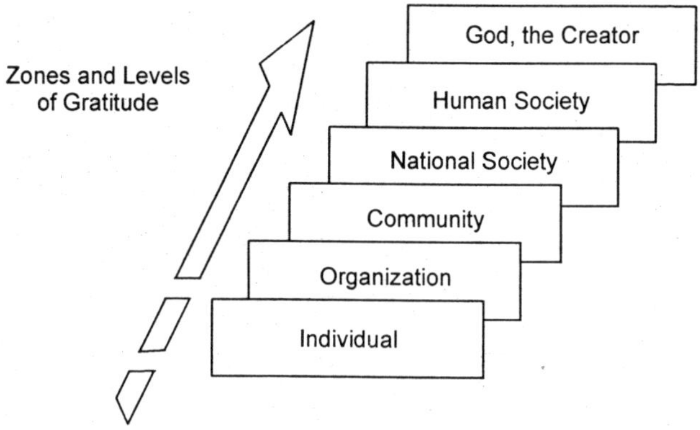

Gratitude to individuals who have been helpful is minimum and at the lowest level; gratitude to God who has not only helped us visit this world as His children (*amritasya putraha),* but also created the beautiful world for us to live in, is the highest form. Importantly, as we move from the lowest or minimum level to the highest level in gratitude gradient, the object or reference point of gratitude becomes more and more abstract.

In organizations, there are conflicts between individual and organizational obligations. Most of the people in leadership positions (heads of institutions) serves individual obligations; institution builders serve organizational obligations. Individual obligations are visible and concrete; organizational obligations are abstract; one needs a special ability to recognize them. According to leadership ethics, organizational obligations are higher than individual obligations.

Securing a leadership position like the head of an institution may require explicit or tacit support of other people. With increasing politicization of education this is almost becoming almost the rule of the day. Even when someone is selected on merit, there are people behind who try-to seek a non-meritorious person onto the job.

The heads of institutions, whether they come through the pull and push of unholy nexus or by the persuasion of well-meaning people—people in leadership positions—are pulled between individual and organizational obligations. As a matter of general ethics, the individual should feel obliged and grateful to those who facilitated his/her positioning in the leadership status.

The problem starts when the obligation to the individual is in conflict with the obligation to the institution. For example, in the cases documented here, Buch, Saran, Mukhopadhyays (both senior and junior), Chhaya, and others were invited to head their respective organizations because of their reputation. There are several major incidences, e.g., staff appointments, extending institutional facilities, surrendering the autonomy of the institution by submitting to the wishes of the employers, etc., in the life of these individuals, when they stood against the wishes of their (one time) well-wishers and mentors, to protect the interests of the organization. Every one of them paid a price for their ethical stand.

The institution builders put a higher premium on the obligation to the Institute than the individuals who helped them achieve their position. Their counterparts favour the obligation to the individual at the cost of the institution. In case of a conflict between individual and organizational obligations, the institution builders demonstrate their obligations to the organization above their benefactors. For example, in selection of faculty, it is rather common to receive recommendations for candidates from certain quarters. Institution builders listen to the recommendations, but do not oblige unless the candidate is of merit; often candidates of merit are not recommended. An average administrator concedes to such recommendations, harming the long-term interest of the institute by recruiting undeserving candidates for the sake of his personal gains. Such an act is unethical since it compromises the organizational interest and does injustice to the deserving candidates. There are rare incidences where such recommendations do not matter.

An Episode

I was participating in the selection committee meeting of IGNOU chaired by Prof. B S Sharma, then pro-vice chancellor. During the selection committee meeting, before a candidate came in for the interview, Prof. Sharma announced that the candidate has been recommended from a very important quarter. Out of 13 candidates, this happened four times. When the interviews of all the candidates were over, we got into the business of short-listing and selecting candidates. Incidentally, not a single recommended candidate figured in the final list. Prof. Sharma was silent. All the experts and the chairman signed the papers, the papers were sealed in our presence, and meeting was called to an end.

At this stage, I asked the chairman about the recommended candidates. With a broad smile, the chairman said, "I've to serve my university and uphold its interest; we need good candidates to build up our university."

I asked, "Wouldn't those who recommended ask what happened to their candidates?"

Prof. Sharma, at the best of his wit, laughed and said, "I'll tell them that I had informed the selection committee, but the members did not agree." We all shared his wit and admired his ethics.

Similar conflicts of obligations are also visible in areas of financial transaction. The national institutes have reasonably good funds for annual maintenance. The common practice is to assign the work to CPWD. There are instances where CPWD is obliged with assignment at a much higher cost with lower efficiency and quality of work, although Ministry of Finance, Government of India has short-listed several organizations (about 27) for both construction and civil maintenance works. In such cases, institutional interest is sacrificed. In sharp contrast, Ranajit Basu withdrew the contract from PWD, and carried out the construction by a committee of parents and teachers making optimum use of the funds available to the college, to the extent that he was able to mobilize one of the retired engineers of PWD to provide voluntary, supervisory support. The institution builder's obligation was towards the college making the best use of money; for their counterparts, obligation was to the individuals to benefit out of the institution's resources.

The issue of contrast in obligation can be extended further, when the obligation to institute conflicts with the obligation to the larger society. Universities and the national institutions being autonomous and think-tank of the civil society, need to take ethical positions, which may or may not match with the political agenda of the party in power. There are several instances of conflict between national interest and institutional position. Sometime in the not so remote past (April-May, 2006), there was a massive upheaval against the announcement of quota for OBCs in medical and other professional institutions. The announcement was made by the head of the system in the government. It sharply divided people in the major national institutions. Many heads of institutions took the safe position of supporting their employers, many others in the academia questioned the wisdom of the decision. More than 100 professors of IIT Kanpur decided to resign, a decision that they are proud of. The case of AIIMS stands out. Although, with the intervention of the Supreme Court, the crisis was averted, the minister in the UPA (I) government continued his crusade against the director of AIIMS and those who stood for the interest of national development in the context of global competitiveness. The issue may be the difference of opinion and conviction, but the important lesson is how people put their gratitude to the country above their affiliation to the institute.

Management of Coterie

Formation of coteries is rather common in organizations. Administrative heads maintain a coterie; members of coteries derive additional advantage at the cost of institutional interest. Institution builders carefully decimate coteries. Swami Atmapriyananda has mentioned how he made efforts to keep the coterie away. His main contention was that 'you may have to depend on some people more than others in managing your institution. You must also be careful that they do not form a cordon around you and use your office for their benefit; in turn, you derive personal benefits'.

There were servant quarters attached to the staff quarters of an institution. When these quarters were allocated, Prof. Moonis Raza requested his colleagues not to keep servants in the servant quarters though the allottees were entitled to. His argument was two fold: this small self-contained units can house the bachelor faculty members coming from outside Delhi. Indirectly, this will help manage the ecology because otherwise, these small single room tenements will be occupied by 4/5 member-families of the servants (which is the case today—2010-11). All the occupants agreed, appreciating his concern for the Institute. Compared to this, it is quite common for head of institutions to allocate quarters out of turn, on one pretext or the other, to people who provide support to their personal interest. This, again, is the difference between institution builders and their counterparts.

It is rather common to constitute committees to advise and assist management of large institutions. In one such large university (not included in the case studies in this book), the new vice-chancellor constituted 26 committees on various areas of functioning of the university. One head of the department was found to be a member of as many as 24 committees. Compared to that, Saran promoted matrix organization (structure) in TTTI, where members of the faculty had the choice to identify areas (task forces) in which they wanted to work. Also, they had to change the task force after two or three years. This kept every member of the faculty involved in activities of his choice, but equidistant from the principal, since he himself was not a member of any task force. There are several instances that are different with Saran. Just to remind, he constituted a group of four professors to prepare a plan of action for a particular state. The three senior professors prepared the document without involving the fourth who was a junior professor. Saran asked them to go back and involve the fourth professor, before submitting the document.

Institution builders need to draw the best of everyone in the staff; the coterie blocks the vision of the head of the institution, and colours his or her understanding of the strengths and weaknesses of the individual staff members. The institution, then, misses out on the contributions of many capable staff members. Kotter and Rothbeger's (2006) now famous book, *Our Iceberg is Melting* is a beautiful case of how unknown (in this case the small penguin) can make important and meaningful contributions.

Austerity vs Grandiose

The head of an institution enjoys power to corner and use the institutional facilities for self or to share with others. Ethics that differentiate between institution builders and their counterparts is by the attribute of sharing with others vis-à-vis cornering facilities for self. Bhagavat gives an important dictum. "Human beings have the right to only that much of food that fills the stomach. Whosoever wants more is a thief and deserves to be punished (*Yavad bhriyate jatharam, twavat swattam hi dehinam; adhikantu yo bhi manyate, sa steno, dandamarhati*)". Acharya Vinoba Bhave described Prakriti, Vikriti and Sanskriti in the following terms:

- When one is hungry and eats, it is *prakriti* or nature;
- When one is not hungry but still eats, it is *vikriti* or perversion; and
- When one is hungry, still gives away his/her food to another hungry person, it is *sanskriti* or culture.

In our assessment, institution builders are men and women of '*sanskriti*'. Let us take a few examples to illustrate difference between austerity as values in organization and grandiose as dis-values and how they influence or affect the process of institution building. NIEPA provides a very interesting backdrop in this regard. After joining NIEPA, Moonis put up a partition in the rather large Director's office. He, thus, converted his office into two small rooms, curbing out a committee room. Since there were not enough rooms for group exercises during the training programmes, this was a great help. The subsequent three directors coming from similar scholarly background honoured this arrangement. Later, one of the directors removed the partition and created a huge office for him; he also spent a large sum of money to create an impressive office with expensive furnishings. Moonis spent a fairly large amount of money in converting the conventional classrooms into modern classrooms; and of course his all time favourite place, the Library. These classrooms have been used for over 20 years.

The episode of the eminent scholar Prof. Amlan Datta is worth sharing. When he joined as vice-chancellor of Viswa Bharati (Rabindranath's Shantiniketan), his office sought his permission to fix air-conditioners in his office (in summer Shantiniketan gets very hot). He politely turned down. When this was insisted, his argument was "universities are run by teachers; they teach; so we are here. You did not give me AC when I was performing the important job of teaching." When his office pointed out the important administrative role of the VC, he argued, "University administration actually rests on the shoulders of registrar, controller of examinations, finance officer, and other such important officers. I only advise them. We cannot provide ACs to all such important officers. So let me not have AC in my office. I'll let you know as and when I need." That 'need' never came.

Institution builders care for public space (classrooms, libraries, etc.) and practice austerity in private space; their counterparts ignore public space and practice grandiosity in their private space.

After serving as vice chancellor of Jammu University, (Late) Prof. Satya Bhushan shifted to Delhi and joined as Joint Director and then as Director of NIEPA. At the first instance, he disconnected the STD facilities from his residential phone. When asked, he clarified: 'we have recently shifted from Jammu; our children are young, all their connections and friends are in Jammu. They would like to use the STD facilities to talk to their friends; we would not be able to maintain the records. So, it is safe to disconnect the STD facilities. Whenever they need, they can go to a STD booth. If I need for official purposes, I can walk up to the office which is nearby.' In sharp contrast, there are many who not only maintain multiple telephone connections, but even connect their official telephone lines to an instrument at home so that personal calls are also dumped onto the official phone number.

There are many such contrasting cases. The basic issue of ethics is setting examples and models for others to follow. The head of an organization who exploits organizational resources for personal benefits creates that as the organizational norm; others create value based norms as models. The exploitation based models eat the bone marrow of the organization.

Academic Integrity

Academic integrity of the head of an academic institution is another ethical dimension in institution building. Academic integrity of the person inspires his or her followers to make personal academic contribution to the academic growth of the institution. In the reverse case, the heads of institutions exploit the junior colleagues; in the process they not only learn the technique of exploitation, but also become immune to the ethical aspects of academics.

Let us take two contrasting pictures to illustrate the issue. I was, then, a junior research fellow in the M S University of Baroda. Dr. Buch, my Ph.D. guide goaded me on to write a research paper on management of change. I drafted a review paper, after a hard struggle for nearly two months. As per the convention, I put Dr. Buch as the first author and my name as the second author. I gave him a copy for his comments and suggestions. He called me on the third day, and gave me back my paper with extensive corrections and editing. He had also edited his name out with the same pencil. When I asked him about this, he told me: 'the paper is good, it would be published on its own merit. If you put my name, you lose the credit which is yours.' With his usual 'mischievous smile', he said, "I'd have put my name if the paper was of poor quality; but that is not necessary." I asked again, 'you have taken so much pain to do such meticulous and extensive corrections. What about that?' His response was: "I am elder to you in age, senior to you in the department, and I am your teacher. What's the use of being elder, senior and teacher, if I can't build up my juniors?" In sharp contrast, there are plenty of heads of institutions that insist on including their names in the publications of their juniors, which they have not even read once. Such unethical behaviour of stealing the credit from others also works as a model for the younger people. As they grow up in the profession, they would believe that it is an acceptable behaviour. And, they would exploit their juniors. The institution builders support their colleagues and feel credited with the honours bestowed on their colleagues. Their counterparts exploit their colleagues and feel credited. To quote Dr. Buch, 'it's the buoyancy phenomena. You grow as much as you can, and I will facilitate. But remember, I am the cork, and you are water in the glass. More you grow in stature, higher I will reach, not because I want, but that will happen because of buoyancy.'

Walking the Talk

Another important leadership ethics is walking the talk. Gandhiji exhorted his countrymen to do what he does, not what he says. This is the genuineness and transparency. The most common ethics of academic institutions is maintaining the intellectual tradition of reading, thinking and articulating through oral communication, written articles, papers and books. The ethical behaviour of a leader in an academic institution is maintaining the intellectual tradition and contributing to that. In other words, the heads of academic institutions must necessarily be academic leaders. And, that should be demonstrated by reading, quality of teaching and research, oral and written articulation in the form of papers, articles, monographs and books. Institution builders, almost all in the cases presented in this book, are head and shoulders above their colleagues in their academic distinctions, combined with their personal modesty and inspiring quality.

There are several contrasting experiences of walking the talk. Institution builders invariably display their genuineness; they are either outstanding scholars or make extraordinary efforts to cope with the demands of their job. Their counterparts, however, maintain the quality and duplicity between walking and talking. They sit in judgment and supposedly advise their colleagues in research and writing, when they are incapable of researching or writing themselves. Similarly, they profess honesty, punctuality, discipline, commitment to the institution, etc. without practising it.

Public Attendance

By public attendance, I mean interface of the head of the institution with the local community; may be for inaugural or valedictory speeches, keynote addresses, participating in meetings, etc. These are important occasions and opportunities for building organizational reputation. The ethical question in this context is preparedness for public presentation—both in content and style. Institution builders are perceptive of the image of the Institute when they speak, they do not necessarily do advocacy for their organization. Many of the leaders of the institution documented in this volume were good orators. More importantly, they always prepared themselves well before presenting themselves. NIEPA conducts, on an average, 50 programs a year. Moonis was scholarly, articulate and an orator; yet, he insisted on inviting other scholars to inaugurate the programmes which he would chair. His basic contention was, irrespective of the level of scholarship 'how can one deliver 50 inaugural addresses on a wide variety of subjects requiring a variety of specializations?' But, there are many heads of institutions who with their weak flow (oration) and substance, present themselves repeatedly, and unhesitatingly.

When we were young students in the university, our head of the department would always come well prepared for any public addresses. Besides the concern of the image of his university department, he had another important ethical question, "When you address a public gathering for say 30 minutes and 200 people are listening to you, there are 100 person hours are involved. Who should be responsible for 100 man hours of the audience and your own 30 minutes? His emphasis was: 'it is not 30 minutes'. 'Now, if you prepare well you can make meaningful use of 100 hours of others. If you don't, you are responsible for wasting valuable 100 hours. One may need a few hours of preparation to make effective presentation. But that can save 100 hours of others. Isn't that a good economics?"

Universities and major national and state level institutions are involved in various committees. Such invitations are extended to the heads of the institutions. Institution builders depute the faculty on the basis of their specialization and subject of the meeting for the committee. Their counterparts use all such invitations for their personal presence. What is important is to recognize is that institution builders send specialists to such meetings to indicate the capability of the institution above their personal agenda, and also to ensure best contribution for the larger cause. Their counterparts practice the reverse; they participate in every meeting irrespective of the kind of specialization needed to make a meaningful contribution. For example, NIEPA was involved in various committees of the Ministry of Human Resource Development, Planning Commission, UGC, etc. Although all correspondences were received by the Director, Moonis would nominate senior faculty members to various committees depending upon their specializations. When asked, he said: "I can't be the best in everything. I'm good at overall policy making. When it comes to finance, technical education, projectization, etc., we have outstanding scholars and specialists who are better than me. What is important is to provide our best services to the country and best image of the institute." During the policy making in 1986, a senior official in the Ministry of Human Resource Development lamented that except 'so and so', there is no one in India who specializes in educational technology. I confronted her and asked about her familiarity with a few names in the same institution. I also asked her whether she was familiar with the All India Association for Educational Technology that has more than 1200 members. She was kept completely in the dark by the 'so called' expert. Institution builders play team game. They put the best foot of their institute forward.

Lessons Summary

- Ethical dimension in institution building is locked into the positioning of self vis-à-vis the organization.
- Institution builders position themselves behind the organization they lead. They get known and earn respect and fame because of the organizations they build. Their counterparts position their own selves before the organization. They exploit the organization for personal benefits.
- Institution builders work for reputation of the organization. Their counterparts work for personal name and fame, and gratification at the cost of the institution.
- Institution builders nurture organizational ambition; their counterparts nurture personal ambition.
- Institution builders build institutions with their blood and sweat. Their counterparts build their own career on the blood and sweat of the organization.
- Institution builders work for the organization; their counterparts work for themselves.

Ethics and values are the core of human beings. The quality of an organization is also determined by ethics and moral values, particularly in management.

Conclusion

Institution building is a process; it is an endless journey. It has overt as well as covert processes; it has an internal and a public image. An educational institution's internal image as honest, academically competent and performing organization, generates corresponding public confidence and reputation. The leader being the pacesetter, his/her own personal behaviour, and clean (ethical) image, influence others. An institution is built-up, when all members contribute their best; an institution is destroyed when members exploit the Institute for their personal advantage, often led by the head of institution. It is this dichotomy of contributing versus exploiting the Institute that is the main contention of ethics in management and leadership.

Since people in leadership positions show the way, when they tend to exploit their organizations for their personal advantages, people tend to follow their trodden path. Organizations stand exposed and exploited. On the contrary, institution builders not only contribute to the organizations, but also mobilize others to contribute. They create a different organizational culture—culture empowered with self-esteem and positive confidence. The conventional administrators put self above the organization; institution builders put the organization—above self. It is the quality of ethics, personal and professional life that distinguishes institution builders from their counterparts.

NOTE

1. *Chapter 3, Verse 22.* Lord Krishna said, "O son of Prtha, there is no work prescribed for Me within all the three planetary systems. Nor am I in want of anything, nor have I need to obtain anything—and yet I am engaged in work".
   Chapter 3, Verse 23. "For, if I did not engage in work, O Partha, certainly all men would follow My path".
   Chapter 3, Verse 24. "If I should cease to work, then all these worlds would be put to ruination. I would also be the cause of creating unwanted population, and I would thereby destroy the peace of all sentient beings".

19
LEADERSHIP FOR INSTITUTION BUILDING
Indian Model

Introduction

Institution building is the process of developing internal capacity of an organisation to be resilient through an ongoing process of change management. In this chapter, we would examine how this process capabilities are developed in educational institutions. We will build a model or a strategy for institution building within the Indian cultural and institutional ethos.

In a fast changing world, challenge of institution building is developing the capability of change management on a continuing basis. Most important enabler of change is innovation. It is the process of adoption and institutionalization of innovation that makes change happen. Adoption of innovation once in a while in a sporadic manner does not create the mechanism of change management. Process of institution building is developing the capacity so that an institution innovates and manages change rather automatically. The implication is independence of the process of change from the leader. In a way, institution building implies coming out of "around the man approach". Thus, strength of institution building process is the self renewing capabilities of the organization.

We will look at 'institution building' through the prism of change management, especially for sustainability of the process of change. There are many instances where an innovative institution relapses back to near innovation-illiteracy with the change of the person in leadership position. IIM Ahmedabad provides a fine example of sustainable self-renewing capability. It continues to maintain its leadership position among the business schools in India despite periodic changes in the position of directors.

Let us first revisit the stages in the life of an institution; strategies for adoption of innovation, change management and institution building; and the leadership styles that distinguishes some heads of institution as institution builders from others.

Stages in the Life of an Institution

We referred to the classification of organisations by Clark in terms of State of growth in chapter 2. Let us revisit the classification to derive implications for the cases in this book.

- *Formative Period:* Shreyas School, Udang High School, DAV Public School belong to this category. Though all three schools began from the scratch, they differ from each other in terms of their goals and missions. Shreyas was a personal initiative of Shri Rajni Jani inspired simultaneously by social commitment and entrepreneurship. DAV School was rather thrust upon as a challenge to Ms. Anita Makkar by the DAV College Management Committee. One rented room, one chair and a table to start with. Udang high school was set up by the Village leaders of Udang; headmaster Late Shri Nrisinha Prasad Mukhopadhyay was invited and brought from another village to head the school. Common factor was their youth—all in their late 20s or early 30s—when they took charge of their respective schools
- *Rapid Growth Period:* Kathmandu University and National Open School belong to this category. Though NOS was born only three years before the period of its case documentation, it inherited academic traditions and cultures developed over 12 years of its existence as project school in the CBSE. Within the first three years, the first chairman had given a complete shape to the institution that decided its own curriculum, developed self instructional material, delivered programmes through distance education mode, examined students and certified; certificate that was recognized by other boards and universities in the country. During the second term, it

experienced qualitative change along with rapid expansion. Appointment to the post of the chairman of National Open School is done by the Appointments Committee of the Cabinet.[1] chaired by the Prime Minister of India.

- *Period of stability:* NIEPA, TTTI, Rama Krishna Mission Vidyamandir, Jai Hind College, and Smt. Parvatibai Chowgule College belong to this category. In this category, NIEPA is an apex institution of international repute that was started with UNESCO collaboration. Prof. Saran was previously a teacher, then head of the department and principal in the local polytechnic funded and managed by the Madhya Pradesh state government is one of four regional institutions for technical teachers training is run by the union Ministry of human resource development. Prof Saran was recruited through the normal procedure of recruitment to head the TTTI. Jai Hind and Smt Parvatibai colleges are well established institutions. Rama Krishna Mission Vidya Mandir Belur is a reputed institution of higher education in West Bengal popularly rated as next to Presidency and St Xavier's Colleges in Kolkata.[2]
- *Period of decline and decay:* Bharatiya Vidya Bhavan and the Kendriya Vidyalaya and Mrinalini Devi Mahavidyalay belong to this category. Bharatiya Vidya Bhavan is a well established institution and one of the notes of a chain of such institutions in the country setup with the inspiration of K M Munsi. The institution was steadily losing out on quality and also the values which are cherished in Bharatiya Vidya Bhavan. Dr. Chhaya was originally recruited to head one of the Bhavan schools in Mumbai; he was placed in Delhi because of crisis. Dr. Ranajit Basu was also serving as a college teacher somewhere else. He was selected as a principal in the normal chatter of selection. Mrinalini Devi College was affecting of general decay of the society and educational institutions in the state. It makes an interesting study how one could make a turnaround when the social and educational decadence is almost all pervasive.

A careful analysis of the situation occurring in the institution experiencing decay and degeneration, a stage comes when its very existence and functioning is threatened. I prefer to consider that as the fifth stage—stage of crisis. We have not included any case on such an institution in this book, though we have referred to episodes and instances to illustrate.

Roger Allen (2009) provides another useful classification of organizations. He classified organizations into three stages—state of chaos, state of stability and state of high performance (www.centerod.com). In this framework,

Stage I: Chaos (*Fire-Fighting Mentality*) is indicated by Crisis/short-term focus, Lack of clear direction and goals, Shifting priorities, Unclear policies and procedures, "Us" vs. "them" attitude, Blame and lack of ownership, Alienated work force. These characteristics can be found either in newly established institutions that are still struggling to find their feet or among the institutions that are decaying and degenerating where established policies and procedures are marauded.

Stage II: Stability (*Back to the Basics*) as indicated by Clarity of goals and direction, Consistency in priorities, Well-defined policies and procedures (technical and personnel), Agreement on roles and responsibilities, Basic management processes rewarded and practiced (goal-setting, performance reviews, etc.).

Stage III: High Performance (*Outstanding, sustainable results*) characterized by Clear statement of mission that creates sense of esprit de corp, Well defined values which result in distinctive culture, Respect for people that is a deeply ingrained part of culture, Good communication and information sharing systems, High involvement and empowerment of people, Design (work flow, structure, systems) that supports mission and values

In this model, there is a dynamism. Roger paints institutions on the move—(a) 'from chaos to stability' and (b) 'from stability to high performance'. Among our cases, Udang, Shreyas and DAV on one hand and Mrinalini Devi College, Bharatiya Vidya Bhavan, Kendriya Vidyalaya on the other hand are on the move from chaos to stability. NIEPA, TTTI, NOS, Rama Krishna Mission, CASE, Kathmandu University are on the move from stability to high performance.

Interestingly, institution builders vary widely in their entry into the position of leadership. Some came through normal process of selection; some came on invitation; some entered the position through their enterpreneurship; and two of them came through high-profile process of the ACC. Hence, we are not able to find any significance implication or relationship between entry into the leadership position and capability to build institutions. Their personal style vary widely except converging on issues of ethics and values that has been dealt separately in the next chapter. Let us look at a few other issues.

Visioning

Vision is celebrated concept in the literature of institution building. People tend to equate institution builders with men/women of vision. 'Vision' is used by different people to mean different things. According to John Gordon (1994) "vision is a word variously construed" and "vision is the operational definition of values." In the institutional context, I consider vision as *seeing things that does not exist now*, the way a painter visualizes a picture in a blank canvas or a site planner or architect visualises a township or a building in a place dotted with bushes and stones without an iota of any habitation. Visioning, hence, is creative and not distributed 'normally' among the people in leadership positions. While distinguishing leadership from positional authority (administrators, in my paradigm), Gordon (1994) prefers to see 'role of vision in how energy is used within a group. Positional authority—typically hierarchical power—exercised without vision, diffuses and dissipates energy. With vision, energy is focused and directed towards a desirable future'. Visionary leadership is the first and the most effective leadership style in Goleman's (2002) resonant leadership paradigm too.

James MacGregor (2004), in his foreword to the book by Joanne B. Ciulla's Ethics: The Heart of Leadership wrote, "*We think of vision as an overarching, evocative, energizing, moralizing force ranging from broad almost architectural plans for a new industry, say to an inspirational, spiritual, perhaps morally righteous evocation of future hopes and expectations of a political movement. Visions are often projected by charismatic leaders calling for mass mobilization and action over the long run on many fronts, perhaps even for a revolution. To the extent Vision is transformational—that is, calls for real change—must it not embody some kind of supreme values in some kind of hierarchy? Otherwise, would vision not be a kind of loose cannon lurching back and forth as the visionary leaders follow their own guiding stars?*"

Members in an organization use words like 'visionary' to admire their leader. They attach high value to visioning. Visioning has a compelling effect on the followers. Institution builders hence, are invariably associated with visioning. In the journey of institution building, vision inspire the journey illuminating the path ahead.

There are different kinds of visioning that are effective in different stages of the institution's growth. In the pre-formative period, institution builders define medium-term and long-term vision, projecting five to ten years' perspective. They define what kind of organization they want to create. They derive components of their vision from their own imagination; as well as from other institutions that they want to emulate. For example, while designing the Andhra Pradesh Open University as well as Indira Gandhi National Open University later, (Late) Prof. G Ram Reddy's vision was informed and inspired by UK Open University, as he shared with me in a personal discussion.

During the formative stage, a qualitatively different visioning is a distinct possibility by synthesizing visions and vision statements filtered through one's own imagination. National Open School (NOS) presents an interesting case. National Open School was functioning as an 'open school' for little more than three years in its new structure and format. It inherited another about 12 years of meaningful existence and experience as a unit of Central Board of Secondary Education. Before I took charge, NOS did an excellent job as a 'delivery institution' of school education, developing its own curriculum, instructional material and programme delivery through printed material and personal contact programmes. During my discussion with the Search Committee chaired by Prof. G. Ram Reddy, then Chairman of UGC, I shared my vision. After I took charge of NOS as its chairman (also CEO), I analyzed vision or vision-like statements in all the available documents, comments by various people and developed a synthesis of vision and filtered through my imagination and my initial vision; carried out SWOT analysis (to understand what was possible). My vision, rather imagination at that stage was re-conceptualizing and reconstructing NOS as a R&D organization for a leadership role in open schooling within the country, and internationally.

From a delivery institution to global leadership role needs a paradigm shift in visioning. I opted for collective visioning with leaders in the system. As an initial input, with my colleagues within NOS, I developed a perspective document on open schooling in India spelling out our 'local imagination'. With the approval of the idea by the Education Secretary, we constituted a committee comprising Dr. Chitra Naik (then member Planning Commission), Prof. G. Ram Reddy (then chairman, UGC), Prof. Ram G. Takwale (then vice chancellor Y.C. Maharashtra Open University), and Sri S.V. Giri (then Union Education Secretary). Through several meetings, the document was finalized leading to reconceptualization of NOS as National Institute of Open Schooling which it is now.

Visioning undergoes qualitative change as the institute enters into the rapid growth and the mature period. In the mature period, visioning becomes incremental, more in the style of political leadership (Baddaracco and Ellsworth, 1989). In reality, leaders identify a few improvements or innovations that can be carried out in the given situation, conscious of the possible resistance of the system and the people. The interesting dynamics is that such incremental visioning and action create an innocuous entry point in the organization; it then becomes a continuous process, an endless journey by venturing into more and more new ideas. Success begets success; leaders tend to move to larger and complicated visions with larger ramifications and long-term implications.

The contrary situation makes an interesting study. I asked one of the heads who succeeded Dr. Buch as head of CASE –'what's your plan to take CASE further?' His response was, 'this is already a good and reputed institute, nothing more can be done'. There is more concrete example. In one of my workshops for school principals, one principal (of a girls' school) proudly stated, 'my school is national champion in Basketball'. We all congratulated her for the distinction. I asked her when the din of clapping came down, 'why is your school not Asian or World Champion?' There was a silence. Principal said, 'I was happy with national championship. It did not even occur to me to try for the next level'. Those who lack this imagination/vision don't build institutions.

Cases of TTTI Bhopal, NIEPA New Delhi and Rama Krishna Mission College (Belur) under the leadership of Prof. Y. Saran, Prof. Moonis Raza and Swami Atmapriyananda respectively are interesting cases that illustrate this qualitative change of vision. All the three institutions were already well-established before these persons came to lead the respective institutions. Institutions had good traditions, but also well entrenched into the traditions (past). Saran, Moonis and Swamiji initiated innocuous innovations slowly opening up the institutions to tolerate change. End product was the paradigm shift in both the organizations' perspectives, reputation and social contribution. In such cases, the organization experiences continuous improvement.

In case of organizational decay and decline, and organizations at risk, vision is restricted to putting the organization back to its path first. It's more like a surgery to remove the cancerous growth. Then, there is the post-operative period where health is restored back, followed by development of physical strength. In such cases, there is neither a long-term vision, nor incremental vision; vision is putting back the organization on the track. Bharatiya Vidya Bhavan under M. P. Chhaya, Kendriya Vidyalaya under Savita Kapoor, Mrinalinin Devi College under Ranajit Basu are some of the examples. Their first job was to bring the institution to normal functioning (stable in Roger Allen's classification). Hence, limited vision is restoring normalcy; then add qualitative vision of moving towards high performance.

Let me get back to the issue of incremental visioning that is common with stable organizations. The important feature of incremental visioning is the 'involved thinking and micro visioning'. The institution builders think continuously about the institute; they tend to live in the romantic world of 'improvement-ideas'. This leads to visioning in smaller subsets of the institution as a process of lateral thinking, exciting further creativity. The improvement or development of ideas may begin in one of the rather innocuous domains of the organization. Using such an entry point, new ideas spread into nerves and arteries of every department of the organization. The impact over a period of time is holistic change in the organization.

Organizational visioning is actually additive—the leader adds on incrementally to the vision; and followers sum it up to credit their leaders with a long-term vision. The staff or the followers take every move of the leader as important and strategic. "...everything the leader may do, however casual, may be taken by staff as planned and meaningful" (Latchem and Hanna, 2001). Although actions flowing out of vision are often seen as strategic actions of the political leadership style, I found very little evidence of any strategic planning. On the contrary, institution builders seem to be inspired by the joy of creation, like a painter or a musician, often oblivious of the externalities. In fact, it is the followers who sum up the organizational experience, as if there was a long-term vision, which was strategically implemented in small steps and measures.

Another important determinant of visioning is the concept of space and orbit. Although institutions are national by definition, visioning tends to provide a larger space and a different reference group. A local institution re-orbits itself at the national level, a national institution develops its reference point with international institutions.

In our assessment, visioning is a quality that is attributed by the followers to their leaders. Among the cases that have been documented here in this book, there is none that had a vision document or a formal statement of vision. Further, for translating the vision, vision needs to unbundled into missions, missions into goals and goals and targets. To achieve the goals and targets, organisations need to have a strategic plan and strategy management approach that is significantly emphasized in the Baldridge model. I did not come across any institution that had spelt out its vision, missions, goals and there was any strategic plan except that the institutions registered under Societies Registration Act have spelt out a few objectives as required under the Act. Instead of setting the vision in advance, and moving towards that, most Indian institution builders nurture evolution of a vision through lateral thinking. Involved positive thinking by the leader is what helps in the evolution of a vision. In the language of total quality management, it begins with Kizening in one area and then slowly spreading into different departments of the institution; finally creating a holistic impact in culture of the institution.

Innovations and Strategic Management of Change

There are a wide variety of innovations practised in the institutions that have been documented in this book. It is rather difficult to create a repertoire of all the innovations here; also I suspect that may not be of very great relevance because every innovation by an institution builder is essentially situated. The only common thread across all the institution is the emphasis on the human resources, especially teachers. This matches the cardinal principle of emphasis on staff development for total quality management by Crosby (1984), Deming (1988), Juran (1988), and others.

There have been some interesting studies on the nature of innovation that determine their adaptability in the institution. Such characteristics have been classified under two broad heads namely intrinsic characteristics and extrinsic characteristics. Intrinsic characteristics include scientific status of the knowledge (innovation), value, the visibility, complexity and communicability. Extrinsic characteristics are compatibility of the innovation into the culture of the institution and relative advantage. It will be interesting to examine each innovation in terms of their implementable characteristics.

As strategy, almost every institution took one small step at a time to innovate and build change brick by brick. The only exception was Saran's TTTI that brought a quantum shift in the organisations through massive project funded by the UNDP. The massiveness of the concept was such that the Government of India asked him to take it up for all four TTTIs, though original proposal was for TTTI Bhopal only. This brings us to the scientific concept and strength of the concept of Kaizen that finds a prominent place in the strategic management of change. We realize from our study that the members of the institution, especially in India, where professionalisation of the educational personnel has still not happened, need to tolerate innovation, and then experiment with them. This is precisely what happened in most of the institutions.

Bennis, Benne and Chin (1973) mentioned three strategies of change management, namely Rational-Empirical, Normative-Reeducative and Power-Coercion, based on the nature of members of the human organizations. Later, Fred Nickols (2010) added another strategy, Environmental-Adaptive.

Rational-Empirical	People are rational and will follow their self-interest—once it is revealed to them. Change is based on the communication of information and the proffering of incentives.
Normative-Reeducative	People are social beings and will adhere to cultural norms and values. Change is based on redefining and reinterpreting existing norms and values, and developing commitments to new ones

Power-Coercieve	People are basically compliant and will generally do what they are told or can be made to do. Change is based on the exercise of authority and the imposition of sanctions.
Environmental-Adaptive	People oppose loss and disruption but they adapt readily to new circumstances. Change is based on building a new organization and gradually transferring people from the old one to the new one

Source: www.openlearningworld.com

These strategy definitions are derived out of 'what works'. Most conclusive understanding is that no single strategy is good enough. It needs a strategic combination of all four. Strategies of change management varied widely among the selected institutions depending upon the nature of the institution and style and stature of the leader. Those who enjoyed high stature (personal style and not the positional authority) faced very little resistance when they introduced innovation. People were rather keen to get closer and provide support to the initiatives. We may call this as charismatic effect. It seems to be a curious, rather optimal combination of Rational-Empirical with Normative-Re-educative approaches.

Persons who built institutions from the scratch also had lesser resistance because every new entrant was their choice/recruit who fell in line. Environmental-Adaptive Approach was in full display. Yet, there are plenty of occasions where the leader used poer-coercion and normative re-educative strategies.

Distinctly different were the strategies in case of institutions that were in the state of decay and degeneration. They rightly resorted to Power-Coercive style. Their immediate challenge was to bring the institution back to normal functioning. As they say, 'you don't consult or discuss or put to vote what to do when house is on fire'. This is what happened in case of Ranajit Basu's, Savita Kapoor's, MP Chhaya's cases. But once the crisis was over or the degeneration was arrested, the leaders adopted multiple strategies like Rational-Empirical helping people to see reason to change, and then supported by normative-reeducative strategies.

In case of established and well run institutions like NIEPA, TTTI, NOS, strategy was to help people imagine and open a new horizon to the vision of the organisation; indeed, a twinning combination of Rational-Empirical with Normative-Reeducative. Once, the members of the institution saw reason to believe larger possibilities for the organization and self, they had to be reeducated and set new norms.

Institution building does not work in such cut and right manner. It often requires a combination—adopting one strategy in one area, another in some other area.

Let me illustrate this with NOS which I was personally involved with. NOS was located in Wazirpur—a highly polluted industrial area for several years. All the employees had settled down around that area. High degree of pollution and shortage of space prompted me to decide to change the location to a more habitable place. NOS administration found a place in South Delhi. Though there was no agitation, there was murmur against this policy. I asked my office to go ahead; but added free office transport to all staff members from their respective areas of residence. This was Power-Coercive combined with Environmental-Adaptive Strategy.

Members of the NOS community had associated their concept zone within 'school framework'. I decided to upscale; I planned to recruit candidates with doctorate degrees and to have Vice chancellors and heads of national institutions in the selection committees. My colleagues in academic and administrative departments expressed their apprehension of the response to my initiative. When the interviews were over and we succeeded on both the counts of candidates and selectors, the perception changed. Similarly, when my colleagues were able to participate in international conference in New Zealand for the first time and drew applaud for the quality of their paper, they rationalized their self-concept and capabilities. My helping them in writing the papers and simulation exercise of presentation was normative re-educative, but their presentation and rediscovering their academic self was rational-empirical.

Important conferences were held by my predecessor before I took charge. I called upon my younger colleagues to edit the report, and we got it published under their names as editors. During a series of international workshops, I deliberately separated out the academics from the organisational chores so that they reconstruct themselves as academicians.

In NOS library books were under lock and key as is the case in normal schools. I converted it into open self library which is common in higher academic and research institutions where academicians can access books by themselves. These are just a few examples to illustrate how we change the horizon of the members of the institution to think big, and think better through strategic combination of normative-reeducative with rational-empirical strategies.

The important trick of institution building is to adapt and change the strategies with the change of the culture of the institution. One can use Power-coercion where people fail to respond to good gestures; once this stage is overcome, leaders take to rational-empirical to help people see reason. This is followed by normative-reeducative strategy that builds new capabilities and sets new norms. As these strategies succeed, institution builders resort to delegation and facilitation.

Since educational institutions are human intensive systems, success of innovation, management of change, and also transition of vision is directly related to and dependent upon the involvement of the people. The literature on total quality management emphasizes involvement of people at every stage and every occasion. Because, it is the people in the organisation that either facilitate or resist adoption of innovation and change.

This analysis also reflects on the resistance and resistance management. Everett Rogers classified people with respect to their reactions to innovation into five categories. These are innovators, early adopters, adopters, late adopters, and laggards. Every institution has all these categories of people. Challenge of the leader and institution builder is to convert and laggards into late adopters (reluctant adopters), late adopters into adopters, adopters into early adopters, and ideally early adopters into innovators. As we move from laggards to innovators, our strategic choices shift from power-coercion to delegation and facilitation through normative-re-educative strategies.

Leadership Styles

There are several paradigms with which we can map leadership styles. There is a strong body of literature on leadership skills. One such list mentions

1. Understanding the needs and Characteristics of the post,

2. Knowing and using the Resources of the group,
3. Controlling group performance,
4. Evaluating, Representing the group,
5. Communicating,
6. Planning,
7. Setting the example,
8. Sharing the leadership,
9. Counseling,
10. Effective teaching (www.lifelonglearning.org).

Situational Leadership Theory by Hershey and Blanchard identifies four styles—directing or controlling, selling or coaching, participating and delegating. This is based on the combination of concern for tasks and concern for relationships. Leaders may have higher concern for either task or relationships. According to this classification, directing style represents high concern for task and low concern to people, selling style represents high concern for tasks as well as high concern for people, participating style represents high concern for people but low concern for task, and the delegating style represents low concern for task as well as low concern for people. No single style is better than the others. Every style has a place in managing an organization. On the basis of choices of actions against a given situation, leadership skills are measured in terms of style preference (one of the four styles becomes dominant), style flexibility (ability to adopt all four styles depending upon the situation) and style effectiveness (choice of style with respect to the demand of the situation).

Goleman classifies leadership styles into two broad categories, namely resonant and dissonant styles. In the repertoire of leadership styles, he mentions visionary, coaching, affiliated, democratic, pacesetting, and commanding. The pacesetting and commanding styles can be dissonant; hence Goleman advises us to sparingly use this to styles.

I have presented a hierarchical structure of leadership—how to move from the lower end of transactional to higher end of L-5 leadership in brief in the Prologue at the end of this book.

Depending upon the situation specially the complexity of the task and the capabilities of task maturity of the employees, a leader had to choose different styles in different situations, according to the situational leadership theory. But the situational leadership is restricted to management—day-to-day operations of the institution. For institution builders, the challenge is reduction in the frequency of choice of high task oriented styles and transcending to low task orientation and low people orientation so that through delegation, the organisation can run without much intervention of the leader.

In the paradigm that I have presented, there is a transcendence of leadership style from managerial to elusive style through transactional, transformational, primal and inspirational. If those styles are the front end leadership styles, cognitive intelligence, emotional intelligence and spiritual intelligence forms the back-end. Just as leaders need to transcend in their overt style, they also need to transcend at the covert back-end intelligence.

Our fundamental contention is institution building can be sustainable only when leader is able to achieve the level of delegation; in the words of Jim Collins, level V leadership. To achieve that level, a leader has to learn to delegate which warrants preparation for delegation.

In all the models, leadership style is seen in either static or semi-permanent changing the followers to achieve organisational goals. In this model, there is a simultaneous journey of the leaders and followers. As the same followers mature in a variety of personal and task criteria, leader also changes from lower order to higher-order styles with the ultimate objective of making himself or herself irrelevant to the situation. In Chinese proverb, 'where leaders presence and absence does not matter'.

In the cases presented here, almost every institution, except IIM Ahmedabad, receded on their stature and style of change management with the departure of the institution builder. This indicates the incompleteness or fragility of institution building process undertaken by the leaders. This can be partly situational, but partly inadequate skills and styles of the leaders. For example, if Ravi Mathai, credited for success of IIM Ahmedabad was there eight long years as director, there are also others in these cases who were there in the same institutions for more than two decades. There are several reasons why institution building are not sustainable. Besides these are built 'around a man approach', the leaders did not have a strategy of exit and sustainability of innovations and change management.

Inspirational Leadership

John Adair (2009) and Lance Secretan (1999) contributed the concept of Inspirational Leadership. An inspired person is self-propelled, does not wait for others to lead. It fits in well as step towards Level-5 leadership of Jim Collins. Inspired people are committed to a mission that they have accepted. Secretan refers to Mother Teresa, Gandhi, Nelson Mandela and others who inspired. So, being inspired is affiliating to a cause, a mission and a vision. Accomplishing the task is motivation-part of personality. Inspiring leaders are able to create that affiliation.

An interesting effect of inspiring leadership can be seen in the followers. The empowered followers scale new heights in their own profession; they themselves emerge as leaders. For example, many of the young scholars who worked in CASE, Baroda, turned out to be academic leaders in their own sphere in many Indian universities. Graduates of IITs and IIMs of India lead corporate houses all over the world. How does it happen?

For institution builders, inspiring is not a strategy. They do not either decide or plan to inspire. They behave in their own natural style. They are genuine and not artificial. We felt inspired by the personal styles of Prof. Buch or Prof. Raza or Sri Nrisinha Prasad Mukhopadhyay with whom I have been personally associated. They did not try to inspire. It happened. "*When I think about inspirational leadership, I think of people in my life that pushed me beyond what I imagined and I was extremely thankful for it. It was a math teacher in 6th grade, a basketball coach in 8th grade, a business professor/mentor in college, a manager at AT&T, an early investor in my first startup, a board member today. All of whom I wanted to work beyond what was expected and excel at a higher level for. They always believed you were capable of more. They always believed you could be excellent*" (Al Pacino at www.inspiredstartup.com/inspirational-leadership/15 Sep 2010).

Rajesh (2009) [www.slideshare.net] proposed a 10pt formula for inspiring leadership. These are:

1. Provide an inspiring vision, and strategic alignment and launch a crusade
2. Help people connect their personal goals to business goals
3. Make relentless innovation a religion

4. Encourage entrepreneurial creativity and experimentation
5. Involve everyone, empower and trust employees
6. Coach and train your people to greatness
7. Build teams, promote teamwork and leverage diversity
8. Motivate, inspire, energize people and recognize achievements
9. Encourage risk taking
10. Make business fun

There remains, however, a large number of unanswered questions. Though institution builders are, by and large, inspiring, their inspiration does not have the same or similar effects on all members of the organisation. Inspiring is neither an easy solution nor a formula for leadership. Wherever the behaviour of the leaders resonate with the ambitions and styles of the followers, the followers stand inspired. Resonance can be generated only with those who share the same set of human values. In Indian educational institutions, inspirational leadership flourishes in paternalistic organizational climate.

Organizational stability and growth depend on task accomplishments. No wonder that leaders are task-oriented; and are characterized by production emphasis. There is an apparent autocratic behaviour among the institution builders, unless we explore the hindsight of the process. The 'ruthless task masters' turn out to be soft and humane like the caring mothers, when their followers are in difficulty. They forget the official relationships; they go out of the way to alleviate the condition. This combination of task orientation and production emphasis with personal concern provide unique personal characteristics to leaders. J B P Sinha (1980) called this Task-Nuturant style. This personal concern creates a resonating-emotive relationship between the leader and the followers. The followers tend to give their best in such situations and to such leaders. Amazingly, the style resembles the style of a typical head of an Indian family. In the intellectual domain, they show their superiority; in the emotive domain, they indicate their affiliation and concern for others.

Behavioural Determinism in Leadership Styles

Although many of the leadership theories profess strategic decision for enhancing leadership effectiveness, style preference seem to be semi-permanent, if not permanent behaviour. Such behaviour gets repeated like habits. Hence, there is some kind of determinism in leader behaviour. They seem to be compelled to behave in a particular fashion repeatedly, though situations change.

We come across leaders who headed more than one institution with similar leadership behaviour, creating differential impact on the institutions. It should be evident from the analysis presented above that, depending upon the stage of development of the organisation, institution building needs different kinds of visioning, power building, paternalization etc. The institution builders, with great reputation, bring themselves to the other institution with the same or similar stock of skills, competence, beliefs, and even vision. Consequently, they make a differential impact. This consistency of behaviour, despite difference in situations, is what is construed as determinism in behaviour. For example, Prof. Moonis Raza was a very successful nurturant leader in NIEPA. However, same style did not fit well when he led Delhi University as Vice-Chancellor. When he took charge, NIEPA was a small organization with a few retired professors and administrators. He recruited bright young faculty who needed all the inspiration of a nurturant leader. In sharp contrast, Delhi University is a well-established institution with large number of distinguished scholars. Hence, it needs much more Delegative-facilitative style. Same was true for Dr. Buch who successfully built CASE with young bright scholars, but not the well-established Department of Education in the University that he himself headed. My personal experience in NOS versus NIEPA corroborates the same. Those who are nurturant leaders can do a great job in budding institution with young faculty.

There is another interesting feature of determinism. Leaders tend to use their previous experience and vision into the new organisation. First chairman of the NOS was principal of one of the top end schools of Delhi and also later chairman of the CBSE. He beautifully combined these two experiences to create a NOS combination of a good school and a board of examination. I took charge from him. I carried with me my experience and ambition of apex national institutions that are simultaneously leader of the sister institutions in the country and India's interface to the world. Hence, over a period of time, I developed the perspectives of open learning system in the country with a network of 20 open schools and NOS upgraded to NIOS to lead the movement in the country. One of my successor coming from the NCERT—another major national institution—converted my perspective into reality. Similarly, Moonis Raza came from Jawaharlal Nehru University with a distinguished record of scholarship. His compulsive thinking was to make NIEPA another distinguished academic research organisation. He recruited bright young scholars and converted them into leaders in the field of educational planning administration both nationally and globally.

Both Indian and western schools accept the possibility of behaviour modification through involved action and practice. Several techniques like T-group sessions, sensitivity training, data-feedback, transactional analysis are used for behaviour modification. Indian traditional knowledge also highlights the possibility of behaviour modification and the methods like meditation and inculcation of new habits (Ch 6. Abhyasayoga in The Bhagavat Gita). Changing behaviour, rewriting the life-script is possible, though difficult. It needs a dedicated student within, to be able to re-learn and re-write the life-script.

Conclusion

Institution building is building self-renewing capability of the organization. Hence, it is building the process capabilities that can sustain change and make an institution resilient. In a way, it is an effort to help an institution gain freedom from the leader and be self-propelled. Apparently, it is a contradiction. Leadership for institution building is person centric, but goal of institution building is freedom from person centricity. There is actually no contradiction. It is like propelling a rocket in space. It needs lot of energy and push to launch, but once it is in the space orbit, it moves on its own. Role of leadership is to place the institution in that orbit where is moves on its own.

NOTES

1. Appointments of heads of national institutions is done by the appointments committee of the Cabinet. The ministers of human resource development appoints research committee to identify potential candidates for the position. The search committee usually recommends 3 to 5 names to the Minister.

Minister for HRD chooses one of the names and forwards it to the Department of personnel and then to the Prime Minister. Chairman of NOS and director of NIEPA were selected through this process.

2. After the study, I was convinced that the college has matured and have all the potentialities to occupy the top position among the higher education institutions in the state. Hence, I titled The case as 'Changing the Orbit'. One day, Swami Atmapriyananda, called me on the phone and informed me that my prophetic statement has come true. The institute has been granted deemed university status. Incidentally, this tradition of the institute was announced in the making of the ministers of education in the country chaired by union Minister of Human Resource Development in Bangalore which I happen to attend; and I inform Swamiji that I'm witnessing the formal announcement of the tradition of the college into the deemed university.

20
EPILOGUE
Graduation in Leadership[1]

'Leaders are born' or 'are made' is the age old debate. If leaders are only born, world must wait for those special constellations when leaders would be born; and leave institution building to chances and accidents. According to science of management and experience, leadership is a 'Learned Trait'. Leaders who build institutions evolve. They learn and equip themselves with new skills, competencies, values and attitudes. They learn to believe that they can change themselves and can change their followers. In this epilogue, my effort is to map the pathway to develop leadership skills and style to reach the highest level, what I would call as 'Graduation'.

On the basis of research evidence and experience of institution building, it is safe to conclude that delegation is the key to the leadership for institution building. Delegation is not allocation of responsibility. Delegation is devolving rights with responsibilities; devolving authority. When initiatives and innovations emerge from different levels; and become a bottom-up process, when innovation and self-renewal becomes a culture of the institution, institution building can be said to have happened. From transactional to L-5 is a seven stage journey. Not everyone needs to begin from the lower level. There are lateral entrants at higher levels depending upon one's entry behaviour and style.

Leadership has been defined in many ways. For us, leadership is the process of influencing one or more people—groups, teams and crowd—to achieve certain socially desirable goals synergizing organizational goals with individual and group goals. Leaders derive their inspiration from imagination of the future. They live and lead organizations within a set of rules and regulations, but do not get tied down to rules and regulations. Let us see the nature and styles of different levels of leadership.

Graduation in Leadership

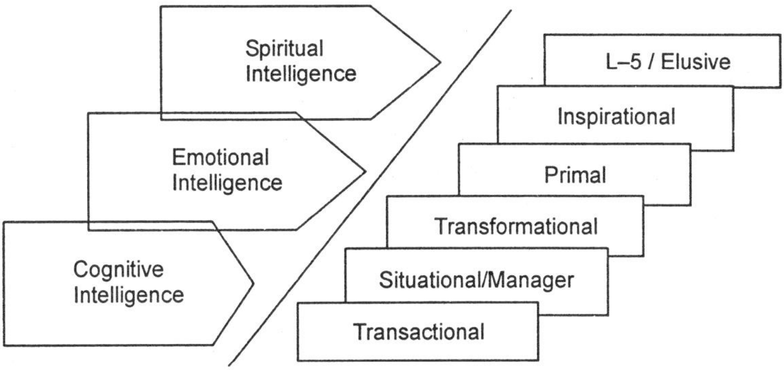

Transactional Leaders: Bass, Burns [Leadershipchamps. wordpress.com] and few others have contributed to give shape to the concept of transactional leadership. It is based on the concept that people work only for rewards. Hence, in this style there is a transaction—work transacted against material benefits. According to Bass, "the transactional leaders work within the organizational culture as it exists; the transformational leader changes the organizational culture". Taking it further, transactional leadership expects work against compensation according to rules. In this style, concern is almost exclusively about task, and not people. To that extent, this resembles administrators; and I prefer not to classify under leadership.

Situational Leaders [Managers]: Situational Leadership Theory is contribution of Hersey and Blanchard (1992). Its primary emphasis is on managing people and tasks in the organization for smooth running of the organization. Concern for people finds place in this style of leadership. Instead of past, emphasis here is on the present and tends to live on day-to-day basis. Although they do not ignore past, their strength is: they are not embedded in the past. Since they tend to live almost exclusively in the present, for them future is often a subject of little relevance. For me, this is management, a stage before leadership.

Transformational Leadership: Transformational leaders cultivate leadership skills and qualities in their followers. They transform others to take charge and perform leadership roles in the smaller organizational subsets. The person in the leadership position shares both responsibility and rights with the followers mentoring them to take over leadership functions in the organization. [www.mindtools.com]

Primal Leadership: Primal Leadership theory is contribution of Daniel Goleman (2002) known for his theory of emotional intelligence. Primal leadership is leading with emotional intelligence. He classified leadership with emotional intelligence into two broad categories, namely resonant and dissonant styles. In resonant style, leader and followers vibrate at the same wave length creating a resonance. In dissonant style, leader and follower may run into cross purposes missing the resonance.

Inspirational Leadership: John Adair, Lance Secretan (1999) and others are the main contributors to the theory of Inspirational Leadership. I prefer Lance Secretan's formulations. The basic thesis is: if the followers can recognize their worth and their potentiality, they would move on their own for personal and organizational self-actualization. Primary role of leader is to create that inspiration among the followers to recognize their potential, and move on their own.

L-5 or Elusive Leadership: L-5 leadership was proposed by Jim Collins (2001) in his book, Good to Great. The concept was articulated by a Chinese scholar in 6th Century BC in the following language—'Leader is good if his presence is felt, leader is better if his absence is perceived, and Leader is best if his presence or absence does not matter'. L-5 leadership is when leader becomes omnipresent without any visible presence. It is the stage where organizations learn to auto pilot.

Leader-Follower Positioning

In the proposed process of graduation in leadership, positioning of leader and follower changes. At the lowest level, namely transactional leadership that works on hiring-firing basis, leader is the boss with large distance from the followers. Leader is much taller and uses position and authority to get work done.

In situational leadership, the gap reduces because there is concern for people and relationships without conceding on task concerns. Yet, leader stands taller than the followers.

Primal leadership is about resonance. Resonance can happen only at the same or complimentary wave lengths. Hence, in this type of leadership, leader and follower come to the same level and share the same platform. Leader and follower share the same height.

Inspirational leadership is a complete turnaround where instead of instructing followers, leader asks, 'can I help you?' Having developed the followers, he/she changes her position to an assisting person. Thus, in Inspirational Leadership, so-called followers stand taller than the designated leader. Beautifully expressed, Secretan terms followers as 'Perceners'.

At L-5 level, leader becomes elusive where his/her presence or absence does not matter. In this model, followers as leaders everywhere, the designated leader is almost missing in the scene. Ricardo Semler's Maverick provides an interesting case of this style.

It should be evident that as a leader moves up in the ladder, he/she reduces her visibility, relegating himself to the background. Instead of leading from the front, she inspires from behind allowing others to take charge.

Leadership Styles and Nature of Intelligence

Intelligence has been described in very many ways starting with Alfred Binet and others. Latest ones are Gardner's multiple intelligence, Goleman's Emotional Intelligence, and spiritual intelligence by Dana Zohar and Marshall. I find some interesting relationships between guiding intelligence behind the styles of leadership. At the lowest two levels, leadership decisions are taken logically that requires algorithmic thinking or cognitive intelligence. As we move on to transformational leadership, along with cognitive intelligence comes emotional intelligence because of the affiliation of the leader with the follower. Primal leadership is predominantly guided by emotional intelligence.

Spiritual intelligence is still being debated—what's its nature? There are different definitions and descriptions forwarded by different scholars. From Indian scriptural point of view, spirituality is awaking into the consciousness beyond self; recognizing self as a spec in the vast cosmic consciousness; perceiving the universe as a dream-game of the omnipresent and omniscient consciousness called God. Since nature of inspirational leadership and L-5 leadership is rediscovering self by inspiring and promoting others putting self in the background, these styles of leadership are fuelled by spiritual intelligence.

Pathway to Graduation

First important step is to diagnose one's own leadership style and map it in the ladder; because the journey starts from there. I have seen how Dr. Buch used his transformational style; Prof. Moonis Raza or Prof. Y Saran used primal and inspirational leadership. Those were their respective entry leadership behavior. Goal for every graduate student is the same—reaching L-5. If one is at Transactional style, has to walk up six steps; if one is at Transformational, he/she has four steps to reach.

Process is collaboration between the leaders and the followers. One important role of the leader trying to graduate is to prepare the follower so that from learning to act against rewards, they learn to affiliate with work and then moves on to learn to lead small activity groups, departments/units in the organization to take charge of large and complex functions in the organization. The other simultaneous role of the leader is to slowly but definitely withdraw him/her to the backyard of organizational operations and position himself/herself to assist others. Something very obvious in this process of transition is reconstructing and reducing ego or 'I'-ness (that's spirituality); shifting from the limelight to behind the light. Best practical example of this leadership graduation is what an Indian mother does to her daughter.

Conclusion

In this prologue, I have made an effort to flag the idea very briefly. I shall make a detailed presentation on this subject in my next book on educational management. My fundamental theses is leadership is a 'learnable skill and competence', not necessarily an inborn or inherited trait. My second assumption is if leadership can be learned, it should be possible for many to become institution builders.

NOTE

1. From Leadership for Institution Building in Education by Marmar Mukhopadhyay

REFERENCES

Adair, John, 2009, The Inspirational Leader: How to Motivate, Encourage and Achieve Success,

Allen, Roger 2009, 3 stages of organizational development, centre for organizational design, (www.centerod.com).

Baddaracco, J.L. and Ellsworth, RR., 1989, *Leadership and Quest for Integrity*, Harvard Business School Press, Boston, MA.

Bennis, W.G., Benne, K.D. & Chin, R. 1969, The Planning of Change. New York:. Holt, Rinehart, & Winston.

Chowdhry, Kamla, 1977, Institution Building: Two Approaches in Contrast, in Ravi Mathai, Udai Pareek and 1V Rao (eds), *Institution Building in Education and Research: From Stagnation to Self Renewal*, All India Management Association, New Delhi:

Ciulla, Joanne B. 2004, Ethics: The Heart of Leadership, Westport: Praeger

Clark, Donald, *Big Dog's Leadership Page*. Retrieved from http://www.nwlink.com/-donclark/leader/leader.htrnl

Collins, Jim, 2001, *Good to Great*, New York: Harper Collins.

Cornette, Zane J. and Thomas, Jack Ward, 1995, Integrity in Professionalism: Ethics and Leadership in Practice, Presented at Society for American Foresters National Convention, Portland.

Covey, S.R. 1995. Ethics of total integrity. Executive Excellence 12(8):3-4.

Crosby, P.B. 1984, *Quality without Tears*, Singapore: McGraw Hill, 1984.

DeBono, Edward, 1985, *Tactics:* Art *and Science of Success*, Harper Colins, New Delhi.

Deming, W.E. 1986, *Out of the Crisis*, Cambridge: Cambridge University Press.

Dewan, R. 2004, Women Leaders in Education, NIEPA, New Delhi (mimeo).

Ezman Milon, J. and Blaise, Hans, C., (1966), *Institution Building Research: The Guiding Concepts*, IURPIB, University of Pittsburgh, Pittsburgh.

Fry, Louis W. 2003, Toward a theory of spiritual leadership, Tarleton State University-Central Texas, 1901 South Clear Creek Road, Killeen, TX 76549, USA.

Frye, Jonnathan, The Correlation of Ethics and Leadership, www.leadershipjot.com

Goleman, D. et al. 2002, *The New Leaders: Transforming art of leadership into science of results,* Little Brown, London.

Gordon, J.C. 1994. From vision to policy: A role for foresters. J. of For. 92(7):16-19.

Havelock, R.G. et al. 1973, *Planning for Innovation through Dissemination and Utilization of Knowledge,* University of Michigan, Ann Arbor, Michigan.

Hersey, P. and Blanchard, K.H. 1992, *Management of Organizational Behaviour,* Prentice Hall of India, New Delhi.

James, M. and Jongeward, O., 1978, *Born* to *Win,* Signet, New York.

Juran, J. 1988, *Planning for Quality,* New York: Free Press, 1988.

Kaiser, A. 1985, Organisations, in Kuper, Adam and Kuper, Jessica *The Social Science Encyclopaedia,* Routledge, London:

Kalam, A.P.J. Abdul, 2002, *Ignited* Minds: *Unleashing the power within India,* Penguin Books, New Delhi.

Kidder, R.M. 1994. Shared values for a troubled world: Conversations with men and women of conscience. Jossey-Bass Publishers, San Francisco. 332 p.

Kidder, R.M. 1995. How good people make tough choices. William Morrow and Co., Inc., New York. 241p.

Kotter, John and Holger Rothbeger, 2006, *Our Iceberg is Melting,* MacMillan,

Latchem, C. and Hanna, D. 2001, *Leadership for* 21st *Century Learning: Global Perspectives from Educational Innovators,* Kogan Page, London.

Lynton, R.P. and Thomas, J.M. 1979, The utility of institution building: Scrutiny for strategies and methodologies of consultation. In Sinha, D.P. (ed.), *Consultants and Consulting stifles,* Vision Books, New Delhi.

MacGregor, J. 2004 Foreword (to the book), *Ethics: The Heart of Leadership* ed by Ciulla, Joanne B. Westport: Praeger

Mitra, C.R and Mankad, P. 2003, *Higher Education: A Knowledge Enterprise,* Sanskriti, New Delhi.

Mitra, C.R. 2007, Technical Education: Poised at a New Crosssroads, in Mukhopadhyay, Marmar and Parhar, Madhu, *Education in India: Dynamics of Development,* New Delhi: Shipra.

Mukhopadhyay, Marmar, 1981, *Barriers to Change in Secondary Education,* Education Books, Udang.

Mukhopadhyay, Marmar, 1989, Management of Change in Education: In Search of Indian Model, NIEPA, New Delhi (mimeo).

Mukhopadhyay, Marmar (ed.), 2004, *Value Development in Higher Education,* Viva books, New Delhi.

Mukhopadhyay, Marmar, 2005, *Total Quality* Management in *Education,* 2nd Ed. New Delhi: Sage.

Nickols, Fred, 2010, Four Change Management Strategies, (www.nichols.us)

Nisbette, R., 2003, *Geography of Thought,* Nicholas Brealey, London.

NOS, 1995, Open Schooling: Perspectives, NOS, New Delhi (mimeo)

Pacino, Al, 2010, Inspirational Leadership, www.inspiredstartup.com/inspirational-leadership

Pareek, Udai, 1981, *Beyond Management,* Oxford and IBH Publishing, New Delhi.

Pareek, Udai, *Institution building: the framework for decision-making,* in Ravi Mathai, Udai Pareek and TV Rao (eds), *Institution Building* in Education *and Research: From Stagnation* to *Self Renewal,* All India Management Association, New Delhi.

Parsons, T. 1964, *Social Systems,* Free Press, New York.

Rao, T.V. 1990, Institution Building and Self Renewal Needs of Education Systems, www.eric.ed.gov ED331772

Robbins, H. and Finley, M. 1997, *Why change does* not *work,* Orion Publishing, London.

Sanders, J. O. 2007, Spiritual Leadership: Principles of Excellence for Every Believer, Kindle Ed.

Sceinder, L. 1964, Institution, in Gould, J and Kolb, W.L.. (eds.), A *Dictionary of the Social* Sciences, Tavistock, London.

Schein, E.H. 1992, *Organizational Culture and Leadership,* San Francisco: Jossey-Bass.

Secretan, Lance, 1999, *Inspirational Leadership: Destiny, calling and cause,* Toronto: Macmillan Canada.

Seligman, Peter, M. 1990, *Learned* Optimism: *How to Change your* Mind *and your Life,* New York: Pocket Books.

Selznick, Philip. 1957, *Leadership in* Administration, Evanston: Row Paterson.

Sinha, J.B.P. 1984 A Model for Effective Leadership Style in India, *International Studies of Management and Organization*

Terry, R.W. 1993. Authentic leadership: courage in action. Jossey-Bass Publishers, San Francisco. 316p.

UNESCO, 1982, A Training *Module* on *Institution Building and Institutional Management,* Bangkok: UNESCO.

Wallis, Roy, 1985, Institutions, in Kuper, Adam and Kuper, Jessica *The Social Science Encyclopedia,* Rutledge, London:

INDEX